Great Smoky Mountains Folklife

Lynwood Montell, General Editor

FOLKLIFE IN THE SOUTH SERIES

Great Smoky Mountains Folklife

Michael Ann Williams

University Press of Mississippi   Jackson

Library of Congress Cataloging-in-Publication Data

Williams, Michael Ann.
    Great Smoky Mountains folklife / Michael Ann Williams.
        p.   cm.—(Folklife in the South series)
    Includes index.
    ISBN 0-87805-791-9 (cloth: alk. paper.—ISBN 0-87805-792-7
(pbk.: alk. paper)
        1. Folklore—Great Smoky Mountains (N.C. and Tenn.)   2. Great
Smoky Mountains (N.C. and Tenn.)—History.   3. Great Smoky Mountains
(N.C. and Tenn.)—Social life and customs.   4. Great Smoky Mountains
National Park (N.C. and Tenn.) I. Title.   II.   Series.
    GR108.W585   1995
    398'.09768'89—dc20   95-13341
                                                                CIP

British Library Cataloging-in-Publication data available

In Memory of Estelle Bennett Carpenter

Contents

Folklife, a familiar concept in European scholarship for over a century, is the sum of a community's traditional forms of expression and behavior. It has claimed the attention of American folklorists since the 1950s. Each volume in the Folklife in the South Series focuses on the shared traditions that link people with their past and provide meaning and continuity for them in the present, and sets these traditions in the social contexts in which they flourish. Prepared by recognized scholars in various academic disciplines, these volumes are designed to be read separately. Each contains a vivid description of one region's traditional cultural elements—ethnic and mainstream, rural and urban—that, in concert with those of other recognizable southern regions, lend a unique interpretation to the complex social structure of the South.

The Great Smoky Mountains, at the border of eastern Tennessee and western North Carolina, are among the highest peaks of the southern Appalachian chain. The folklife of this region has been uniquely shaped by historical events, including the Cherokee Removal of the 1830s and the creation of the National Park a century later. In this book Michael Ann Williams presents a comprehensive look at the traditional culture of the region and the manner in which it has been defined and changed by scholars, missionaries, the federal government, tourists, and the people of the region themselves.

William Lynwood Montell
SERIES EDITOR

A c k n o w l e d g m e n t s

As do many Americans, I first became acquainted with the Smoky Mountains as a tourist. My family visited the Great Smoky Mountains National Park when I was seven, and I returned eleven years later for a backpacking expedition on a college spring break. In 1980 I moved to southwestern North Carolina to conduct historic sites surveys, and in 1982 I became the folklife specialist for the Mountain Heritage Center at Western Carolina University. The first job gave me an understanding of the history of the region; the second introduced me to the folk arts and folk artists of western North Carolina. It has been my pleasure in writing this book to renew acquaintances and friendships. Special thanks go to Doug and Jack Wallin and to Louise Goings for their help and cooperation.

Also during the early 1980s, I conducted research for my doctoral dissertation on the use and meaning of folk housing in southwestern North Carolina. In conducting over fifty tape-recorded interviews with individuals who grew up in the region, I received far more information on life in the mountains and how it has changed than I could use in my study. I was delighted to be able to return to these interviews and use material that did not fit into the dissertation, which I revised into my book *Homeplace*.

In conducting new research for this study, I found a number of archives and special collections to be invaluable in providing information. Thanks to Peggy Harmon of the Appalachian Room at the Memorial Library at Mars Hill College (which houses the Bascom Lamar Lunsford Collection). Gayle Peters of the National Archives Center at East Point, Georgia, was a great help with the Tennessee Valley Authority relocation files and the records of the Cherokee Indian Agency, as well as pointing me in the direction of the Industrial Surveys, which provided a wonderful record of Cherokee housing in the early twentieth century. As always, Kitty Manscill, archivist for Great Smoky Mountains National Park, was a pleasure to work with and an enormous help in my research. Thanks as well to Bonnie Meyers of the Great Smoky Mountains Natural History Association for sharing her unique perspective on the park. Of course, the conclusions drawn in this book are my own and do not necessarily reflect those of the people who aided me in my study.

One of the pleasures and problems of writing a book with as broad a topic as this one is that the author is forced to go well beyond her own area of expertise. Many people helped along the way. As I was starting, Robert Cogswell of the Tennessee Arts Council and Jan Davidson, now director of the John C. Campbell Folk School, provided a number of useful leads and suggested valuable themes to pursue. Others who supplied important information along the way were Jane Harris Woodside of East Tennessee State University; quilt historian and folklorist Laurel Horton; Suzanne Hill McDowell, curator of the Mountain Heritage Center; and Beverly Patterson of the North Carolina Arts Council. Thanks also to Bill Lightfoot of Appalachian State University for his comments on the manuscript.

My colleagues in the Department of Modern Languages and Intercultural Studies at Western Kentucky University were supportive as always. Special thanks to Lynwood Montell, for getting me on this project in the first place; to Jim Wayne Miller, who shared his considerable expertise in the verbal traditions of the region; and to Erika Brady for her helpful comments on the music section of this study. Thanks also to my department head, Larry Danielson, and to David Lee, dean of Potter College, for their support and encouragement.

A number of past and present graduate students in folk studies helped me with this project. Jim Nelson provided considerable guidance as I began the music research and located a number of articles on musicians from the Smokies. Thanks also to Rebecca Jones, who provided an insightful perspective on the National Park Service, and to Lynn David, who played tourist with me at Dollywood. Several graduate assistants gave help at various points along the way. Thanks are owed to Janice Molloy, April Frantz and Anna Fitzgerald. Finally and most importantly, without the help of my two current graduate assistants, I would never have finished this book (more or less) on time. Both read the manuscript more times than they probably care to remember and still managed to be enthusiastic about the project. Hillary Glatt acted as my right-hand woman, helping to research and edit the manuscript. David Baxter, a park descendant himself, conducted tape-recorded interviews and allowed me to use his family as part of the story. Thanks to all his family for their cooperation.

Another park descendant (of the Bennetts of Little Cataloochee), my husband, David Carpenter, as always provided help and encouragement. His insider's point of view was invaluable and his companionship much appreciated in my research. David accompanied me on a hike along Hazel Creek and went with me to two Old Timers' Days, the Headrick's Chapel singing, the Cosby Ramp Festival, the Cherokee Fall Festival, and the homecomings at Cataloochee and Little Cataloochee, although, in the case of the last, perhaps I accompanied him. (He did, however, refuse to go to Dollywood.) I hope he had as much fun as I did.

On a summer evening, cars crawl along the loop road through Cades Cove on the Tennessee side of the Great Smoky Mountains National Park. The pace is about the same as that of a rush hour in a major city. A minor traffic jam is caused by a raccoon at one point and by a deer at another; but the major holdup, requiring the assistance of park personnel, occurs because of a bear up a tree. Why are all these people here? Certainly the opportunity to see wildlife close up is one draw, particularly for urban folks. A view of the stunning broad valley in the midst of high mountains is itself worth the trip. However, the attraction of Cades Cove, which is the most popular spot in the park, is that it seems to provide a glimpse of life in the past. Visitors to the preserved log homes, churches, and agricultural structures believe that they are seeing what life used to be like.

On the North Carolina side of the mountains, in Cherokee, traffic can get equally congested. Tourists have the opportunity to be photographed with contemporary Cherokee in Sioux bonnets or to purchase Indian souvenirs made overseas. Others looking for more authentic experiences can visit the Museum of the Cherokee Indian, the Oconaluftee Indian Village, or the craft shop maintained by the Eastern Band of Cherokee.

According to an article in a 1990 issue of *American Demographics*, as many as 37 million people have visited the Great Smoky Mountains at some time in their lives. Yearly, the park receives more than twice as many visitors as any other national park. While this is partly due to the beauty of the mountains and to the park's accessibility to major urban areas in the eastern United States, it is clear that many visitors are also here to witness a culture or cultures different from their own.

Although the irony of the situation probably does not occur to most visitors, it is perhaps obvious to some members of families removed during the creation of the park and to many members of the Eastern Band of Cherokee. With some tenacity, the Cherokee hung on to a small fragment of their original land as white settlement pushed most of the tribe off the land and west to Oklahoma on the Trail of Tears. Subsequent white settlers lost their claim to the land a hundred years later, when their homeplaces were redefined as national park. Now, tourists by the millions come to the park and hope as part of their itinerary to experience the cultures

GREAT SMOKY MOUNTAINS REGION

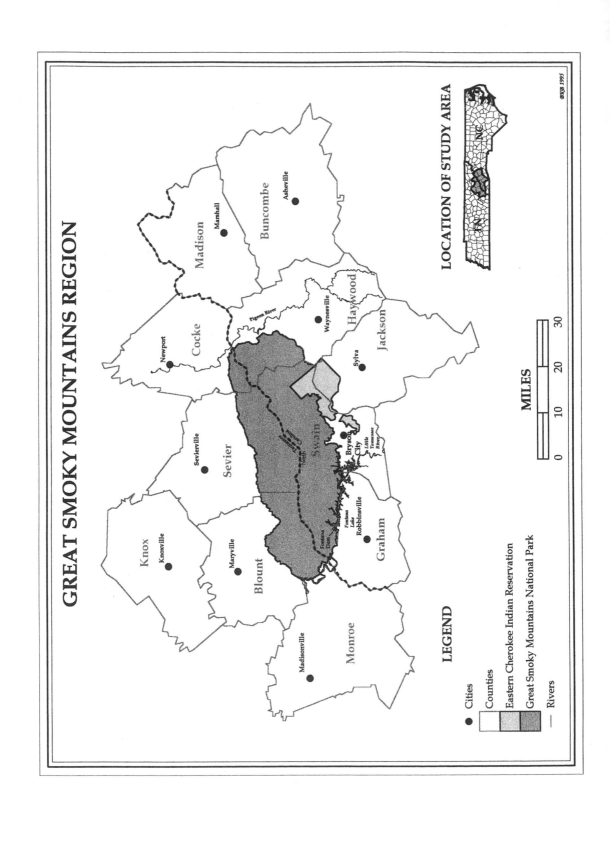

LOCATION OF STUDY AREA

©KJB 1995

MILES

| 0 | 10 | 20 | 30 |

LEGEND

● Cities

Counties

Eastern Cherokee Indian Reservation

Great Smoky Mountains National Park

— Rivers

that have been so rearranged and disrupted. Visitors now value the cultures that were once seen as expendable in the efforts to lay claim to the mountains or preserve them for the benefit of others.

What did it used to be like? Many visitors now ask this question. This study, however, only starts at that point. The folklife of the region is not dead nor is it solely preserved in amber in museum displays and living history reconstructions. What it is like now and how it got that way are equally important questions to ask about the folklife of the Great Smoky Mountains. How has Smoky Mountains folklife been defined by those who are themselves holders of traditions? By those who have chosen to comment on, study, or market it? By the historical events that have shaped it?

If a man and woman living a hundred years ago in the Great Smoky Mountains were somehow transported to the present day, they would indeed be mystified by much of what is now presented as authentic traditional mountain culture. As they watch young clogging groups, the couple might ask why these children are dressed in identical outfits, the little girls with so many petticoats that you see their underpants (discreetly made to match their dresses) when they turn, or why they are clogging in uniform step in square dance figures. Listening to the music, the couple might find some of the tunes to be familiar, as would be the fiddle and probably the banjo, but the rhythm and the pacing of the music, as well as several of the instruments in the band, would be strange.

If the bewildered couple were to venture into a crafts store, even one purporting to sell authentic mountain crafts, much of what they would see would be unrecognizable to them. It is quite likely that they would never have set eyes on the Appalachian dulcimer (more often purchased than played by those modern folks who wander into the crafts store). The handwoven coverlet, that enduring symbol of Appalachian craftsmanship, might be more familiar, although some of the designs and colors would seem odd to the couple, as would the perfectly matched seams.

If our imaginary couple were Cherokee, their bewilderment would be even more profound. The selling of the culture to the tourist, who often cares little about how the Cherokee are distinct from any other Native American group, has led to a baffling array of images. Today a strong degree of pan-Indianism—the identification of the Eastern Cherokee with other Native American cultures—has shaped the folk arts from within as well.

These differences are, to a degree, appropriate. Folk arts change; they are supposed to. They do not stay immutably the same across the decades or centuries. Particularly in this century, when certain arts have found mass appeal with the help of the media (as in the case of traditional Appalachian string music contributing ultimately to the development of bluegrass and modern country-western), changes are inevitable. However, perhaps no region of the country has been culturally so defined by outsiders as has Southern Appalachia. In fact, in recent years it has often been argued that "Appalachia" did not exist until it was discovered, or perhaps "invented," by those who wished to preserve or transform it.

Within Southern Appalachia, which is often portrayed as a unique region, the area of the Great Smoky Mountains is to some extent also distinct, not so much because it is different culturally from the rest of that part of the world, but because certain historical events have led to its particular visibility. Although outside—especially federal—intervention has been extensive throughout Appalachia, it has been felt the most in the Great Smoky Mountains region. The removal of the majority of the Cherokees in the 1830s and the reconfiguration of those who remained behind into the Eastern Band have contributed uniquely to the folklife of the region. In the twentieth century the government created a national park that encompassed most of the Great Smoky Mountains. If, before that, the Smoky Mountains region was not the best known part of Southern Appalachia, it would become so by the second half of the century. No region of Southern Appalachia has been so defined by tourism.

Writing of the "Great Smoky Mountains region" is, of course, in itself problematic. Is it a cultural region or can it be defined only in terms of its geography? The geographical definition is certainly the easier. The southern Appalachian Mountains stretch southward in two roughly parallel chains. To the east, the Blue Ridge reaches from northern Virginia to the top of Georgia. The western chain is the Alleghanies. The southern extensions of the Alleghanies, which form the western wall of the Shenandoah Valley in Virginia, are sometimes referred to as the Unakas. Forming the boundary between Tennessee and North Carolina, they run southwest to northeast, from Georgia to Virginia. The Great Smoky Mountains, located between the Little Tennessee and Pigeon rivers, form one segment of this chain. With the exception of Mount Mitchell, the tallest mountain east of the Mississippi, which is located nearby in the North Carolina Blue Ridge, the Smokies are the highest peaks in the Appalachian chain. Horace Kephart, in *Our Southern Highlanders*, referred to the Smokies as the "housetop of Eastern America."

While the Great Smoky Mountains can be defined in physical terms as a specific chain of mountains, defining the region as a cultural entity is more difficult. The Great Smoky Mountains National Park encompasses most of the range of mountains defined as the Smokies. But clearly the region includes land immediately surrounding the park as well. To some extent, what constitutes the Smoky Mountains region has been defined by outsiders, and today the name is often used by commercial interests catering to the tourists. Seen in these terms, the region is expanding, as businesses wish to associate themselves with a popular tourist destination. The degree to which individuals who grow up in the shadow of the great mountains describe themselves as being "from the Smokies" depends on many factors. They may also (or may not) see themselves as Appalachians, or (more likely) as Tennesseans or North Carolinians, or as natives of any of the several counties that adjoin the park.

This study will examine the ways in which the Great Smoky Mountains region has been culturally defined. Since its boundaries are constantly being shifted and negotiated, no attempt will be made to name any that are absolute. However, for the convenience of those unfamiliar with the region, a brief description of its layout is included.

The boundary between Tennessee and North Carolina runs along the crest of the Smokies. The Great Smoky Mountains National Park was carved out of six counties: in Tennessee, Blount and Sevier counties and a small portion of Cocke County; in North Carolina, Swain, Jackson, and Haywood counties. Immediately adjacent to the park are Monroe County, Tennessee, and Graham County, North Carolina, at the west end of the park. Madison County, North Carolina, is located just to the east of the park boundaries. Although this is a somewhat arbitrary designation, these counties form the heart of what may, for the sake of convenience, be referred to as the Smoky Mountains region. The two urban bookends of this region—Knoxville in Knox County, Tennessee, and Asheville, in Buncombe County, North Carolina—should not be excluded, since it was the business interests of these two cities that did much to promote the visibility of the Great Smoky Mountains as a region.

The two sides of the mountains are different topographically. While a couple of small chains of mountains parallel the Smokies on the Tennessee side, the land levels out into the Tennessee valley, which stretches to the Cumberland Plateau. On the North Carolina side, the terrain remains mountainous. A number of transverse ranges stretch southeast to the Blue Ridge. The area between the Smokies and the Blue Ridge, particularly around Asheville, has been labelled by promoters for over a century as the "Land of the Sky." Culturally, it is impossible to distinguish where the Smokies end and the Blue Ridge begins.

Federal ownership of land in this region is not limited to the national park. The Cherokee and Pisgah national forests are found on either end of the Great Smoky Mountains National Park. The Tennessee Valley Authority has built several large reservoirs in the region, and the TVA's Fontana Lake forms the southeast boundary of the park. Neither are the Cherokee lands in private ownership. The main portion of the reservation, referred to as the Qualla Boundary, surrounds the principal entrance to the park at the south end. Other lands of the Eastern Band are located in southwestern North Carolina in Swain, Graham, and Cherokee counties. In some of the counties adjoining the park, less than half of the land is in private ownership.

If the Great Smoky Mountains region can be described loosely in terms of geographical boundaries, it can also be described historically. The folklife of the region may not be unique, particularly when compared to that of the rest of Southern Appalachia or the Upper South, but it has been shaped by unique historical circumstances. This study will focus, in part, on the manner in which these circumstances defined and transformed the traditional culture of the region. The aim is not to winnow the unauthentic chaff from the authentic grain of tradition. "Authenticity" is in the eye of the beholder and may be defined in very different terms depending on whether one is a Cherokee craftsperson, a promoter of revival crafts, a folklorist, or a tourist.

This book is divided into three sections. The first is a historical overview examining both the nature of settlement and displacement in the Smokies and the manner in which the folklife of the region was discovered and defined during the late nineteenth and early twentieth centuries. The second section looks at various folk traditions and how they have changed in the past century. It is impossible to be comprehensive here; the rich musical tradition of the Smokies alone warrants a volume (or two). Therefore the approach to the material is selective, with those traditions that are richest or best documented receiving particular attention.

The final section focuses on aspects of folklife specifically generated by the creation of the park and on the development of tourism in the region. Not only did the park bring new occupations and occupational lore to the mountains, but the act of displacement generated new forms of folklife as former residents struggled to redefine their relationship with the region. The concluding chapter addresses the question of why authentic folklife cannot be completely separated from touristic portrayals of folklife, examining three "displays of culture": the Cosby Ramp Festival, the Cherokee Fall Festival, and the Dollywood theme park.

Historical Overview

Settlement and Removal

Today the Smoky Mountains speak of wilderness. It is easy for the casual observer to believe that it has always been so—that this land was miraculously snatched up and preserved before it was besmirched by human occupation. Strictly speaking, however, much of the wilderness is a product of reconstruction rather than of preservation. For some, the Smokies have been home, not wilderness; the mountains have been domesticated, and their natural resources exploited, by humans for a very long time.

The Great Smoky Mountains region has supported human habitation not only for centuries but for millennia. By the time of European contact, the Cherokee had come to dominate not only the Smoky Mountains region but a considerable expanse of land (some forty thousand square miles) extending into present-day Kentucky, Georgia, and Alabama. The Smokies, however, were the traditional heartland of the Cherokee; the ancient capital, Kituah, was located near present-day Bryson City, North Carolina. After European contact, the Cherokees living closest to the mountains were the most likely to maintain traditional beliefs and lifestyles, and it was this group who would become the core of the Eastern Band.

European contact began in the sixteenth century with Spanish adventurers, and sustained trade began with the English in the final quarter of the seventeenth century. Within a hundred years these new interlopers had substantially eroded the Cherokee Nation's holdings. In 1791 the Cherokee ceded the first piece of the Smokies, and by 1819 they had lost most of the mountains, although they still retained control of land immediately on the other side of the Little Tennessee River. In the two decades before their removal west, the Cherokee owned a small portion of southwestern North Carolina, southeastern Tennessee, and northeastern Alabama. The largest section of the Nation's holdings was in northwest Georgia. As the Cherokee clung to this small fragment of their once-expansive territory, the United States government moved closer and closer to the position that the Indians should be moved to territory west of the Mississippi. The discovery of gold on Cherokee land in Georgia and the election of General Andrew Jackson to the White House in 1828 made this removal seem even more inevitable.

Historically, the Cherokee Nation has been known for its cultural adaptability. By the time of their removal to Oklahoma, the Cherokee had not only a written language but also a tribal newspaper and a constitutional government. However, this willingness to change may have only been a veneer. The most acculturated Cherokee were predominantly upper class and most were of only partial Indian descent. Acculturation may also have been a calculated move to stave off removal by the United States government. If this was the case, the effort backfired. The Cherokee were perceived as an even greater threat by many non-Indians, and the development of plantations in the nonmountainous regions made their land even more desirable. Eventually a small elite group of the Cherokees decided they should succumb to pressure from the United States and give up their land in exchange for a cash settlement and lands west of the Mississippi. Despite opposition from the majority of the Cherokee Council, the federal government forced the signing of a treaty with a small minority faction. No North Carolina Cherokee were present at the signing, and Cherokee leader John Ross, who opposed removal, was held prisoner so that he could not attend. The terms of the Treaty of New Echota, ratified by the Senate in 1836, stated that the Cherokee were to cede all their eastern lands in exchange for government land in Indian territory and a cash settlement of approximately fifty cents an acre. The Cherokee Removal began in 1838. An estimated four thousand individuals died en route to Oklahoma.

Oral tradition holds that many of the North Carolina Cherokee eluded removal by fleeing into the mountains when United States government troops arrived and began placing the Cherokee in stockades to await removal. Many did indeed flee. However, a group of Cherokee families living along the Oconaluftee and Soco creeks applied for exemption from removal due to their legal status. After the 1819 land cession these "Qualla Indians" were granted property on former Cherokee lands and claimed citizenship of the United States. Other Cherokees also applied for certificates permitting them to stay. Although they were only a tiny fraction of the total number of Cherokee, those who eluded removal, either "legally" or by fleeing, were largely from the Smoky Mountains region.

As the Removal wore on, the United States government tired of searching for every last fugitive. However, it is probably true that if the mountainous land had been perceived as more desirable, the Qualla Indians and the fugitives would have been forced onto the Trail of Tears. As former Cherokee land came up for sale, some of the remaining Cherokee began to purchase land back through non-Indian agents. The United States government did not officially recognize these Cherokees' right to remain in the East until 1842, and pressure on them to consent to be removed lasted for decades. So too did the Eastern Cherokees' legal limbo. In 1889 the Eastern Band was granted reservation status, but questions about their citizenship continued into the twentieth century.

The specific circumstances of the Removal explain the dispersed nature of the Eastern Band's lands in North Carolina. The largest portion of land is the Qualla Boundary, a 45,413-acre tract in Swain and Jackson counties. It includes the town of Cherokee, now a major tourist haven, but also the traditionalist community of Big Cove, one of five townships at Qualla. Near Qualla is the smaller Thomas tract. Further to the southwest, in Graham and Cherokee counties, are a number of individual tracts, intermingled with land owned by non-Cherokees. Although they live close by their non-Indian neighbors, the Snowbird Indians in Graham County are among the most traditional of the Eastern Cherokee, with a higher percentage of fullbloods and speakers of the Cherokee language.

Even before the Cherokee Removal, non-Indians were settling in the Smoky Mountains region. Explorers came first, followed by traders and missionaries. As former Cherokee lands were "opened up," white settlers flocked into the region. Even then, much of the land was hardly wilderness. The Cherokees had cultivated the land for centuries and by the time of the Removal had adopted European-derived agricultural techniques and architectural technology. Some of the new settlers moved directly into Cherokee-built homes, which were generally indistinguishable from the dwellings the white settlers would have built themselves.

Many of the new settlers were of English descent. Others were "Scotch-Irish," descendants of lowland Scots who had settled on the plantations of northern Ireland in the seventeenth century and left for America in the next century in search of economic and religious freedom. However, the stereotypical notion that the white settlers who came to Southern Appalachia were of pure British stock is sheer nonsense. Many nineteenth-century settlers were of central or northern European ethnicity—Swedes, Finns, French, Dutch, and Germans. Typically these groups entered America through the port of Philadelphia and eventually followed the great wagon route down the Valley of Virginia into the piedmont of North Carolina or the Tennessee Valley. Due to the presence of the Cherokee and the limitations of topography, white settlement west of the Smokies preceded settlement of the mountains themselves.

In the Smoky Mountains region, the broad river valleys, which were most suitable for agriculture, were settled first. Only as this easily accessible land became more scarce and costly were the inner reaches of the Smokies settled by European-Americans. In the early years of the nineteenth century, whites settled along the Oconaluftee close to the Qualla Indians. By the 1820s, white settlement had begun in Cades Cove on the Tennessee side of the mountains, and a decade later families were moving into the Cataloochee Valley and Hazel Creek. By mid-century, a number of the smaller creeks in the Smokies had been settled by European-Americans.

African-Americans have never lived in any great numbers in the Smoky Mountains. However, their history and cultural contributions cannot be discounted. Historian Theda Perdue notes that escaped slaves sometimes took refuge in Cherokee territory, and that the Cherokee themselves traded in captured black slaves. Therefore it is possible that the Smokies had residents of African descent before there was permanent white settlement.

Contrary to popular belief, slaveholding did exist in Southern Appalachia. In the Smoky Mountains region, slaveholders were found particularly in the broader river valleys. These slaveholders might own up to twenty or thirty slaves, although many owned only one or two. Within the deeper reaches of the mountains, slaveholding was considerably less common. In Cades Cove, Tennessee, local opposition apparently led those who had owned slaves to give them up before settling in the community. However, Cataloochee, on the North Carolina side of the mountains, did accept slaveholding, and a small slave cemetery still exists there. Another slave cemetery found within what is now the national park is on Mingus Creek, also on the North Carolina side. Ironically, the owner of these slaves was Abraham (or Abram) Enloe, reputed by local legend to be the "real" father of the Great Emancipator, Abraham Lincoln.

Slaveholding was not unfamiliar to the Cherokee. An indigenous form of bondage that made use of captives of warfare did exist, though it was far different from the American system that some Cherokee elite would embrace as one of the trappings of assimilation. As with non-Indians, slaveholding among the Cherokee was less common in the mountainous region and, overall, fewer than 10 percent of the Cherokee held slaves in the years immediately before the Removal. Among the few conservative Cherokees in the mountains who were slaveowners was Chief Yonaguska, although he was reputed to have treated his one slave, Cudjo, as his brother.

The Civil War strongly divided the loyalties of people in the Smoky Mountains region. While few battles were waged there, civil disruption was great, as members of families and communities were pitted against each other. Nonslaveholders were not necessarily inclined to support the interests of the slaveholding elite, but many felt their loyalty split between the state and the federal government. Generally, support for the Union was strongest on the Tennessee side of the mountains and in communities where there were no slaveholders, though divisions were seldom neat. The Qualla Indians mostly supported the Confederacy, out of loyalty for William Thomas, who had acted as their agent, and out of distrust for the United States government, but other Eastern Cherokee fought on the side of the Union. The divided loyalties in the Smoky Mountains region left a legacy that endured in oral narratives (as well as political affiliations) well into the next century.

In areas where slaveholding had been most common, some small African-American communities sprang up, but these were more likely to be found just south of the Smokies in Henderson, Macon, and Cherokee counties in North Carolina. In most of the more mountainous communities, the African-American population was almost negligible. While some have argued that racism is less virulent in Appalachia than elsewhere in the South, it is perhaps just of a different order, the result more of ignorance than of entrenched social and economic orders. Still, African-American culture helped shape the folklife of the Smokies, particularly in song, dance, and narrative traditions. The folklife of the Smokies represents a cultural hybrid exhibiting not only the influence of various European traditions but also the mixing of Native American and African-American cultures.

Throughout most of the nineteenth century, the economy of the Smoky Mountains region was based on agriculture. The construction of roads such as the Buncombe Turnpike, completed in 1827, made it possible to get farm products to larger markets. In the fertile river valleys, some larger farms flourished, and, in the decades before the Civil War, these valleys had a more stratified society than was typical within the more mountainous communities. The majority of the farms within the Smoky Mountains region were small, family-based enterprises. To the extent that self-sufficiency was the rule for these farmers, its basis was the rural community, not the individual. Members of these communities exchanged not only specialized products and skills but also free labor. Farmers trading "a day's work" with their neighbors meant that buildings could be built and agricultural tasks completed, and that families could make it through hard times. This ethic of labor exchange remained among some rural people in the region well into the twentieth century.

Among the Eastern Cherokee, the exchange of labor was more formalized. The *gadugi*, or free labor company, arranged cooperative exchange of labor, primarily providing help with agricultural tasks and during times of family crisis. The free labor companies developed even more formal structures during the early twentieth century, though by mid-century many of their responsibilities were usurped by community clubs and federal assistance. The spirit of working together is still maintained by conservative Cherokees today through the maintenance of the traditional values of the harmony ethic.

As the nineteenth century progressed, the Smoky Mountains and much of the rest of Southern Appalachia lagged behind the rest of the country in economic development and industrialization. Despite mixed loyalties, Southern Appalachia shared with the rest of the South the economic aftermath of the Civil War. Furthermore, the terrain made the development of effective transportation routes difficult. Knoxville, Tennessee, was linked by rail to other urban areas just before the Civil War, but the delays of the war left Asheville, North Carolina, without a railroad until 1880. The Smokies themselves were not accessible by rail until after the turn of the century.

Unlike what happened in central Appalachia, mineral extraction played only a minor role in the developing economy of the Smoky Mountains. Although some mining did exist, especially of copper, it was another natural resource that brought industrialization to the Smokies. Commercial timbering came to the area in the final decades of the nineteenth century. At first it was primarily a locally based industry, but, by the turn of the century, northern business interests were purchasing large tracts of timberland in the mountains. It was these large lumber companies that built rail lines into the mountains, linking the lines with existing routes that ran along the river valleys.

The development of the timber industry in the early twentieth century brought profound changes to the lives of people in the Smokies. Many rural people for the first time found "public work," that is, paid employment away from home. The timber wages were a strong temptation, bringing many people more money than they had ever seen before and the luxury of purchasing store-bought goods. However, the boom-and-bust cycle of the timber industry ultimately left many of those who had become dependent on cash wages poorer than ever. Some struggled to maintain their family farms, with women and children often taking up the slack, but others were forced to sell the land that had supported their families for generations. The timber boom was short-lived, and, as it declined, many were forced to leave the Smokies in order to support their families. While some went to the coal fields or the industrial north, the most common destinations were the mill towns of the piedmont and the newly developed timber lands in the state of Washington.

While the timber boom resulted in considerable dislocation among rural people, industrialization did not bring about a significant increase in the cultural diversity of the Smoky Mountains region, as it did in some parts of Appalachia. African-Americans from the deep South and individuals from eastern and southern Europe were actively recruited to the coal camps of central Appalachia, but in-migration to the timber camps of the Smokies was on a much more modest scale. The subsequent era of federal intervention did little to further enhance diversity. In 1935 attempts by the federal government to send four black companies of the Civilian Conservation Corps to the newly created Great Smoky Mountains National

Park were opposed by park officials who feared the reaction of local people. The Tennessee Valley Authority met similar opposition in 1942 with the construction of Fontana Dam at the south end of the Smokies. Although no African-Americans lived within thirty miles of the project, the TVA, under executive order, proceeded to bus African-American workers to the construction site. Virulent protest erupted from some white residents of the region who were joined by some of their Cherokee neighbors. In the end the TVA built three sets of accommodations at Fontana, segregating black, white, and Cherokee workers.

While the short-lived timber boom would profoundly alter the lives of many Smoky Mountains residents, another "industry" would have a more long-term effect on the economy of the region. Even as early as the 1820s, soon after the construction of the Buncombe Turnpike, summer people were being attracted to the scenery and cool climate of the mountains. The railroad brought a greater number and variety of summer visitors. Health resorts flourished; the mountain climate was thought to be particularly effective in the treatment of tuberculosis. The same railroads that took timber out brought tourists further and further into the recesses of the mountains.

Even in the late nineteenth century, a few individuals dreamed of "preserving" the mountains by bringing the land under public domain. The destructive methods of the timber industry further heightened support for federal intervention. While some supported the creation of national forests in the Smokies (which allowed controlled timbering), others supported a national park. Ultimately, it was local business interests that won the day for the park idea. The most effective group of park promoters was the Knoxville-based Great Smoky Mountains Conservation Association. These businessmen and professionals, affiliated with the local chamber of commerce and automobile association, believed that the development of good roads and tourism would be the salvation of the local economy. The Great Smoky Mountains National Park was authorized in 1926. Although the majority of the land acquisition was completed within five years, the park was not officially dedicated until 1940.

The development of national parks, unlike the creation of national forests, entails the removal of the local population. Official histories of the park assure their readers that the majority of the land encompassed by the park was owned by timber interests and that the local people removed were offered a fair price and were ultimately better off. While the majority of land in the Smokies was owned by a few timber companies, over seven hundred farm families (and an unknown number of tenants) also lost their homes. Although some left willingly, other landowners clearly did not think that the price was fair, and they fought through the court system. The fact that most of those displaced lost their land on the eve of the Great Depression heightened the economic hardship these families faced. Aside from payment for the land, virtually no other assistance was offered to those displaced by the park's creation. The residents felt especially betrayed because they had been repeatedly assured by park promoters that they would not be displaced. In communities such as Cades Cove, where local people had extended hospitality, feeding and putting up the supporters of the park, many were shocked to find that their land, too, was to be lost to eminent domain.

A second removal occurred over a decade later with the construction of Fontana Dam at the southwest side of the Smokies. Although some of the families whose land was flooded in the dam construction may have found solace in the fact that their removal was part of the war effort, this was not the case for those whose land was located on the north shore of the newly created Fontana Lake. After the only access road to their communities was flooded, 163 families lost their farms to the Tennessee Valley Authority, who turned over the land to the Great Smoky Mountains National Park.

The legacy of bitterness that the park removals engendered remains today, though it has begun to fade with the passing away of those who were removed as adults. The next generation is perhaps more sanguine. Bonnie Meyers understands the feelings of her mother, who, now in her nineties, still does not like to visit the park. Her mother was one of the many in Cades Cove who extended hospitality to the park creators and was assured that her family would not be removed. After the creation of the park, the family stayed on for several years as tenants but were forced to move to Townsend after the school was closed.

Bonnie Meyers, however, does not carry on her mother's bitterness. Instead she works at the Visitors Center at Cades Cove and has come to terms with the park. "My mother even cooked meals for these people that were dealing for the state. She put them up in her house, fed them, cooked meals for them, and all the time they were saying that we don't want your homes and your farmland. Betrayal, yes, it's sad. But as it come on down to the end of the line, I'm glad that, you know, it's like this for people to see."

Whether or not the park removals were for the greater good, it became apparent that one person's wilderness could be another person's home. Cades Cove is now, in fact, interpreted largely as a cultural rather than a natural landscape. Whether the park removals were fair may continue to be in dispute; opinions differ according to whose vantage point is being used. Clearly, however, the government was remiss in its lack of aid to dislocated families. Finally, even the inevitability and extent of the removals must be questioned. Most of the larger communities consumed by the park were close to the park's boundaries. Had these people had more political and economic clout, the boundaries might have been drawn differently. Recent examination of the historical evidence suggests that the criteria by which the park boundaries were drawn was not necessarily objective. In individual cases, park service officials chose to take property on the boundaries because the owners were seen as undesirable or their property unsightly. The creation of these boundaries also reflected the park service's desire to create a buffer against unsupervised development around the park.

The settlement histories of most regions include instances of displacement. The extent and nature of displacement in the Smokies make this region unique. Certainly the history of European-American settlement of North America is a saga of the displacement of native peoples. However, among the most tragic chapters of this story was the removal of the Cherokee on the Trail of Tears, where thousands died of disease and starvation. Only a small fraction of the Cherokee remained behind in the Smoky Mountains. Less than a century later people all over Appalachia were displaced by industrialization. However, in the Smokies, these people, reeling from vast social and economic changes, were again displaced, this time by the federal government in the largest removal of people by eminent domain for a national park in the United States.

CHAPTER 2

"Discovering" the Folklife of the Great Smokies

The creation of the Great Smoky Mountains National Park in the 1930s brought the region to the attention of the nation. Ironically, it was at the same time that the massive disruptions of the park removals were occurring that the park service began to promote the (supposedly) unique folk culture of the region. However, the same process had already been taking place on a more gradual level during the half century that preceded the creation of the park. As tourism and timbering were changing forever a way of life, scholars, popular writers, and missionaries were starting to "discover" and promote the folklife of the Great Smoky Mountains.

Before the twentieth century, little attention had been paid to the Smokies as a unique region. Indeed, the mountains themselves were usually referred to only as a part of the larger chain, the southern Alleghanies or Unakas. The early chroniclers of the region were mostly naturalists who were attracted by the scenery and unique flora and fauna. Luckily, some also took notice of the people. In the 1760s, Philadelphia naturalist William Bartram described the Cherokee as part of his tour of the southeast. Ninety years later, landscape architect William Law Olmsted ended his grand tour of the Upper South with a stay in western North Carolina.

After the Civil War, writers increasingly drew attention to the singular qualities of Southern Appalachia. Indeed, as has been recently suggested, Appalachia was "invented" in the writing of this period. However, much of this literature focused on the Cumberlands and eastern Kentucky. When Horace Kephart moved to the Smokies in the early twentieth century, he complained that he could find nothing written on the region except a United States Forestry Service publication. With Kephart's writing and the discovery of local crafts and music traditions, the Great Smokies came to be included by those who defined the culture of Appalachia.

Like Appalachian culture, Native American cultures were alternately portrayed in negative terms, as being degraded, and in positive ones, as representing preserved cultures of the past. While scholars and popular writers were "inventing" Appalachia, so too were writers racing to define

Native Americans. However, writings on Appalachia, intent on arguing the pure English or Scotch-Irish heritage of the region, only occasionally recognized the Native American culture in the region. Therefore the literature on the Cherokee was (and still is) quite separate from the work that focuses on Appalachia. Two of the most influential writers about the cultures of the Great Smoky Mountains region, James Mooney and Horace Kephart, did recognize the importance of studying both the Cherokee and non-Cherokee cultures of the region, but each only dabbled outside his own area of expertise. Still, taken together, the writings of Mooney and Kephart present an important early attempt at ethnographic description of the cultures of the Great Smoky Mountains.

THE EARLY ETHNOGRAPHERS: JAMES MOONEY AND HORACE KEPHART

Although passing travellers had left brief accounts of the peoples of the Great Smoky Mountains, serious study of the cultures found there did not begin until the late nineteenth and early twentieth centuries. Two men did much to define these cultures to readers outside the region: James Mooney, who lived among the Eastern Cherokee in the 1880s, and Horace Kephart, who settled on Hazel Creek in Swain County, North Carolina, in 1904. Superficially, the two men were quite different. Mooney was an employee of the Smithsonian Institution, collecting data for scholarship, while Kephart was escaping a scholarly life and writing for a popular audience. However, although their approaches differed somewhat, Mooney and Kephart were both meticulous scholars as well as romantics, drawn to the Great Smoky Mountains in search of something they could not find in their own "civilized" existence.

James Mooney, the son of Irish immigrants, was born in 1861 in Richmond, Indiana. His father had died before his birth, and his mother instilled in him a deep love of Irish folklore. As a schoolboy, Mooney also developed a deep and abiding interest in American Indians. After brief stints in teaching, journalism, and Irish nationalist politics, Mooney decided to pursue his Indian hobby on a professional level. He lobbied unsuccessfully for a job at the Smithsonian's Bureau of Ethnology and then moved to Washington, D.C., where he was able personally to impress upon the bureau director, John Wesley Powell, his capabilities and his desire for a job.

Mooney joined the Bureau of Ethnology in 1885 and the following year was appointed to the position of ethnologist. In 1887, he was finally able to conduct his first field research on American Indians. His assignment took him to the Great Smoky Mountains to observe the religious practices and customs of the Eastern Cherokee. Mooney's interest in the Cherokee had developed through contact with Quakers in his hometown (the Quakers ran schools among the Cherokee) and through meetings in Washington with N. J. Smith, chief of the Eastern Cherokee. The field-work Mooney conducted among the Cherokee in the late 1880s came at a time of great cultural change for the band. Much traditional lore was slipping away, and its disappearance was actively encouraged by the federal government.

In his attempts to study Cherokee beliefs, Mooney encountered a great deal of secrecy. Not only were the rituals traditionally kept secret within Cherokee society itself, but the federal government was actively discouraging their practice. Mooney, however, was not above trickery to obtain what he wanted. Once, after claiming to be a shaman in his own right, he faked a ritual using Gaelic formulas. One of the greatest strokes of luck on his first field trip was the revelation by a Cherokee shaman, Swimmer, of the existence of a notebook containing various ritual prayers, songs, and prescriptions. A storehouse of traditional knowledge, Swimmer also provided Mooney with about three-quarters of the Cherokee myths later published in his collection in 1900. Swimmer died the year before the "Myths of the Cherokee" was published, and Mooney noted his passing with these words: "Peace to his ashes and sorrow for his going, for with him perished half the tradition of a people."

Along with collecting sacred formulas and myths, Mooney also studied medical practices and Cherokee ballplay (which he documented photographically). As a man of his day, Mooney did not question the evolutionary principles of nineteenth-century anthropology or the belief in the superiority of his own culture. But his identification with Ireland led to a sympathy with Native Americans, and he brought to his work more respect for the people he studied than many of his contemporaries did. He also insisted on the importance of immersing oneself in the culture being studied, living with the people and learning their language. In light of the active discouragement of ritual activity by the Bureau of Indian Affairs, perhaps Mooney can also be credited with validating for members of the Eastern Cherokee the importance of their traditional beliefs. A man such as Swimmer perhaps needed no such validation, but it was through Mooney that Swimmer was able to preserve his traditional store of knowledge for posterity.

Mooney only briefly turned his attention to the non-Cherokee inhabitants of the region. In his article "Folk-Lore of the Carolina Mountains," published in the *Journal of American Folklore* in 1889, Mooney wrote that the "notes here given were picked up incidentally while engaged in other work, and are but stray leaves of the volume which the industrious collector may yet gather among this primitive people, as yet unchanged by immigration and uncontaminated by the modern civilization." Although an evolutionary anthropologist, Mooney found the non-Cherokee inhabitants of western North Carolina to be as primitive and exotic as the Cherokee. However, as Kephart would do later, Mooney insisted that he was writing only of the "mountaineer proper" and not of the inhabitants of the region's towns or villages. Whatever its limitations, Mooney's article is the first scholarly consideration of the non-Cherokee folk culture of the Smoky Mountains region.

By 1890, Mooney's interests were drawing him west of the Mississippi to other Indian cultures. A decade later he would again turn his attention to the Eastern Cherokee in order to complete his monograph "Myths of the Cherokee." However, this work was based mostly on the fieldwork Mooney had conducted from 1887 to 1890. While he did not find time to complete any more extensive fieldwork among the Eastern Cherokee, Mooney's work was an important record of the Eastern Band in the late nineteenth century. At his death in 1921, Mooney left behind a great deal of unpublished material. Among this material was his analysis of the Swimmer manuscript, which, revised and edited by Frans M. Olbrechts, was published in 1932.

Although any number of anthropologists and Cherokee scholars followed Mooney, he not only made his own reputation with his studies of the Cherokee but also established the scholarly study of the band. His reputation among the Cherokee was such that, when Olbrechts began fieldwork in Qualla in the 1920s, he found that Mooney's name "served as the best introduction I could have desired."

Horace Kephart was born a year after Mooney, in 1862, in Pennsylvania, although he spent much of his youth in Iowa. He returned east for college and embarked on a library career, first at Cornell University and later at Yale. In 1890 Kephart accepted a job at the St. Louis Mercantile Library, where he proceeded to develop the institution's collection of western Americana. Ultimately, however, reading and writing about frontier history did not satisfy Kephart's restless nature. In the early 1900s, he experienced what today might be called a mid-life crisis of massive proportions. Bouts of ill health and alcoholism finally led Kephart to leave his job and family in search of a new frontier.

In 1904 Horace Kephart left the "tame west" and settled in "this wild east," the Great Smoky Mountains. "I had a passion for early American history," Kephart wrote, "and, in Far Appalachia, it seemed that I might realize the past in the present, seeing with my own eyes what life must have been to my pioneer ancestors of a century or two ago." Settling in the "back of beyond," Kephart escaped his life as a scholar but did not give up scholarship. Though he wrote for popular audiences, he always kept meticulous notes and took his research seriously.

Our Southern Highlanders was first published in 1913 and was updated and expanded in a 1922 edition. Although the book purports to be about Southern Appalachia as a whole, most of it draws on Kephart's experience living in the Great Smoky Mountains region. From 1904 to 1907, Kephart lived on Hazel Creek in Swain County, North Carolina, and his experiences here became the basis for much of his classic work. Leaving Hazel Creek in late 1907, he travelled to other parts of Appalachia to check his generalizations about the region as a whole. By the time he returned to the Smokies, the W. M. Ritter Lumber Company had begun operations on Hazel Creek, so Kephart settled in Bryson City, the seat of Swain County, where he would remain until his death.

Horace Kephart
(Photo courtesy of Great Smoky Mountains National Park)

A popular book in its time, *Our Southern Highlanders* today finds an ambivalent reception. Allen W. Batteau in *The Invention of Appalachia* (1990) calls Kephart's work "probably the most vigorous and honest book written on the Appalachian South." However, in 1988 Durwood Dunn described *Our Southern Highlanders* as the "nadir of Southern Appalachian stereotypes" and made the refutation of Kephart's representation of mountain life a major objective of his own study, *Cades Cove*.

Kephart recognized and attempted to correct many negative stereotypes and overly romanticized portrayals of the southern mountains. However, his own need for adventure drew him to the wildest characters and the most uncivilized aspects of life. Before the book settles down to a somewhat more sober consideration of life in the mountains, Kephart takes the reader on jaunts of bearhunting, moonshining and manhunting. Kephart was not much interested in town life and, having escaped domesticity himself, had little understanding of the lives of the women in the region. Although defying stereotypes, he also tended to give the readers what they wanted. Thus while noting on several occasions that the Smokies were not a region known for feuding, he devotes a chapter to blood feuds elsewhere in Appalachia.

Despite the proximity of Bryson City to Qualla, the Cherokee receive only passing mention in *Our Southern Highlanders*. Kephart wrote a few articles on the Eastern Cherokee, most notably a series titled "The Strange Story of the Eastern Cherokees," published in three 1919 issues of *Outing Magazine*. After Horace Kephart's death, Laura Kephart (who had remained his wife despite his absence of three decades) reworked these articles into a small booklet, *The Cherokees of the Smoky Mountains*, which is still in print. Kephart's Cherokee writing is largely derived from Mooney's scholarship and contains none of the firsthand description characteristic of Kephart's other writing. In fact, he wrote little about the Eastern Band as it existed in the early twentieth century. Still, Kephart transformed Mooney's writings, published in scholarly ethnological journals, into material available to the average reader.

For good or ill, Kephart's other major contribution to the Great Smokies was his campaign for the national park. During the 1920s, he was a leading spokesman for the North Carolina promotion of the park, serving as chairman of the Great Smoky Mountains, Inc. He also wrote a considerable amount of promotional material for the proposed park, in pamphlets and magazines such as the *Tarheel Banker*. Ironically, although Kephart made his name writing about the residents of the Smokies, this promotional material touted the Smoky Mountains as an "empty wilderness."

Surely Kephart's motives were different from those of the Knoxville businessmen who also promoted the park, though he worked hand-in-hand with them. In *Our Southern Highlanders*, he wrote of the encroachment of the forestry industry: "Slowly, but inexorable, a leviathan was crawling into the wilderness and was soon to consume it." Kephart believed that the creation of a national park was the only way to protect the wild beauty of the mountains, though it would also disrupt forever the lives of the "highlanders" who lived there and would ultimately serve to "civilize" the mountains. Much of the campaign for the park focused on promoting decent roads into the Smokies. Despite his active involvement,

Kephart must have felt some ambivalence about the campaign's success. In a letter to his son, Kephart wrote, "Within two years we will have good roads into the Smokies, and then—well, then I'll get out."

Kephart did not live long enough to flee civilization again. In 1931, returning by taxi with a companion from a visit to a local bootlegger, he died in an accident. Hundreds of people came to Bryson City for his funeral, including members of his estranged family. While two months before his death the United States Geographic Board had honored Kephart by naming one of the high peaks of the Smokies after him, the National Park Service declined to allow his body to be buried in the Great Smoky Mountains National Park. His final resting place is a hill overlooking the town of Bryson City.

THE CRAFTS REVIVAL

Handicrafts are to many Americans the most visible evidence of a distinct traditional culture in Southern Appalachia. A simplistic interpretation of events is that these crafts were discovered just in time by outsiders, who, through heroic effort, managed to preserve this part of the region's tradition. The story, however, is more complicated than that, though crafts were indeed "discovered" in the 1890s, and a handicraft revival, well-documented in Allen Eaton's classic 1937 study, *The Handicrafts of the Southern Highlands*, spread throughout much of Appalachia.

Eaton began his study with two of the earliest and most influential "workers in the revival." During the 1890s, both Dr. William Goodell Frost of Berea College in Kentucky and Frances Louisa Goodrich, a social worker for the Home Mission Board of the Presbyterian Church stationed near Asheville, North Carolina, discovered traditional weaving in their regions and made it the centerpiece of new programs. These "fireside industries," as they were labelled by Frost, were designed not merely to preserve a beautiful traditional art but to provide social and economic benefits to the craftspeople and their communities.

The handicraft revival in Appalachia created such powerful images that the reality of the situation has been all but obscured. By the 1890s, handweaving and many other craft practices were in decline as the railroads made mass-produced items more available and affordable. Rural communities were also being drawn into a market economy and were relying less on production within the community itself. Not only was the weaving tradition vestigial when discovered by Goodrich and Frost, it had never actually existed as it was portrayed in the revival's romantic images.

Handwoven coverlets were common in many rural homes in the Great

Smoky Mountains region when Goodrich was first presented with one when she worked as a missionary in Brittain's Cove in Buncombe County. However, it is a false notion that there was once a time when every mountain home held a loom at which an old lady sat producing beautiful coverlets. For one thing, the large bulky looms did not fit into many traditional houses, especially if the family who lived there was large. If the family did own a loom it was often accommodated by some sort of a shed addition or separate "house." Some loom houses were converted to kitchens, since cookstoves and separate kitchens became popular about the same time as store-bought cloth. Furthermore, weaving was not practiced in every home. Even before the arrival of the railroad, it was a specialized craft within the rural community. Some weavers who did have looms were not skilled enough to produce coverlets. Nor can it be assumed that the individuals who did make the coverlets were always women. The European-American settlers of the Great Smokies region came from traditions in which weavers were frequently professional and male.

Nevertheless, having discovered a weaving tradition in western North Carolina, Goodrich commissioned three coverlets to be sold up north. The weavers she turned to, the Angel family on the Paint Fork of Ivy, perhaps illustrated the typical production set-up that still survived in the region at that time: a small home-based industry consisting of the combined labors of a husband, wife, and children. The skills were passed through families, though not all families. When Goodrich began her work, she identified a few master weavers, but, under the crafts revival, the continuation of the tradition quickly ceased to be a matter of family-based training.

Little is known about the weaving tradition in the Great Smoky Mountains before the beginning of the handicraft revival. Jan Davidson, in an introduction to a recent reissue of Goodrich's *Mountain Homespun* (originally published in 1931), notes that in preparing a display of forty coverlets from western North Carolina for an exhibit, it was discovered that the revival coverlets always had matched center seams, while the older ones did not. Perhaps, he suggests, the older looms made it difficult to produce an even beat, unlike the smaller efficient looms brought in by the missionaries. It is also possible that the older coverlets were frequently taken apart for washing or that matched seams were simply not an aesthetic priority. Whatever the case, Frances Goodrich and the subsequent craft school in the area maintained strict "quality control."

After discovering the weaving tradition in Brittain's Cove, Frances Goodrich persuaded the Home Mission Board to move north to the Laurel Country, a section of Madison County. There, at the community of Allanstand, she began her crafts work in earnest. In 1908 Goodrich took advantage of the tremendous growth in Asheville, due partially to the flood of tourists brought by the railroad, and opened the Allanstand shop on Main Street. The craft shop, which featured weaving as well as a number of other handicrafts, became a model for many other revival efforts in Southern Appalachia. In 1928 a number of these revival workers came together to form the Southern Mountain Handicraft Guild (later changed to Southern Highland Handicraft Guild, a name thought to be more elegant) and two years later an aging Goodrich turned over the Allanstand shop to the guild.

Several early North Carolina proponents of the national park wished to include Madison County's Laurel Country within its borders. Although logging had already begun to take its toll in this region, Goodrich did not think that the park would ultimately benefit the local people, and she campaigned early against the Laurel Country being included in any such plans. As it turned out, the crafts program most closely tied to the future of the Great Smoky Mountains National Park was not to be Allanstand but rather a craft program started by the Pi Beta Phi Settlement School in Gatlinburg, Tennessee. In 1910 the women of the national Pi Beta Phi Fraternity had decided to begin an education project among "mountain whites." The community of Gatlinburg in Sevier County, Tennessee, was chosen as the most worthy, and in 1912 a school was opened at the base of the Great Smoky Mountains. Partly as a result of Goodrich's success at Allanstand, crafts became a part of the school's agenda, and the weaving program began within a few years of the school's opening. By 1924 the Fireside Industries was paying for itself, and two years later the program became more formalized with the opening of the Arrow Craft (later Arrowcraft) Shop. With the creation of the Great Smoky Mountains National Park and the subsequent development of Gatlinburg into a boom town, Arrowcraft thrived and spawned other crafts operations in the town.

The operations at Arrowcraft and Allanstand, as well as in many of the other craft revival programs, were similar. Mountain women were taught a craft that presumably was part of their own tradition, but those who ran the programs retained firm control over aesthetic decisions. Most of the women who made such decisions about design and color, and who kept a strict eye on quality, were trained in northern schools. Goodrich herself studied at the Yale School of Fine Arts. Some of the teachers introduced nontraditional designs as well as new products, especially smaller items such as placemats that would sell well. At both Allanstand and Arrowcraft the market initially consisted of northern urbanites who wished to support a philanthropic endeavor, but both organizations quickly adapted to the growing tourist trade.

What were the motivations of the weavers themselves? While their philanthropic patrons may have had social, moral, and aesthetic uplift in mind, many of the weavers were clearly driven by economic need. The early twentieth century was not a prosperous time for many rural people in the Great Smoky Mountains region. More and more men were drawn to paid work away from the farm. Women took up the slack and in some cases sold their domestic space or skills. Many of the weavers during this period did not learn to weave from family or community members. However, the training provided by the crafts programs allowed them to bring in much-needed cash for their piecework.

As in most cases of revivalism, the question exists as to whether the traditional form was truly preserved or was reinvented. If handweaving stopped being a folk art in the Great Smoky Mountains (and this point is arguable), it was not so much because of the standardization of product and the introduction of new techniques and designs as because the products stopped reflecting the collective aesthetic preferences of the community that produced them. The pieces ceased to have artistic or utilitarian meaning for that community and became tourist arts.

As the market for tourist arts grew, the craftspeople of the Great Smoky Mountains region did not stay forever under the benevolent thumbs of the settlement schools. Perhaps some craftspeople regained a sense of personal aesthetic freedom, even if the community aesthetic was lost. Also, revival arts have a way of reintegrating themselves into community values, and in a few instances we now see second- and third-generation craftspeople being trained within the family, even though the family tradition might have originated in the settlement school or crafts program.

While weaving was perhaps the most emblematic of the folk revival crafts, it was not the only handicraft to be marketed through the settlement schools. White oak baskets were another popular item sold by Allanstand and Arrowcraft. As with weaving, basketry was probably never practiced on every homestead, and basketmakers operated on a professional or semiprofessional basis. Basketry was not as moribund as handweaving when the revival workers arrived in the Great Smokies region. Since the settlement schools did not totally usurp the traditional means of passing down the craft, basketry was perhaps less changed by the revival than weaving. However, the revival workers did introduce new forms (including a half-basket design from Germany) and induced the makers to include some color in their baskets. While they were more likely to be traditionally trained than the weavers, the basketmakers also became pieceworkers filling orders for the shops. This does not mean, of course, that the craftspeople did not reap economic benefits from this arrangement, particularly as their wares came to be seen not as practical items with a market in the rural community but as aesthetic ones sold to affluent tourists.

As tourism boomed in the region, the shops created by the settlement schools prospered. Some traditional craftspeople, including basketmakers, chairmakers, and broommakers, took the opportunity to market directly to the tourist. The settlement school programs also spawned a new type of craftsperson such as O. J. Mattil, who came to the Pi Beta Phi School to teach woodworking and ultimately started his own shop for the making of reproduction furniture. New generations of professionally trained craftspeople, who have either attended schools in the region or been drawn there by the interest in crafts, now dominate much of the craft market.

The discovery of folk crafts in the Great Smoky Mountains and elsewhere in Appalachia represented in some sense a turning point for those who defined the region in terms of what it lacked culturally. For the first time, benevolent workers began to portray the region as having a positive indigenous culture. If it was perceived that mountain people had to be taught their own culture, at least such a culture existed.

Although receiving only passing mention in most accounts of the crafts revival in the "highlands," the Eastern Cherokee also experienced a crafts revival. As elsewhere in the Great Smokies region, the cash economy at the turn of the century had led to a significant decline in spinning and weaving, and the federal government generally discouraged the perpetuation of traditional crafts. This attitude began to change in the early years of this century after the Superintendent of Education in the Indian Office suggested that crafts could be a source of additional income for Indians. The viability of Cherokee crafts as a market was provided by the tourists who were beginning to stream into western North Carolina. The Cherokee Fair, organized in 1914, became another important outlet for the marketing of crafts.

As the promotion of crafts grew with the Cherokees' increasing economic reliance on tourism, the revival of Cherokee crafts received an official boost with the advent of the "Indian New Deal" of the 1930s. Franklin Roosevelt's new Commissioner of Indian Affairs, John Collier, encouraged the preservation of tribal cultures, including traditional arts and crafts. Some within the Eastern Band of Cherokee, including traditionalists and the most acculturated, were suspicious of this change of federal government attitude, and at least one critic suggested that it was an effort to enhance tourist interest in Cherokee, North Carolina, now the southern entrance of the new national park. In any case, along with promoting traditional crafts, the Cherokee Indian Agency organized a crafts guild in 1933 as an auxiliary of the new Southern Mountain Handicraft Guild.

As with European-American crafts, the "revival" changed, as much as it preserved, the nature of Cherokee crafts. Some crafts, such as weaving, had already been strongly influenced by European-American tradition, and the pottery that was made for tourists originated in part with the Catawba Indians. The carving of small wooden animals became a popular handicraft among men, as it was in non-Indian crafts programs. However, one of the most popular of the early tourist items was the handmade blow gun, the use of which had remained a traditional skill among some Cherokee.

Although the European-American craft revival in Appalachia has received a greater amount of scholarly attention, the promotion of Cherokee crafts has perhaps had a more enduring effect on the craftspeople. Far more than was the case among white Appalachians, the products of Cherokee traditional culture became a commodity to be bought and sold, and the effect of tourism on the local economy was more profound than that of the settlement schools and craft programs. While the selling of culture is viewed with ambivalence by some Cherokees, revival crafts have begun to be seen as traditional. Although many older Cherokee craftspeople were also taught their cultures by outsiders (in their case this often occurred in federal boarding schools rather than in settlement schools), family crafts traditions have grown, and aesthetic control and creativity now reside within the community.

THE "DISCOVERY" OF MOUNTAIN MUSIC AND DANCE

The revival of mountain crafts was accompanied by a corresponding "discovery" of an indigenous music and dance tradition. However, music and dance were not as successfully co-opted by those with philanthropic interests, so the situation took a somewhat different form. Although the settlement and folk schools did make some attempts to present traditional music, the initial attention to Appalachian music and dance was more scholarly than philanthropic in nature.

After Mooney's article in the second volume of the *Journal of American Folklore*, the folk song tradition of the Smoky Mountains region received occasional notice in the pages of that journal. Earlier folk song scholarship in America tended to focus on manuscript sources and the English tradition. In the early twentieth century, American folklorists were just beginning to discover a living folk song tradition in their own country. The person perhaps most responsible for focusing early attention on the Southern Appalachian tradition was Olive Dame Campbell, the wife of John C. Campbell, Director of the Southern Highland Division of the Russell Sage Foundation. Campbell, in travelling with her husband through the region, had been impressed by the folk songs she heard and began to collect them. Wanting this work to be continued by the "most competent" person, Campbell approached English folk song collector Cecil Sharp. The outbreak of World War I had dampened Sharp's work with the folk song and dance revival in England, and the noted collector was in America to make a living and stir up some interest in the revival in this country. At Campbell's urging, Sharp set forth with his assistant, Maud Karpeles, to follow up on Campbell's pioneering work.

If Kephart came to the Great Smoky Mountains region to discover America's lost frontier, Sharp found, in Karpeles's words, the "England of his dreams." Instead of having to confine his collecting to the elderly, as he had done in England, he discovered that in the Laurel Country of North Carolina singing among all age groups was "as common and almost as universal a practice as speaking." Sharp was thrilled to find a vigorous folk song tradition. Between 1916 and 1918, Sharp and Karpeles would spend forty-six weeks conducting fieldwork in the southern Appalachian Mountains.

Although their travels would take them to Virginia, Kentucky, and West Virginia, as well as to North Carolina and Tennessee, Karpeles would subsequently write in her preface to the second edition of Sharp's *English Folk Songs from the Southern Appalachians* that the most fertile ground for folk songs was "on either side of the big mountain range (known as the 'Great Divide') which separates the States of North Carolina and Tennessee." Sharp and Karpeles used Asheville as their jumping-off point, as would subsequent generations of ballad collectors, and much of their early work was conducted in the North Carolina counties of Buncombe and Madison. However, the team also collected elsewhere in the Great Smoky Mountains region, in Haywood and Jackson counties in North Carolina, and in Knox County and Sevier County, Tennessee.

Karpeles believed that the Great Smoky Mountains region was the richest source of folk songs in Appalachia because it was less touched by the forces of modernization and industrialization than Virginia, West Virginia, and Kentucky. However, it was no coincidence that Sharp had been led to Goodrich's Laurel Country in Madison County. Under the guidance of Olive Campbell, Sharp used the network of mountain philanthropic organizations for board and lodging in his travels and in western North Carolina specifically relied on the hospitality of Presbyterian missionaries. One of his first destinations was Allanstand.

Although Sharp appreciated the support of the various philanthropic organizations, and sometimes found common ground in their interest in the preservation, or revival, of folk traditions, he was skeptical about the intent of the missionaries. The rural people of the Smoky Mountains region were sometimes undereducated, but they were definitely not, in Sharp's mind, uncultured, and he was concerned about tampering with traditions. The rural people Sharp worked with seemed to appreciate his attitude. He wrote that many "assumed that strangers like ourselves could have but one object and that to 'improve', and their relief was obvious when they found that we came not to give but to receive."

Perhaps because Sharp was not American, he was remarkably free of the prejudicial attitudes that characterized most assessments of Appalachian culture during the period. His great respect for the culture was not double-edged; if anything, he deliberately overlooked any negative aspects of it. However, Sharp's romanticized descriptions contributed to other cultural stereotypes. Although his documentation of a living folk song tradition derived from England and Scotland was significant, Sharp contributed to the image of Appalachia as a repository of pure Anglo-Saxon culture. Sharp and other folk song collectors were not interested in many of the region's forms of music that were cultural hybrids, although, to Sharp's credit, the second edition of *English Folk Songs from the Southern Appalachians* did include lyrical songs, hymns, nursery songs, jigs and play-party games, as well as traditional ballads. However, noting a total absence of songs of a ritual nature, Sharp overlooked the religious song tradition, except for five hymns included in his collection. He also found the dance tradition to be decadent and, according to Karpeles, the instrumental tunes that accompanied the dancing were judged to be of little value.

If Campbell and Sharp brought national attention to the Southern Appalachian folk song tradition, the person most responsible for promoting Appalachian music and dance in the Great Smoky Mountains region was Bascom Lamar Lunsford. Unlike Mooney, Kephart, Goodrich, and Sharp, Lunsford was a native of the region whose culture he helped define and promote. Born in 1882 in Madison County, North Carolina, to a fairly well-to-do educated family, Lunsford engaged in a variety of occupations including teaching, selling trees, and marketing honey, before obtaining a law degree. His childhood in Madison and Buncombe counties and his early travels throughout western North Carolina had instilled in him a deep interest in the music and dance of the region. Already a collector of folk music, Lunsford began lecturing on and performing the music he loved soon after receiving his law degree. Several years later, Lunsford, in a stint as a special agent for the Justice Department during the First World War, travelled to Washington, D.C. He met Maud Karpeles there, and she introduced him to scholarly folklorists and collectors.

Lunsford served academic folklore as both a collector and an informant. While he collected folk songs from traditional singers in western North Carolina, a number of prominent folklorists collected songs directly from him. Columbia University and the Archive of American Folk-Song at the Library of Congress eventually made extensive recordings of

Bascom Lamar Lunsford with legendary banjo player Samantha Bumgarner (Photo courtesy of Lunsford Scrapbook, Photographic Archives, Mars Hill College)

his repertoire. Lunsford also acted as local guide for a number of visiting folklorists. In 1925, on the first leg of what was to be an extensive folk song collecting trip throughout America, Robert Winslow Gordon arrived in Asheville and was guided through the region by Lunsford in order to record songs on wax cylinders. When Gordon began his duties as the first director of the Archive of American Folk-Song in 1928, he appointed

Lunsford as a district collector. In 1930, Dorothy Scarborough of Columbia University made a field trip to Virginia and North Carolina in search of ballads. On arriving in North Carolina, she made straight for Bascom Lamar Lunsford, the man "who is doing more than any one else in the region to bring people to realize the interest and value of the native folk arts, singing, fiddle-playing, dancing and so forth."

Lunsford's primary contribution, however, was not as a scholar or even as a writer, but as a promoter. Following the lead of the philanthropic organizations, the Asheville Chamber of Commerce was learning that mountain culture was a commodity that could be sold. In 1928, the group organized a Rhododendron Festival to attract tourists and asked Lunsford to present a program of folk dances and music. The next year he separated the program from the Rhododendron Festival and created the Mountain Dance and Folk Festival. While this was only one of a number of festivals and programs Lunsford was to organize, it was the most successful. Lunsford presided over it until his death in 1974, and the festival still continues today. Although created in part for tourists, the Mountain Dance and Folk Festival received support from the region and was not simply a presentation for outsiders. Lunsford's festival was influential in the development of other festivals both in and outside of the region; Sarah Gertrude Knott, founder of the National Folk Festival, especially, credited Lunsford's influence.

Unlike most of the folk song collectors who trooped through the Smoky Mountains region, Lunsford, perhaps because he was a native, had a broader vision of the folk song tradition there. Although he had a more encompassing view of folk music than many, Gordon was little interested in the instruments more recently introduced to the region or in stringband music. Scarborough wrote that it would be interesting to record a "complete song chart of a small, isolated section" but did not live to carry out that project and on her ventures to North Carolina restricted herself to English ballads. Lunsford was more open to newer forms of music, and he particularly promoted dance and stringband music. He was himself a two-finger banjo picker.

Of course, Lunsford also had his biases in what he promoted. He documented African-American and Cherokee traditions in the Great Smoky Mountains region but seldom featured them at his festival. His own aesthetic preferences often ruled at the festival and he emphasized the competitive element of local song and dance traditions. Local dance traditions were especially changed by Lunsford's efforts, and he is often credited with (or blamed for) the popularization of team clogging. While Lunsford was said to have mildly resisted clogging, he did permit it, and it became an important feature of the festival, eventually altering the perception of traditional Appalachian dance.

By the 1920s, interest in Appalachian music was beginning to diverge down two separate paths. The most intriguing aspect of Lunsford's career was that he followed both. Academic folklorists continued to seek and document what they defined as "traditional." Their efforts found added support during the 1930s with the popularism and public works of the New Deal. However, traditional Appalachian music also began to find a popular outlet through commercial recordings and radio. Not only did Lunsford work with the academic folklorists, he also did much to popularize regional stringband music. His festival featured several of the early "hillbilly" musicians recorded by commercial labels, and Lunsford himself was recorded by Okeh and several other commercial recording companies. Lunsford also wrote the original version of "Mountain Dew," popularized by Lulu Belle and Scott Wiseman. In the 1930s, Lunsford collaborated on several projects with Kentuckian John Lair, creator of the Renfro Valley Barn Dance. While Lunsford eschewed the costumes and other trappings of "hillbilly" music, he did not deny the authenticity of the music itself.

In the 1950s, Karpeles returned to western North Carolina to see if she could find some of Sharp's former singers. Later, in her biography of Cecil Sharp, she wrote, "The region is no longer the folk-song collector's paradise, for the serpent, in the form of the radio, has crept in, bearing its insidious hill-billy and other 'pop' songs." However, the music of the region, never "pure" to start with, was a major influence in the creation of hillbilly (and later country-western) music. Perhaps Lunsford understood that Appalachian music transformed popular music as much as it was in turn transformed.

While western North Carolina is one of the best-known areas for the collection of traditional music, the other side of the "Great Divide" was not neglected by the ballad scholars. Another native of the region, Mildred Haun, was from Cocke County, Tennessee, and was educated at Vanderbilt University, where she came under the influence of the members of the English Department associated with the Fugitive movement. In 1937, under the direction of Donald Davidson and John Crowe Ransom, Haun completed her master's thesis, "Cocke County Ballads and Songs." Collecting mostly from her own family, Haun produced a work that was one of the first studies to focus exclusively on the Tennessee ballad tradition. Subsequently, Haun put her energies into fictionalized accounts of the community in which she was raised. Her collection of short stories, *The Hawk's Done Gone*, was published in 1940.

George Pullen Jackson, a professor of German at Vanderbilt University, focused on the religious song tradition, which was usually neglected by the folk song collectors. Although his work was not based as extensively on fieldwork, Jackson devoted much of his career to study of the "shape note" singers of the Upper South. While his work covered an area vastly larger than the Smoky Mountains region, without his scholarship this component of the religious song tradition might have been neglected in the folk music scholarship of the region. Though some of his conclusions have since been challenged, Jackson's *White Spirituals in the Southern Uplands*, first published in 1933, is a classic study of the "fasola" and "dorayme" folk.

Although the full significance of their contributions have only recently been recognized, two husband-and-wife teams documented the folk song tradition on the Tennessee side of the Great Smoky Mountains region during the 1930s and 1940s. Edwin Kirkland, who held a Ph.D. in English literature from Northwestern University, came to the University of Tennessee in 1931. During the middle and late 1930s, Kirkland and his wife, Mary, made extensive field recordings of folk music in Knoxville itself and in areas that could be reached in a day's drive, including Gatlinburg, Sevierville, and Townsend. About the time that the Kirklands' work was winding down in the early 1940s, Mary Elizabeth Barnicle and Tillman Cadle settled in Townsend. A professor of English at New York University, Barnicle had had extensive fieldwork experience during the 1930s collecting African-American folklore in the South with Alan Lomax and Zora Neale Hurston and recording traditional and protest music in mining communities in southeast Kentucky. In Kentucky, she met former miner and union activist Tillman Cadle, whom she married.

Both teams of collectors had fairly broad notions of what to collect in east Tennessee. Edwin Kirkland's motto was "collect everything," and he felt that rural mountain folk were not the only bearers of tradition in the region. The Kirklands made extensive use of informants in the professional and academic community in Knoxville and also recognized the merits of the local radio stations in discovering the traditional music of the region. Barnicle and Cadle recorded the religious song tradition as well as the humor and narrative traditions of Southern Appalachia.

Although their intentions were different, the ballad scholars, like the craft revivalists, helped convey to the rest of the world the idea that a pure culture had been preserved in the Great Smoky Mountains region, at the same time helping to transform that culture into a marketable commodity.

Changing Traditions in the Twentieth Century

CHAPTER 3

Music and Dance

CHEROKEE SONG AND DANCE

The music and dance tradition with the deepest historical roots in the Great Smoky Mountains region is that of the Cherokee Indians. Song and dance were an integral part of the traditional belief system of the Cherokee people. Religious ceremonies incorporated dance, and even social dances had sacred elements. Ritual dance was believed to insure the welfare of both the individual and the community. Nineteenth-century pressures on the Cherokees to acculturate to white ways, however, took their toll on traditional music and dance. Even before the Removal, the establishment of a secular form of self-government separated political and religious leadership. Christian missionaries attempted to eradicate traditional ritual, and, as many Cherokees converted to Christianity, the pressure to dismantle traditional belief systems became internal. Baptists, in particular, opposed dance in general and especially dance linked to rival belief systems.

The death knell has been rung for traditional Cherokee dance many times; still it has persisted, undergoing a number of revivals during the past century. The person most responsible for bringing traditional Cherokee dance into the twentieth century was Will West Long, the son of a Cherokee minister. Born about 1870, West Long, along with many other Cherokees of his generation, was sent off to boarding school against his will. After returning to Qualla, West Long's abilities and intellect were noticed by anthropologist James Mooney, who hired him as an aide and interpreter. His association with Mooney inspired West Long to conduct his own study of traditional Cherokee culture. After spending nine years away from his home studying at the Hampton Institute and pursuing his career, West Long returned to Qualla to dedicate his life to preserving the traditional culture of the Eastern Band.

Under Will West Long's leadership, traditional dance continued at Qualla, especially in the Big Cove community, through the first several decades of the twentieth century. During the 1930s and 1940s, West Long not only provided leadership for the continuation of the tradition among his own people but also collaborated with anthropologists Frank G. Speck

Cherokee dancers led by
Will West Long, 1937
(Photo courtesy of Great
Smoky Mountains National
Park)

and Leonard Broom in the scholarly study *Cherokee Dance and Drama*, first published in 1951. Working with West Long, Speck and Leonard were able to describe traditional dances still extant, as well as those which survived only in West Long's memory.

Speck and Broom found a high degree of allegorical drama in Cherokee ceremonial dance. They believed that by the twentieth century the dramatic and performative elements of the dance had eclipsed the magical or curative value, although the degree of belief in the efficacy of dance varied with the participants. Dancing was accompanied by the singing of chants and the use of a few instruments: gourd rattles, a wooden water drum, and turtle shell leg rattles worn by women dancers. A "driver" was appointed by the host of the dance to direct the course of the dances. The dance style consisted of a low shuffling gait with the knees bent and the body inclined forward. Dramatic gesture was used only at specified moments in the dance.

The dances documented by Speck and Broom included various social and animal dances that could be held at any time of year, as well as those performed in a specific season. The Booger, Eagle, and Bear dances were only danced in the winter, while the Green Corn and Ballplayers' dances

Women dancing the
Green Corn Dance at the
Cherokee Indian Fair,
1926 (Photo courtesy of
Great Smoky Mountains
National Park)

were performed in the summer. The ethnologists seemed especially fascinated by the Booger dance, in which masked men portray various types of non-Indians. The dance is particularly noted for its use of lewd humor and clown-like behavior.

Will West Long died in 1947, leaving behind a vacuum in leadership regarding the preservation of traditional dance. In the years immediately after West Long's death, Speck and Broom were not optimistic about the survival of traditional Cherokee dance. In *Cherokee Dance and Drama* (p. 6), they expressed particular concern about the assault on traditional dance by Cherokee preachers:

Cherokee ceremonials would disappear soon, in any event, out of sheer growth of ignorance and loss of interest, but this energetic attack from within strikes at the self-confidence of the leaders, reduces their prestige with possible participants, and surely hastens the day when the ribaldry of the Booger Dance and the solemnity of the Green Corn Dance will no longer be known. The preservation of superficial aspects of the dances adapted for the entertainment, if not the edification, of tourists will do little to postpone this event.

During the post-World War II era, tourism in Cherokee boomed. The dances were dramatically shortened to a few minutes each, and the number of dancers decreased from the hundreds who once performed to fewer than a dozen. In some instances, Plains Indians costume was incorporated, as were the high steps of Plains "fancy dance," which contrasted with the low shuffling step of traditional Cherokee dance.

To the outsider it would seem that Speck and Broom's prediction has come true. Today traditional Cherokee dance seems to exist only as a much-altered remnant of the past to be performed for tourists and school-children. However, as one dance scholar, Olivia Skipper Rivers, notes, it is important to distinguish between "dances performed" and "dances held." While traditional dancing may not have thrived in the years following West Long's death, in the traditional community of Big Cove, well off the tourists' beaten track, several individuals struggled to preserve dance in a form closer to the original. These were not dances performed for outsiders but were social events held for individuals within the community. In many other parts of Qualla, however, traditional dancing as a social event became only a memory.

In the past two decades, a resurgence of interest in traditional dance and music has taken place at Qualla. The United States bicentennial inspired some early efforts, notably the revival of the Green Corn Dance. However, a more important influence has been the renewal of ties between the Eastern and Western Bands of Cherokee. At the first gathering of the bands in 1984, a new leader in the preservation of dance and music emerged. Walker Calhoun, a half-nephew of Will West Long, achieved public attention as a ceremonial singer at this gathering and was soon organizing his children and grandchildren into a group known as the Raven Rock Dancers. Four years later, at a gathering of the Eastern and Western Bands, Calhoun became the first recipient of the Sequoyah Award, created to honor contributions to the preservation of Cherokee culture. Calhoun has also gained recognition for his efforts from non-Cherokees. In 1989 he received a North Carolina Folk Heritage Award and in 1992 was designated a National Heritage Fellow by the National Endowment for the Arts.

Both the performance of traditional dance and the holding of traditional social dances have been revitalized. The dance grounds at Big Cove have been resanctified and, at the annual Cherokee Fall Festival, the number of dance performances has swelled. Dances performed have been aimed more directly at Cherokee audiences, rather than exclusively at tourists. The annual gatherings of the Eastern and Western Bands have provided an important venue for Cherokee dance. Cultural exchanges have also taken place on a more intimate level. Walker Calhoun travelled to Oklahoma, where he participated in a stomp dance, and he has since been active in working with Cherokee dancers from the Western Band in reviving the stomp dance religion.

Pan-Indianism has also played a role in reviving interest in dance, as well as in altering traditions. The growing number of pan-Indian pow-wows and dance festivals provides another arena for Cherokee dancers as well as exposure to other cultural styles. While the showy Plains Indian dance styles and costumes have been used to attract tourists (many of whom associate all American Indians with Plains Indians), the pow-wows have inspired a growing audience for "fancy dance" styles among Cherokee audiences. The festivals and pow-wows also add a competitive aspect to the dancing, as cash prizes are usually awarded.

While the financial rewards of dancing for tourist dollars or prize money lead to a greater emphasis on individual skill, Cherokee dancers have generally valued the feeling of group harmony that comes with dancing in unison. The degree to which dance is still linked to traditional belief systems varies from dancer to dancer and is a private matter often not shared with outsiders. However, leaders such as Walker Calhoun have helped reinfuse traditional Cherokee dance with a spiritual quality. To some extent the sacred quality of dance today lies not in the belief in specific rites but in the link to tradition and the past.

Not all of Cherokee music and dance has roots in the pre-Removal era. Fiddle playing, banjo picking, and ballad singing were all adopted by the Cherokees from their non-Indian neighbors. Since the 1930s, clogging has been popular among some Cherokees (and it is possible that Cherokee dance influenced the development of clogging in this century). Cherokee clogging groups compete with non-Indian groups at festivals within the Great Smoky Mountains region, and clogging, as well as traditional dance, is featured at the Cherokee Fall Festival.

Among the musical forms that derive from non-Indian sources, one of the most important among the Cherokee is the singing of hymns and gospel songs. While the tunes may be familiar to non-Indians, the songs are often sung in the Cherokee language. For some members of the Eastern Band, hymns provide a contact with the language that is no longer spoken among many families and communities. As with the non-Indian communities in the Great Smokies, gospel quartets are extremely popular. They perform at regular services, funerals, baptisms, and other special occasions as well as at yearly singings.

One such event is the annual Trail of Tears Singing held at Snowbird in Graham County, fifty miles west of the Qualla Boundary. The three-day event was begun in 1968 and was modelled after a similar singing in Oklahoma. Before the gatherings of the Eastern and Western Bands were established in the 1980s, the two Trail of Tears singings provided an opportunity for exchange between Oklahoma and North Carolina Cherokees. Today, the Trail of Tears Singing is attended by Oklahoma Cherokee and Cherokee from Qualla (the small Snowbird population is, in fact, outnumbered by Cherokee participants from elsewhere). Non-Indians also attend the event, both as audience and as performers. A number of non-Indian gospel groups perform and, as with most contemporary gospel, much of the singing is backed up by electric instruments. The Cherokee groups also perform with electric instruments, though the majority sing at least some of their selections in the Cherokee language. The event celebrates both the shared ethnic traditions of all Cherokee and the shared religious beliefs of Christian Cherokee and their non-Indian neighbors.

The Trail of Tears Singing as a celebration of tradition differs from those events that feature traditional Cherokee song and dance. While many outsiders might see the event as "less traditional," this is not the conclusion of one anthropologist, Sharlotte Neely. In *Snowbird Cherokees: People of Persistence* (p. 115), she wrote: "[T]he crafts, dances, and stickball games at the Fall Festival are often attempts to revitalize such traditions for a younger generation of Cherokees who have no personal experiences with such endeavors. By contrast, the traditionalism at the Trail of Tears Singing need not be orchestrated since the Cherokee tongue is still a living language in Snowbird."

Whether it means singing Christian hymns in the Cherokee language or performing traditional dance, singing and dance among the Eastern Cherokee can be an act of celebrating Cherokee identity. The singing of gospel music is also an assertion of Christian beliefs, while participating in traditional dance is sometimes an assertion of a link to another belief system (though it is quite possible for Cherokees to participate in both Christian and traditional Cherokee belief systems). However, the artistic qualities of these arts are equally important. People attend or participate in singings and dance for the love of the traditions themselves.

THE BALLAD TRADITION

Of all the European-American folk genres in the Great Smoky Mountains region, ballad singing is probably the best documented. For several decades folklorists seemed intent on capturing this tradition. It was of this region, especially the Laurel Country of Madison County, that Cecil Sharp wrote that singing was nearly as universal as speaking. However, his assistant, Maud Karpeles, forty years later pronounced the tradition dead, or at least dying. Has the twentieth century witnessed the death of one of the Great Smoky Mountains' major folk traditions? Or were Sharp and Karpeles merely overstating their cases?

Traditionally, ballad singing was a private, rather than a public, event. It took place primarily within the context of the family, and it was there that the tradition was learned. Singing was unaccompanied and was largely performed solo. Part of the appeal of ballads is that they are narrative songs. They tell stories, which, more often than not, center around love and tragedy.

Collectors were particularly fascinated by songs surviving in the southern mountains that were of English or Scottish origins, especially those that were versions of ballads collected from manuscript sources in the 1880s by Harvard scholar Francis James Child. The so-called Child ballads did change as they were passed from generation to generation in the southern mountains. Generally, the songs were shortened, supernatural motifs were often lost and Christian morals were tagged on, local place names were sometimes added, and antiquated language was made comprehensible. What is remarkable, however, is that overall the songs changed so little. Ballads about kings and queens and sailing on faraway seas that continued to be sung in the mountains were easily recognized as variants of songs in Child's *English and Scottish Popular Ballads.*

The English ballads were only a fragment of the traditional singer's repertoire. Then, as now, the two main categories of songs among traditional singers in the region were love songs and sacred songs. The category "love songs" covered the whole spectrum of secular song. (As one ballad singer commented, they are more often about murder than love.) While they included the Child ballads, these antiquated ballads hardly exhausted the category of love songs.

While sacred songs were the songs of church and the singing schools, they were also frequently sung at home (and in some homes were the only songs permitted). These songs were of little interest to Sharp or the other early ballad collectors, except for the few rare cases of English ballads with religious themes. If Sharp turned a deaf ear to the sacred music of the region, he also ignored secular songs that did not fit his narrow definition of folk song. By the time Sharp was collecting ballads in the region, a number of nineteenth-century parlor songs had already entered the repertoire of many ballad singers. It is likely that Sharp politely ignored these offerings.

A song-writing tradition also existed in the Great Smoky Mountains region. As in the English broadside tradition, songs were written about local events. Some of these songs were ephemeral, existing only as long as interest in the event did. Others found a permanent place in the tradition. Ballads written about events in nearby regions, such as the North Carolina ballad "Tom Dula" (or "Dooley," reflecting regional pronunciation of the name), became well known. From an even more distant source, "The Murder of Colonel Sharp," reciting the event surrounding an 1825 murder in central Kentucky, became part of the repertoire of some ballad singers in western North Carolina.

As trains became a fixture in the lives of people in the Smoky Mountains, they (or the tragedies they sometimes engendered) inspired songs. A 1909 wreck of a logging train in the Great Smoky Mountains near Elkmont, Tennessee, which killed engineer Gordon A. Bryson and brakeman Charles M. Jenkins, inspired several songs. The best remembered is "Daddy Bryson's Last Ride," sung to the popular tune "Red Wing."

Ballad writing became a commercial enterprise for some in the Smoky Mountains. In her 1937 thesis, Mildred Haun gave an account of Joshia Adams, an "old bachelor" who lived in eastern Cocke County, Tennessee. According to Haun, Adams travelled by horseback to Newport twice a week to hear the news of the world and to peddle the songs he had written based on the news he had heard during the previous trip. Adams printed the songs himself on a homemade press, sometimes using paper bags and other recycled material, and sold the songs for a nickel a sheet. Country music historian Charles Wolfe calls these rural minstrels who sang at county courthouses and sold their "ballet cards" the "first professional (or semi-professional) musicians of country music."

While songwriting found a commercial outlet, unaccompanied ballad singing as a whole did not. Although much loved by the folklorists and folk revivalists, it did not find the mass media outlet that regional instrumental music did. Perhaps for this reason, the ballad-singing tradition changed less but was less vital in the twentieth century than the instrumental tradition. However, it is clear that Karpeles overstated her case. Ballad singing is no longer common, but ballad singers who learned through traditional means can still be found. Most come from families with strong singing traditions.

The best-known ballad singing community is in the Laurel Country of Madison County, North Carolina, which is not surprising considering the attention the region received from Sharp and other ballad hunters. Despite the fame of Sodom-Laurel as a ballad-singing community, it is evident that the tradition was preserved not so much by the community itself as by an extended family of ballad singers. The question that arises is: did the community simply continue its rich tradition of ballad singing, or did Sharp's attention provide a form of validation, hence helping to preserve the tradition? Perhaps this is not an answerable question. The current Laurel ballad singers are well aware of Sharp, but they have not let his book define their tradition. Many can tell which songs he "missed" or got wrong and persist in singing their own particular versions of the ballads, despite any variance with Sharp's collection.

Among the best known of the current generation of Sodom-Laurel ballad singers is Doug Wallin, winner of a National Heritage Award.

Doug's mother remembered Cecil Sharp's visit to the Laurel Country. Although she didn't sing for him (Doug isn't sure why), Doug's great-aunt, Jane Gentry, was one of Sharp's most important sources of ballads. Doug learned in the traditional manner, simply being around ballads and ballad singers. "Speaking of ballads, I learned from my mother mostly. The ones I know. I was barely paying attention to her when I was about six or seven years old. I learned that there was a story in most of these old songs. I was interested in the story to see how they came out. I learned some from my daddy, too. Maybe some from my uncles." He added, "My mother was singing just about all the time. She'd sing at her work or whatever she was doing. And I was always ready to listen. Strange how none of my other brothers or sister never did take that up. Never could understand that."

Most of the versions of ballads Doug Wallin sings are the ones he learned from his mother, though his father knew other versions of the same songs, probably learned from Doug's father's half-sister. Lee Wallin was also a fiddle and banjo player and though he had a fine voice was not as well known a ballad singer as his brother Cas, perhaps because his taste in songs ran to the humorous. "He was a jolly kind of fellow. He liked the funny songs." Within the family there were also stylistic variants. Cas Wallin had a more ornamented way of singing, a style Doug characterizes as more emotional. "I just believe in raring back and singing."

Doug Wallin's repertoire includes a couple of hundred songs. Some, like his favorite song, "Bed of Primroses," which Doug characterizes as an old Irish ballad, are not in Sharp's collection. Another song he often performs, "House Carpenter," is a version of a well-known Child ballad, "James Harris" (Child 243). Version B in Child, which Doug's version most resembles, dates from a 1785 manuscript in the British Museum. While these songs have passed from generation to generation largely unchanged ("I stick pretty well with the way I learned"), Doug has been known to add a verse of two: "Done that on a few. For instance, that song about Tom Dooley. The last verse there, I made me one for the last verse. Sounded pretty good. About as good as the rest of it." Doug has also tried his hand at writing a ballad about local events.

Unlike Maud Karpeles, Doug Wallin is not concerned about the ballad tradition dying out. "I don't think it ever will . . . it's not like this modern stuff they're putting out. They sung some of them out. Lose their popularity. These old ones, they just keep going back and getting them." Later he added, "You have to learn how to love these songs. What counts more than anything else is when you get them down and they're coming from the heart, that's what counts. Put some feeling in it. Make it realistic."

SHAPE NOTES AND SACRED MUSIC

The sacred song tradition is less well documented than the ballad tradition in the Smoky Mountains region. However, the survival of one form of congregational singing is remarkable. Shape-note singing is believed to have its origins in eighteenth-century New England with the creation of singing schools intended to improve congregational singing in the churches. Itinerant teachers would set up these schools on a subscription basis to teach the principles of singing. While the songs were sacred, the atmosphere of the singing school was more often secular. Although ostensibly religious in nature, the singing schools provided an approved form of socializing in many communities.

The most difficult task the singing master had was to teach the pupils to read musical notation. About 1800, compilers of singing-school books began experimenting with aids to teach the reading of music. One solution was the use of shaped note heads. Initially only four shapes were used, reflecting the traditional English method of singing the scale fa-sol-la-fa-sol-la-mi-fa. The popularity of shape-note books in singing schools took off, and several dozen different song books were published during the first half of the nineteenth century.

Shape-note singing schools became especially popular on the frontier and in the rural Upper South. Musical reformers of the mid-to-late nineteenth century did not approve of the shape-note method, and "modern" forms of teaching music were introduced in public schools in urban areas in the northeast. Urban congregations also began to use standardized hymn books that did not use shaped notes. However, singing schools that used the shape-note books persisted into the twentieth century in many rural areas of the South, including the Great Smoky Mountains region. A singing master would make a circuit through rural communities during the summer. The singing schools in this region typically lasted two weeks, and frequently the singing master's circuit would culminate in an all-day singing in the early fall.

The musical reformers were not without their influence in shape-note singing. During the mid-nineteenth century, some song books introduced a seven-shape system to reflect the more modern way of singing the scale. Although four-note books (especially Benjamin Franklin White's *Sacred Harp*) remain popular in some regions to the present day, most of the new books published after the Civil War used seven shapes.

While the earliest singing schools in the Great Smoky Mountains region were formed decades earlier, the two most influential books in this area were published soon after the Civil War. William "Singing Billy" Walker of Spartanburg, South Carolina, claimed that divine inspiration drove him to abandon the four-shape system, and in 1866 he replaced his thirty-year-old *Southern Harmony* with a new seven-note songbook. Walker's *Christian Harmony* remains the shape-note collection of preference in western North Carolina, although nearby in north Georgia, singers still cling to the four-shape *Sacred Harp*. One of the earliest of the seven-shape books was W. H. and M. L. Swan's *The Harp of Columbia* published in Knoxville, Tennessee, in 1848. In 1867, M. L. Swan published a revised version titled *The New Harp of Columbia*. This book remains the standard song book for shape-note singers (called "harp singers" or "old harp singers") on the Tennessee side of the Great Smoky Mountains.

The singing schools for the most part disappeared in the early twentieth century, although shape-note singings continue in the Great Smoky Mountains region. The most traditional of these take place as annual singings in area churches or schools, usually in the spring or fall. These events combine the older traditional singers with the swelling number of younger revivalists, many originally from outside the region. As with the older singing schools, contemporary singings combine the sacred and the secular. The singings usually take place on Sundays (in some cases replacing the usual church service) and feature morning and afternoon singing with a potluck dinner in between.

For the uninitiated, shape-note singing, particularly as practiced by the traditional singers, can produce a strong response. The music has an eerie, spine-tingling effect that usually either fascinates or repels. As in the southern folk preaching tradition, emotion and volume are valued over formal training, and, in the democratic spirit, all are encouraged to sing, not just those with the best voices. The unusual harmonic effect is produced partially by the fact that the high female voices are not carrying the melody as would be the case in modern congregational singing.

As in the ballad-singing tradition, there is no musical accompaniment for shape-note singing, although a pitchpipe is sometimes used for the initial pitch. The song is first sung through with the singers pronouncing the notes (do, re, mi, etc.), and then the verses ("poetry") are sung. Those used to hearing the standardized hymns of the church choir or gospel songs inspired by various forms of popular music will find this music different. The song books include European psalm tunes, early American hymns, anthems and fuguing pieces, and nineteenth-century spirituals from camp meetings and revivals. The song title is often the name of the tune—frequently a geographic location or the name of a secular song—and does not necessarily have any relationship to the lyric content of the song. However, the singers most frequently refer to the song, not by its title, but by its number in the song book.

Although "demonstration" singings are now sometimes held, the emphasis of the traditional singing is on participation, not performance. Ideally there is no audience. Everyone present is encouraged to participate, though in reality some do come just to listen. In Tennessee harp singing, the main core of singers sit in a square with the song leader in the middle. Members of the lead section, who sing the third line, sit in the front seats or pews facing the leader. To their left is the bass section, singing the bottom line, and to their right is the tenor or treble section, who sing from the top staff. Directly across from the lead are the altos. Except for the exclusively male bass section, women and men may sing any part. Typically, the altos are women and the tenors are usually, though not always, men. Not all the singers sit in the square, however. Latecomers, those new to the tradition, or those less confident in their abilities may fill out the pews or chairs behind the lead section and sing any part.

Usually a single individual presides over the singing. This person is responsible for selecting the song leaders. Anyone is entitled to lead a "lesson." In the past, women did not usually take the role of song leader, but this is no longer true. Regulars often have their own favorite song, which they are expected to lead. Songs may also be dedicated to others (or to the memory of others). Song leaders typically lead a couple of songs before sitting down again.

Wears Valley, just north of the Great Smoky Mountains National Park, is one center of Tennessee old harp singing. Despite its proximity to the tourist boom town of Pigeon Forge, with its encroaching suburban development, the valley still retains much of its pastoral feel and is an apt setting for the continuation of this tradition. Wears Valley hosts three annual singings, all held in the fall. The largest and oldest continuous sing in east Tennessee is the Wears Valley Old Harp Singing, now held at the Wearwood School. This singing had its start in 1898 when some Wears Valley residents asked old harp singers from nearby areas to a singing at the Wears Cove Baptist Church. The singings continued sporadically for the following two decades until 1921, when the singers voted to make it an annual event. In 1987, the singing was moved from the church to the school.

If the Wears Valley singing is the oldest and largest, the singing at Headrick's Chapel perhaps best gives the feel of the events as they once took place. The chapel was built in 1902 in the western end of the valley as a union church, serving Primitive Baptist, Missionary Baptist, and two Methodist congregations. An open belfry was added in 1907. Today the chapel is little changed and has received recent repair thanks in part to money raised at the annual singing. Old harp singing is believed to have begun at Headrick's Chapel around 1910; however, this singing apparently ended in the 1930s. The current singing "migrated" to Headrick's Chapel in 1968 when a group split off from the Townsend Primitive Baptist Church, where singings had been held since 1920.

Headrick's Chapel,
Wears Valley, Tennessee
(Photo by Hillary Glatt)

Older people in the Great Smokies region often like to say that they "don't know a stranger." This is certainly the case at the Headrick's Chapel singing (and most other old harp singings). Song books are provided for newcomers who arrive without one, and total strangers are urged forward to join the singing. And, of course, everyone is given the chance to lead a "lesson." The sense of open hospitality extends to the potluck lunch at the "recess." The singers make sure that strangers feel free to partake, whether they brought food or not.

The morning attendance at the Headrick's Chapel singing is sparse, as many singers choose to attend services at their own churches before coming (and others travel from far distances). However, even for many of the more religious participants, attending a singing is an acceptable activity for a Sunday morning. As one woman who grew up near the chapel stated, she tells her Sunday school teacher that she plans to be absent only once a year, when she "comes home" to the singing at Headrick's Chapel. In any case, by afternoon the ranks of the singers and listeners swell to the capacity of the small chapel.

A singing such as the one at Headrick's Chapel highlights the diversity of those who participate in the activity as well as the dual sacred/

secular character of shape-note singing. Some singers only attend one singing, which serves in a sense as a homecoming. On the other hand, passionate devotees will often travel long distances and attend many singings. Older participants often insist that it is the message of the "poetry" that is important, seeming more motivated by words than by music in choosing their lesson. For many, participating in a singing is a religious act. Still, it would be wrong to view the singings as consisting of two opposing groups of old-timers and revivalists. The love of the music and the act of fellowship bring all the singers together.

Old harp singing in east Tennessee continues to find new venues. The third singing in Wears Valley, at the Wears Valley Methodist Church, began in 1989. Three annual singings are now held in the Great Smoky Mountains National Park: at the Little Greenbriar Schoolhouse (as part of the annual homecoming), at the Cades Cove Primitive Baptist Church, and at the Sugarlands Visitors Center (as part of an annual Christmas celebration). Singings are also sponsored by local historical societies, Maryville College, the Museum of Appalachia, and the Dollywood theme park in Pigeon Forge. The Laurel Theater in Knoxville provides a secular setting for a monthly old harp singing. Efforts have been made recently to reinvigorate the institution of the singing school.

Shape-note singing also lives on in the memory of many older residents of the Great Smoky Mountains who do not participate in local singings. These people learned to read music in singing schools held periodically in their communities. It is not uncommon to find older people who will tell you that they can read shaped notes but not round ones. Some hymnals in Primitive Baptist and other rural churches also use shape notes. One young woman who had been raised elsewhere but had family in western North Carolina became choir director at a small rural church in the region. After the church ordered new hymnals, she was mystified when she began to find strange shapes pencilled in on the notes. Only after she discovered shape-note singings at a heritage festival did the mystery resolve itself.

While in the nineteenth century the singing of sacred music in the Great Smoky Mountains was generally unaccompanied (and this tradition has been continued by shape-note singers and some congregations), the accompaniment of sacred music by any number of instruments has become popular. The commercialization of traditional music that began in the 1920s united both the singing and instrumental traditions, as well as the sacred and secular musical traditions. Early twentieth-century string-band (or so-called "hillbilly") music included songs that were religious in nature. These were generally not the hymns and spirituals of the older shape-note collections but rather popular songs with religious or inspirational themes.

Although the label "gospel" music refers to a whole range of musical styles, it is generally associated with music dealing with religious themes that is set to popular, secular musical styles. Hence, stringband, bluegrass, and contemporary country music have all shaped gospel music in the Great Smoky Mountains region. As with the Cherokee, gospel quartets are popular with non-Indians and now frequently feature electrified instruments. It is remarkable that this is true in a region in which there has been a strong religious objection among many groups to any type of instrumental music. Until recently, local radio stations in the region have also played a role in popularizing gospel groups. Frequently a group would be able to buy time for a regular show on a local station with funds sent in by loyal fans.

Shape-note singing at Dollywood, 1994 (Photo by Hillary Glatt)

Instrumental Music

During the nineteenth century in Southern Appalachia, singing and instrumental music to a large extent developed separately. Singing, whether performed at home or in the church, was usually unaccompanied. Instrumental music, usually performed at dances or other community events, was more social in nature. While singing, especially of short, humorous couplets, sometimes accompanied dance music, the focus was on the music produced by the instrument, not the human voice.

The only instrument generally associated with the home-based ballad tradition is the Appalachian dulcimer. However, there is little evidence that the dulcimer actually existed in the Great Smoky Mountains region until the mid-twentieth century. Many scholars now believe that the dulcimer was a relatively rare instrument, not as widespread as once believed. Nineteenth-century dulcimers were found in certain pockets of eastern Kentucky, western West Virginia and southwestern Virginia but generally not as far south as the Smoky Mountains. These early dulcimers are believed to be variants of the straight-sided Pennsylvania German zither.

If the origins and early development of the Appalachian dulcimer are clouded in mystery, its elevation to the status of a symbol of Appalachian culture is clearly a result of its promotion by the settlement schools, particularly the Hindman Settlement School in Kentucky. Dulcimers were possibly introduced to southwestern North Carolina in the 1930s by ballad collector John Jacob Niles during his tenure at the John C. Campbell Folk School (just south of the Smoky Mountains region). With the increased interest in dulcimers spawned by the folk revival of the 1960s, dulcimer making has become a popular revival craft in the Smoky Mountains region.

Fiddles have a far more enduring tradition in the Smoky Mountains. Violins were brought from Europe to the New World, and their portability was certainly an asset along the migration routes into the Upper South. The repertoire of regional fiddlers derived, in part, from Irish, Scottish, and English antecedents. Changes in the tradition are more difficult to document than with ballad singing because fiddle tunes were generally not recorded in manuscripts. However, distinctive styles and tunes soon characterized the Upland South, and the region was not immune to the influences of other fiddling traditions, especially those that developed among African-Americans. Fiddling, and fiddlers, were not approved of by all communities in the Smoky Mountains, especially as they most frequently accompanied dancing, thought of by some as a sin. In spite of this attitude, many communities did host dances. Most took place in private homes; furniture was "broken down" in one or more rooms to make a space for the dance.

By the end of the nineteenth century, fiddling had developed a competitive aspect, and fiddle contests became common in the Smoky Mountains region. In 1909, Louise Rand Bascom described fiddle conventions in the Smoky Mountains as usually taking place in "a stuffy little schoolhouse, lighted by one or two evil-smelling lamps, and provided with a rude, temporary stage." By this time, banjos were also becoming common in the Smokies. An instrument with origins in Africa, the banjo probably did not become common in the Smoky Mountains region until the late nineteenth century. The introduction of the banjo had a profound impact on the local instrumental tradition. At the turn of the century, the banjo and fiddle were commonly paired. The arrival of the railroad and the subsequent access to mail order goods would bring a wide array of other instruments to the mountains, most notably the guitar, although it was not known in some communities until the 1920s. With the pairing of the banjo and fiddle, and the subsequent addition of other stringed instruments, the stringband began to supersede the lone fiddle in providing dance music in the Smoky Mountains region.

While the early collectors of traditional music initially paid scant attention to instrumental music, it was a lucky fact of history that by the mid–1920s, commercial recording companies were eager to capture this music on disc. Consequently, the music of several legendary fiddlers and banjo players of the region has been preserved for posterity. Of this group, the fiddler who had the deepest roots in nineteenth-century fiddling traditions was Dedrick Harris. Born in 1859 in east Tennessee, Harris moved to western North Carolina after marrying a woman from Cherokee County. The couple initially moved to Whittier, North Carolina, to work in the timber industry. In 1916 they settled in Andrews, where Harris became an influential figure among fiddlers in far western North Carolina. In the early heyday of commercial recording of traditional mountain musicians, Harris was recorded at least twice: in 1924 with the Helton Brothers for Broadway Records in New York and in 1925 for Okeh in Atlanta.

Osey and Ernest Helton, who accompanied Harris, were of half-Cherokee, half-Irish descent. Like Harris, they were raised in east Tennessee, but settled in western North Carolina after they reached adulthood. Based in Asheville, they were among the most professionally active fiddlers of their generation. They played at Bascom Lamar Lunsford's Mountain Dance and Folk Festival and the Old-Time Fiddler's Convention in Knoxville, and they were regulars on WWNC-Asheville after the station began to broadcast in 1927.

Another legendary fiddler from the Smoky Mountains region was also of part-Cherokee descent. Born in 1885 in Jackson County, North Carolina, Manco Sneed moved to Graham County with his family when he was about twelve. It was here that he came under the influence of Dedrick Harris, with whom he began to play. Sneed would eventually attribute a substantial portion of his repertoire to Harris. In 1903, the eighteen-year-old Sneed moved with his family to the Cherokee reservation. To a large

Osey Helton (Photo courtesy of Lunsford Scrapbook, Photographic Archives, Mars Hill College)

extent isolated from the traditional milieu of Anglo-American fiddle music, Manco Sneed focused on the development of more technically complex pieces, rather than on dance music. Until his death in 1974, Sneed was known for his technical skill and for his innovative versions of traditional tunes.

A number of the prominent early twentieth-century fiddlers of the Great Smoky Mountains shared similar sources for their repertoire. One notable source was Robert Love Taylor, who served as Tennessee's governor from 1887 to 1891 and from 1897 to 1899. "Fiddling Bob" Taylor used his skill as a musician to promote the image of a down-to-earth man of the people. Before his move to western North Carolina, Dedrick Harris fiddled for Taylor on the campaign trail. Another fiddler who had ties to Taylor was Bill Hensley. Hensley was born near Johnson City, Tennessee, but moved to western North Carolina as a young boy. The farm on which he was born was adjacent to that of the fiddling governor, and Hensley owned a fiddle for which, he claimed, his father had swapped twenty acres of land with Taylor. Hensley attributed a number of his tunes to Taylor and at least one tune in his repertoire to John Sneed, Manco Sneed's father.

Many of the traditional musicians of this era played both fiddle and banjo. Most are best remembered for their fiddle playing, but this was not the case for one legendary player. Defying the stereotypical notion that instrumental music in the region was a man's art form, Samantha Bumgarner is best remembered for her skill with the banjo. The daughter of a

Manco Sneed (Photo
courtesy of Lunsford Scrapbook, Photographic Ar-
chives, Mars Hill College)

fiddle player, Bumgarner was born in Jackson County, North Carolina, in
1880. As a girl she learned to play both fiddle and banjo. By 1924, her
talents were well known in the region and she was invited, along with Eva
Davis, to New York to record for the Columbia Phonograph Company. On
some pieces, Bumgarner played the fiddle while Davis played banjo, but
Bumgarner also sang and accompanied herself on the banjo. Davis and
Bumgarner were among the first traditional stringband players to be commercially recorded. Although for the next few decades she made no other
recording, Bumgarner continued to be an active performer and she was a
favorite at Lunsford's festival. By the 1950s, she was known to a new
audience of listeners brought to traditional mountain music by the bur-
geoning folk revival.

Sneed, Bumgarner, and many of the other legendary musicians of the
early recording era witnessed a major transition in the social role of traditional string music. They were all born during a time when this music
served predominantly as entertainment for house parties, barn dances,
and workings. However, even during that time, contests and conventions
drew attention to the most skilled. The growing timber industry brought

Samantha Bumgarner as
a young woman (Photo
courtesy of Lunsford Scrapbook, Photographic Ar-
chives, Mars Hill College)

large groups of men together in need of entertainment, providing yet another outlet for players in the region. And, as more rural people began to
move from one place to another in search of "public work," musicians
from different communities became acquainted with each other. By the
1920s, record companies, radio, and festivals were bringing some of these
musicians to the attention of a whole nation. Of course, the vast majority
of Smoky Mountains musicians never achieved fame, but commercial out-
lets did exist for the most talented and ambitious.

While instrumental styles have changed immensely in the past seventy years, musicians who play in the older styles do still exist. An exam-

ple of such a fiddler is Mike Rogers of Graham County, North Carolina. Rogers is from the area between Andrews and Robbinsville, near the old haunts of Dedrick Harris and the young Manco Sneed. Mike Rogers learned from old-time fiddlers, and although he has also been influenced by music on the radio, he has retained an old style of playing. Holding the fiddle on his chest, rather than under the chin, he plays in a "short bow" style. He frequently plays in a traditional position, seated, with his legs crossed. His playing is lively and syncopated. Although it lacks the complex fingering and smooth bowing of more modern fiddling, this style is ultimately danceable. After all, that was its purpose.

Traditional banjo playing, altered by "hillbilly" recordings and later bluegrass styles, has changed even more than fiddling. Still, the old two-finger style can be found. In this style of playing, the index finger plays the melody while a drone is played on the first and fifth strings. Today this style has largely been replaced by rhythmic strumming or the three-finger "Scruggs-style" banjo playing of bluegrass music. Still, Earl Scruggs himself derived his own innovative style from traditional North Carolina banjo players. A musician who has taken local traditions in a different direction is Carroll Best of Haywood County, North Carolina. Best, who learned the two-finger style and a three-finger roll from his father, is known for his elaborate system of fingering (using both two and three fingers) and his note-for-note reproduction of complex fiddle tunes on the banjo.

The banjo has come to rival the fiddle as the instrument most associated with Smoky Mountains traditions. A relative newcomer to the Smokies, the banjo was in the nineteenth century typically associated in popular culture with African-Americans. It is interesting to note that the banjo is now often exclusively associated with southern European-American traditions. In the mountains, the banjo's prominence has resulted partly from the development of bluegrass music and the attention given to the banjo during the folk revival. Banjo music frequently accompanies programs on Smoky Mountains culture, and the media often provide images of banjo strummers in the Southern Appalachians.

DANCING AND CLOGGING

Most mountain fiddle playing and early stringband music, with the exception of competition play, existed to accompany dancing. The traditional dancing found in the Smoky Mountains region during the nineteenth century was similar to that found throughout much of the South. Southern square dance, which has many antecedents in European dance tradition, probably developed in the early nineteenth century. A unique aspect of this tradition was that the dancing followed the chanted instructions of a caller. In the nineteenth century, dances in the Smoky Mountains region took place informally in people's homes. Workings and other community events also provided occasions for dances, or "frolics," as they were often known.

As traditional instrumental music found a commercial outlet in the 1920s, it became more performance-oriented rather than existing solely as part of a social event. Dancing also followed this trend. Western North Carolina, and particularly Bascom Lamar Lunsford's Asheville-based Mountain Dance and Folk Festival, was at the heart of the transformation of traditional square dance to a competitive, performance-oriented genre. Lunsford's festival would also introduce a new form of dance that would become closely associated with the traditions of the Great Smoky Mountains region.

While team clogging as we know it today has existed for only slightly over half a century, it does have roots in the mountains. Flatfoot and the more high-stepping buck dancing existed as a solo dance form long before clogging came on the scene. In form, it has similarities to certain types of traditional Scottish and Irish dance, particularly in the fact that the upper half of the body remains relatively immobile while the feet execute a number of complex steps. Often this type of dancing would take place between sets at a community dance. As a solo dance form it was more performance-oriented and competitive than square dance, since dancers might attempt to outdo one another to impress the audience of assembled square dancers and musicians. While this type of dancing has roots in traditional English, Scottish, and Irish dance, it was also strongly influenced by African-American dance traditions. Minstrel and medicine shows, which often featured white performers in black face, probably contributed part of this influence. However, African-American dancers such as Bob Love also shaped the flatfoot and buck dancing of the Smoky Mountains region.

Before the advent of the Mountain Dance and Folk Festival, flatfoot and buck dancing were only small components of the social dancing of the region. Most dances were small, private affairs of four to eight couples and a couple of musicians paid by donations from the male dancers. The main dance was the "big circle" dance, though dancers might also waltz or fox-trot between sets. In the circle dances, participants used a smooth step with a rhythmic bounce (though not the exaggerated smooth step later used in competition).

Within the competitive atmosphere of Lunsford's festival, the styles of flatfoot and buck dancing were married to the group formations of square dancing, and team clogging was born. One of the greatest influences on the development of group clogging was Sam Queen and his Soco

Gap Square Dancers of Haywood County, North Carolina. Queen, who promoted exhibition square dancing at Maggie Valley, was influenced in his own dancing by African-American caller and buck dancer Bob Love. The Soco Gap Dancers were quite popular at the Mountain Dance and Folk Festival and were frequent winners. It was this group which in 1939 accompanied Lunsford to the White House to perform for the Roosevelts and the king and queen of England.

Soco Gap Square Dance Team (Photo courtesy of Lunsford Scrapbook, Photographic Archives, Mars Hill College)

Some scholars have speculated that dancing in the Great Smoky Mountains region was also influenced by Cherokee dance, especially in its emphasis on the toe-heel movement. This would be especially plausible for the dancers of Soco Gap, which is geographically close to Cherokee. Some clogging groups included members of Cherokee descent, and several championship clogging groups were based in Cherokee. Both the Great Smoky Mountains Square Dance Team, an all-Cherokee group under the direction of Arnold Cooper, and the Cherokee Indian Juniors won championships at the Mountain Dance and Folk Festival during the 1930s.

Standardization of dance routines became common during the years

Great Smoky Mountains Square Dance Team, champion dancers from Cherokee (Photo courtesy of Lunsford Scrapbook, Photographic Archives, Mars Hill College)

after the festival began in 1928. Early on, team members began to dress alike, and western-style costumes became popular in the 1940s. Taps were introduced in the 1930s, though Lunsford and others disapproved of them. Despite these innovations, cloggers and "smooth-style" square dancers competed against each other at the Mountain Dance and Folk Festival until 1959, when separate categories were created. As bluegrass, country music and even rock-and-roll replaced traditional stringband music (and were often prerecorded, rather than live), routines became even more choreographed and synchronized. In the late 1950s, the Blue Ridge Mountain Dancers of Hendersonville, North Carolina, under the direction of James Kesterson, began ending their sets in a line of synchronized steps. Soon "precision" clogging, in which all team members dance in synch, became popular, and teams began to eschew the traditional squares for lines of synchronized dancers. While this form of clogging was banned from the Mountain Dance and Folk Festival, it became standard in many other clogging competitions.

A more recent influence on the style of regional clogging has been that of the Green Grass Cloggers. Originally based in eastern North Carolina, the road team settled in Asheville in 1980. While they have tried to incorporate some of the style of traditional buck dancing, they have added their own innovations, including the use of western square-dance figures and head-high kicks. Although their dancing appears more free-form and spontaneous, all of the dancers perform the same steps at the same time, as is the case in precision clogging.

Clogging is now featured on the Grand Ole Opry and other country

Arnold Cooper, leader of
the Great Smoky Moun-
tains Square Dance
Team (Photo courtesy of
Lunsford Scrapbook, Pho-
tographic Archives, Mars
Hill College)

music shows, and performance and recreational clogging groups have
sprouted up across the country (and internationally). However, western
North Carolina is still the heartland of clogging. One indication of its
popularity is the number of public schools with clogging teams. Most of
these teams compete and are as much a part of standard extracurricular
activities as sports teams and cheerleading squads. The teams of very
young dancers are often the most popular with audiences.

THE COMMERCIALIZATION OF TRADITIONAL MUSIC

The advent of the radio era was the impetus for the commercialization of
Southern Appalachian traditional music. As radio stations spread across
the United States, they discovered, sometimes rather accidentally, that
there was a large audience for "old-time" music. Commercial recording
companies, financially beleaguered by the growing popularity of radio,
were making a similar discovery. In the early 1920s, record companies

had already found a market for African-American music, sold under the rubric of "race" recordings. A few years later, traditional European-American music would become an object of their marketing interest.

The first commercially successful record of traditional European-American music was made in 1923 when Okeh Record Company recorded a north Georgia fiddler named John Carson. Fiddlin' John Carson had already performed on Atlanta radio and had been a well-known performer for decades, since his discovery by Bob Taylor, Tennessee's "fiddling governor." (Consequently, parts of Carson's repertoire were similar to that of Dedrick Harris and Bill Hensley.) Record companies were soon scouring the mountains and hills for new talent.

While a number of traditional musicians from western North Carolina were lured to New York or Atlanta to be recorded, much of the field recording took place in eastern Tennessee. The most famous of these sessions was held north of the Smoky Mountains in Bristol, Tennessee, but Knoxville was also an important site for field recording. By the 1920s, the factories of Knoxville attracted workers from the Smokies and the giant fiddle conventions at Market Hall lured many mountain musicians to the city twice a year. The last of the great field recording sessions of the decade were held in Knoxville in 1929 and 1930 when the Brunswick-Balke-Collender Company recorded 150 sides of blues and old-time music.

Knoxville attracted a number of traditional singers, as well as instrumentalists. Among them was George Reneau, "The Blind Minstrel of the Smoky Mountains." Reneau travelled to New York in 1924 to record for Aeolian-Vocalian Records, though the recording executives found his voice too rough, and a studio singer was engaged to sing to Reneau's guitar and harmonica playing. Reneau was eventually allowed to sing his own music, although within a few short years he was back on the streets of Knoxville singing for nickels and dimes.

The music popularized by commercial recordings and radio was soon known as "hillbilly" music. This label covered a whole range of traditionally derived European-American music and was hardly limited to the music of the Smokies or even Southern Appalachia. However, images of the southern mountains were frequent in the lyrics, and the Smokies contributed a number of prominent musicians to this form of music. The popularization of hillbilly music united the instrumental and vocal traditions of the southern Appalachian Mountains. Vocals became a more integral part of stringband music and individual singers accompanying themselves on banjo or guitar were common. The recording of minstrels such as George Reneau linked this new form of commercial music to the regional broadside ballad tradition. Hillbilly music also drew on the regional sacred song tradition and on sentimental parlor songs, many of which had entered oral tradition.

Humor was also an essential part of many hillbilly acts. Traditional southern humor shaped the nature of these performances, but they were also influenced by minstrel and medicine shows and vaudeville. Self-denigration was part of this humor and perhaps led to the acceptance of the otherwise pejorative label "hillbilly." Some individuals took on stereotypical hick characters when they performed. Among the most popular were Lulu Belle and Scott Wiseman, who performed on WLS in Chicago as the "Hayloft Sweethearts." "Skyland Scotty," who took his show name from the tourist promotions of Asheville as the "Land of the Sky," was college educated and earned a master's degree during his years in Chicago. Lulu Belle later represented her western North Carolina district in the state legislature.

Although the golden age of field recording was short-lived, radio continued to promote traditional and hillbilly music. WWNC in Asheville and WNOX and WROL in Knoxville featured performers from the Smoky Mountains region and in some cases became stepping stones to other stations. A number of "barn dance" shows sprang up across the South and Midwest, some organized for merchandizing purposes. Some of these, such as the Crazy Barn Dance at WBT Charlotte, incorporated the pitch of the medicine show. Begun in 1934 and sponsored by Crazy Water Crystals Company of Mineral Wells, Texas, this show featured a number of western North Carolina acts, including Dr. Bennett's Smoky Mountain Boomers from Bryson City performing "real untarnished mountain tunes sung and played by real mountain boys" ("Dr." Kelly Bennett was a well-known pharmacist), and J. E. Mainer's Crazy Mountaineers.

Mainer's Mountaineers represented a new generation of stringbands who were influenced not only by their local traditions but also by the first generation of commercial recordings of old-time music. J. E. and Wade Mainer were from Buncombe County, North Carolina, and absorbed many of the musical influences of the region (though like many other families of the region they travelled to South Carolina and to Knoxville to work in the mills). After performing at local gatherings and competitions, they were hired by Crazy Water Crystals to play at WBT and in 1935 were recorded by Bluebird in Atlanta. The brothers would eventually split and form separate groups, but their music, especially Wade Mainer's banjo playing, would later be seen as an important link between the hillbilly music of the 1920s and bluegrass music, which developed in the 1940s. Both Mainer brothers later found a new popularity with the folk revival, and in 1987 Wade Mainer received a National Heritage Award from the National Endowment for the Arts.

Another influential group of the 1930s was Roy Hall and his Blue Ridge Entertainers. Hall was born in Waynesville, North Carolina, in 1907. A textile worker like the Mainers, Hall was similarly influenced both by local western North Carolina musical traditions and by recorded music. He was recorded by Bluebird in 1937, and his group was hired by Dr. Pepper to work on radio stations in Winston-Salem and then in Roanoke, Virginia. Unfortunately, Hall, who died in 1943, did not live to see a revival in his style of music. However, the clear vocals, bluesy fiddle, and use of dobro in his group's music contributed to the development of bluegrass music.

The rising popularity of brother duets also played a formative role in the development of bluegrass. One of the best-known teams from the Smoky Mountains region was the Callahan Brothers. "Bill and Joe" (actually named Homer and Walter) Callahan were from the musically rich Madison County, North Carolina. In addition to absorbing local traditions, they were also heavily influenced by recorded music, especially the yodeling of Jimmie Rodgers. At the Rhododendron Festival in Asheville in 1934, they began to experiment with the duet yodeling for which they would become famous. Their radio careers would eventually lead them to settle in Texas, but mountain images, such as those in "Little Poplar Log House," are found in much of their music.

During the 1930s, radio careers took many Appalachian musicians far from home, sometimes as far as the Texas-Mexico border. "Border radio," which broadcast at several times the watts permitted in the United States, was influential in popularizing hillbilly music throughout the country. The pioneer in this form of broadcasting was originally from the Smoky Mountains region. Dr. John R. Brinkley was born in Jackson County, North Carolina, around 1885. In 1916, with a questionable medical license, he set up practice in Kansas where he became famous for an operation reputed to restore sexual potency in men through the use of "goat glands." In order to promote his business and hospital, Brinkley started a radio station, KFKB. Hillbilly musicians were featured on the station (which reached much of the country) and in his campaigns for governor of Kansas in 1930 and 1932. After losing his radio license in 1930, Brinkley moved his business to Del Rio, Texas, and began broadcasting out of Mexico. Several other radio entrepreneurs followed, and by 1938 there were eleven stations operating along the border. Although his career was made elsewhere, perhaps Brinkley's background in the Smoky Mountains region shaped his affinity for mountain music. While he is best known for featuring the Carter Family, one of the first programs sponsored by Brinkley's border station starred Samantha Bumgarner, from Brinkley's own home county in North Carolina.

Incorporating a number of stylistic influences, the "hillbilly" tag gave way to "country-western" or just plain "country." However, even as western influences played a larger and larger role in this music, a new musical form, with its roots in traditional stringband music was emerging. Bluegrass music is commonly associated with Kentucky. The major innovator of the style was Bill Monroe, a native of western Kentucky, and the label "bluegrass" derived from the name of Monroe's band, the Blue Grass Boys. However, the style has strong links to the southern mountains, with its emphasis on acoustic music and "high lonesome" singing. Monroe came into direct contact with performers from this region during the mid–1930s when he was performing with his brother Charlie on the Crazy Water Crystals Barn Dance at WBT in Charlotte and elsewhere in the southeast. Although it was not labelled "bluegrass" until many years later, the distinctive sound of this style developed in the 1940s after Monroe split with his brother and formed the Blue Grass Boys. An early member of Monroe's everchanging band was from the Smoky Mountains region. Guitarist Clyde Moody, born in Cherokee of Indian and Scots-Irish parents, had played earlier with Wade Mainer and Roy Hall's brother, Jay Hugh Hall. In the 1950s, east Tennessee became an important center for the development of bluegrass, especially during the years guitar player Lester Flatt and banjo player Earl Scruggs made Knoxville their base after leaving Bill Monroe's band.

Today, bluegrass music is often associated with mountain traditions, though the style itself is less than fifty years old. The pace is several times faster than that of the older stringband music and the banjo takes prominence over the fiddle. Although rooted in North Carolina musical traditions, the three-finger "Scruggs style" of banjo playing also distinguished bluegrass from old-time mountain music. Instruments not found in old-time stringband music, such as the mandolin and dobro, are often included in bluegrass bands. As is the case with clogging, bluegrass is a relatively recent art form that is now emblematic of mountain heritage.

Among the best-known contemporary bluegrass banjo players in the Smoky Mountains is Raymond Fairchild. Like several other prominent musicians who emerged from the Smokies, Fairchild is of partial Cherokee descent. Born in 1939 in Cherokee, Fairchild attributes his early musical influence to his mother's family, especially an aunt who played banjo left-handed. Although his mother's side of the family represents the Cherokee side of his heritage, Fairchild believes that they were primarily influenced by the number of outsiders who came into the area: "A lot of people would come in here to work in the timber that played instruments, I imagine is where they picked that up from." Like most musicians of his generation, however, Fairchild was also influenced by radio and recordings, especially the music of Earl Scruggs and Don Reno.

Raymond Fairchild began his career playing for tips at a tourist stop

Raymond Fairchild
(Photo by David Baxter)

in Maggie Valley run by Ted Sutton. "He taught me the business end of it. How to deal with people. How to figure people out in a hurry. Now he wasn't a musician, he was a showman. He danced and beat bear-bones." Fairchild has since gone on to win two gold records and awards as world champion banjo player and to design and market his own line of banjos. Unlike many professional musicians, however, Fairchild has preferred to stay close to home, now playing mostly at the "Maggie Valley Opry House." Tradition and innovation are seen in Fairchild's music; he is known especially for his fast, intricate playing and for making the banjo mimic the human voice. Fairchild has eliminated the fiddle altogether from his band, letting the banjo take most of the leads. Despite his own innovations, he is sad to see bluegrass moving away from the music he loved, though he is philosophical about the changes:

Well, the younger generation, you know, it's antique to them. It's got to change . . . Now the music they're playing now is bluegrass, but it's bluegrass different. That's what's going to take the day . . . It's just like, you know, back when I was a young man, my daddy would say, "Son, what do you want to listen to Bill Monroe for? I want to play you something." He'd put on J.E. Mainer. No bass

Statue of Dolly Parton in front of Sevier County Courthouse (Photo by Hillary Glatt)

fiddle in there or nothing. I'd think, "My God, Dad. What's the matter with you?" But to him, that was the greatest, you see. But it had to go.

Within mainstream country music, two stars are most frequently associated with the Smoky Mountains. Roy Acuff was born in 1903, not in the mountains proper, but in the foothills of the Smokies in Maynardville,

Tennessee. The son of a Missionary Baptist minister, he received his early singing experience in church and learned to fiddle from his father. The family relocated to the area near Knoxville, where Acuff attended high school and dreamed of becoming a baseball star, not a musician. When illness prevented this dream from coming true, Acuff turned to show business, touring with a travelling medicine show. Soon he was performing on Knoxville radio with a band, The Crazy Tennesseans, and in 1936, cut his first record. After Acuff finally got his big break on the Grand Ole Opry in 1938, the station manager changed the band's name to the more dignified Smoky Mountain Boys.

Acuff became a leading star of the Opry and, with his role in music publishing, a major figure in the commercial development of Nashville as the home of country music. Still, while country music was being influenced by western styles and electrical amplification, Acuff kept his music strongly rooted in southern mountain traditions. Although resisting the general flow of country music's development throughout much of his career, Acuff was still one of its most beloved performers at the time of his death in 1992.

Dolly Parton, on the other hand, was a bit more eager to stray from her musical roots. Born in 1946 near Sevierville, Tennessee, not too far from the Great Smoky Mountains National Park, Parton also got her start singing in church (her grandfather's Church of God congregation). However, she got a much earlier professional start than Acuff, performing on Knoxville radio when she was ten. By the time she took off for Nashville, immediately following her high school graduation, she already had considerable professional experience. As her popularity grew, Dolly Parton embraced pop material and began to eschew country formats altogether.

Despite Dolly Parton's divergence from traditional country music, she keeps her Smoky Mountains background in the public eye. Her rags-to-riches story is very much part of her public image, and she has utilized her considerable songwriting skills to explore her childhood in songs such as "Coat of Many Colors" and her affinity with the region in compositions such as "My Tennessee Mountain Home." Whatever the country music establishment thinks of her, she is a hometown heroine. The front lawn of the Sevier County courthouse (the county's architectural pride and joy) features a statue, not of a war hero, but of Dolly Parton holding a guitar.

CHAPTER 4

Material Folk Traditions

FOLK ARCHITECTURE

The most emblematic of the material folk traditions of Southern Appalachia is certainly the log house. It is an amalgam of the European folk building traditions brought to the southern mountains, especially central and northern European building techniques and British and Irish house plans. However, by the time European-American settlers came to the Smokies, the signs of distinct ethnicity in architecture had largely disappeared and been replaced by a uniquely American system of building. In the early years of white settlement, the log house in Appalachia also represented a practical response to an abundance of raw material and to the relative scarcity of milled lumber.

The log building tradition in the southern mountains is notable less for its uniqueness—log construction was used at some point in many places in the eastern United States—than for the tenacity of the tradition. While log was no longer generally the preferred method of construction after 1900, a number of families in the Smokies continued to live in houses made of log, and it was still frequently used in the construction of small barns and outbuildings. During the years of the Great Depression, log construction enjoyed a brief revival in popularity, though the log houses of this era were frequently built of small, round timbers, rather than the massive hewn logs of the earlier dwellings.

The continuity of log building in the southern mountains has often been attributed to poverty and isolation. However, it is really more representative of the values and economy of rural communities in the mountains. The log house was frequently the product of community-based work exchange. The community could provide its members with housing with little or no cash exchange. The egalitarian spirit of many rural communities also promoted a conservative architectural tradition. If an individual relied on neighbors to help construct housing, he or she was less likely to hanker after something better than what everyone else had.

The log house has been so closely tied to the stereotypes and romanticism associated with Southern Appalachia that many today deny its prevalence. Of course, earlier writings often overlooked the diversity of housing options in Appalachia, but revisionist architectural history denies the conservatism and continuity of the building tradition. Because it experienced industrialization relatively late, even in comparison to other parts of Appalachia, the Smoky Mountains region had a particularly conservative architectural tradition. Even in the late twentieth century, it is not difficult to locate older individuals who as children had first-hand experience with log dwellings.

The oral testimony of these individuals helps us understand how these houses were used and what they meant. As children, many shared common experiences: waking to find snow, which often managed to defeat the protection of board roofs, covering the blankets; digging out pieces of chinking to create small windows in the wall; learning to read and playing word games using the newsprint that papered the walls. This papering of the walls with newsprint has also been cited as an example of the poverty of the region, but the occupants of these houses insist that a well-papered

Single-pen log house with separate kitchen connected by a covered walkway (Photo courtesy of Great Smoky Mountains National Park)

wall was clean and beautiful. Furthermore, the papering of walls followed clear aesthetic principals and allowed for the artistic expression of the dwelling's occupants.

Oral testimony especially helps us understand how space was used in smaller log houses. Beds dominated most rooms except the separate kitchen, if one existed, but functional space was carefully delineated even within very small houses. While children often shared a bed with several other siblings, they still had their own designated place to sleep in the night and sit during the daytime. And, despite the fact that sometimes very large families lived in very small houses, most individuals who grew up in these houses denied that they felt crowded. Privacy was created both by physical means (the arrangement of furniture or the construction of blanket partitions) and by psychological means (a cultivation of reserve). Most insisted simply that "it was all we knew." Most significantly, these houses accommodated not only large families but the routine overnight visiting of friends and relatives.

Log dwellings came in a variety of shapes and sizes. The single-pen house form, consisting of a single square or rectangular unit, was probably the most common type of log house. In fact, by the late nineteenth century, this type had become predominant among log dwellings as families wanting larger homes became more likely to use frame construction than log. However, the size of even single-pen houses could vary considerably. The larger, rectangular types might have an interior board partition; some had a second story (either half or full), usually used to sleep older children; and some had a separate kitchen, frequently detached from the house. As cookstoves became more common in the late nineteenth century, kitchens were often appended to the single-pen dwelling.

The most common of the larger double-pen log houses was the saddle-bag plan dwelling: two equal-sized rooms on either side of a chimney, known regionally as a "double house" or house with a "double chimney." The dogtrot house, with its open central passage, while not unknown, was uncommon in the Smokies. (Sometimes single-pen houses with covered walkways connecting the dwelling to the kitchen are labeled dogtrot houses, but these are not true representatives of the form.) As with the single-pen houses, the double-pen houses had "the room we lived in," which was where members of the family gathered at night, did chores around the open hearth, slept (particularly the heads of households) and, in the absence of a separate kitchen, cooked and ate. Traditionally, the other room in the double-pen plan was the parlor. While this room might also be used to sleep guests or family members, it was viewed largely as a company room, giving testimony to the importance of socializing among those who lived in the mountains. However, in the early decades of the twentieth century, concerns for privacy overtook the perceived need for a

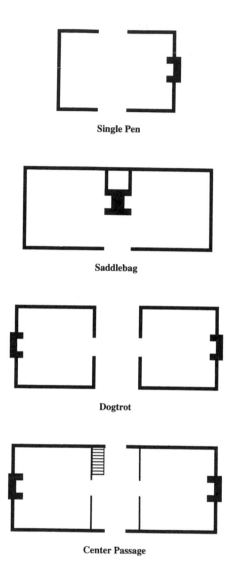

Single Pen

Saddlebag

Dogtrot

Center Passage

Plans of folk house types
found in the Smoky
Mountains region

formal space in these houses, and this space became the "back room" or
bedroom.

Frame construction was, of course, an option after the earliest settlement years. In the decades before the Civil War, frame houses were found
most frequently in county seats and among those who owned prosperous
farms in the broad river valleys. The most common form of frame house
was the two-story, single-pile, center-passage I-house, though two-story,
saddlebag-plan dwellings were also found in frame construction. By the

end of the century, prosperous farmers were experimenting with Victorian trim and beginning slowly to break away from traditional forms.

Although in many rural communities the individuals who owned painted frame houses were better off economically than others, the levelling effects of the Civil War meant that such house owners were not necessarily a separate class. Some families at times moved between dwellings of frame and of log construction. Oral testimony indicates that the use of space within these houses was not significantly different from that in the larger log homes. Although they chose to build center passage dwellings, many inhabitants considered the passage to be wasted space and would try to convert it into a room or to eliminate it altogether.

While some dwellings remain on the landscape as remnants of the folk architectural tradition of the Great Smoky Mountains, the original nature of farmsteads has largely been obscured. Through the early twentieth century, grass lawns were not part of the rural homestead. Yards were largely bare; the tidy housekeeper kept the yard swept with a broom. Native grasses grew in the less-trafficked areas of the yard, and livestock might periodically be allowed to graze so as to keep the vegetation under control (or the area would be scythed). Vines would often be grown to shade front porches, and perennials, both flowers and herbs, would be grown along the edges of the house. Particularly valued plants were grown in the protected spots around the chimney. Up until the early decades of the twentieth century, livestock was often ranged free, so gardens needed to be fenced in. Palen fences, made of vertically placed split boards about two inches wide, were used to enclose vegetable gardens and farm yards.

Farmers in the Great Smokies preferred a scattering of single-use outbuildings rather than a large multi-use barn. A farmstead might include a springhouse, smokehouse, corn crib, hog pen, and perhaps an apple house, among other buildings. In the nineteenth century, kitchens as well were usually thought of as outbuildings. By late in the century, however, most farmers also had a modest-sized barn that combined the function of stabling animals and storing hay. The most common barn type in the Upper South was the gable-roofed transverse crib, with its open drive running from gable end to gable end. However, on the Tennessee side of the Smokies, a distinctive type of construction was used in many barns. These barns consisted of a two-or-four-crib first floor with a much larger frame second story, cantilevered over two or four sides to create a protective overhang. The cribs were used to shelter animals while the upper story was used to store hay (and now tobacco). While antecedents for this type of building exist in folk tradition and a few cantilevered barns are known to exist elsewhere in the Upper South, the quite limited regional distribution of cantilevered barns suggests that these barns were a local

Messer barn, Greenbrier community, 1935, cantilevered construction (Photo courtesy of Great Smoky Mountains National Park)

invention perpetuated by a close family and community network of traditional builders. Over 90 percent of the known cantilevered barns in Tennessee are found in Blount and Sevier counties. However, the overwhelming majority of extant log barns in these two Tennessee counties are cantilevered, so where the tradition existed, it dominated traditional barn-building practices. Only a few examples are known on the North Carolina side of the Smokies. The majority of cantilevered barns that survive today were built in the final decades of the nineteenth century, but the tradition is known to have lasted through the early decades of this century. The latest known construction date for a cantilevered barn in the region is 1938.

Up until 1900, log and frame were the two construction options for most dwellings built in the Smoky Mountains. However, after the turn of the century, a third possibility began to appear in many communities in the region. While vertical-plank, known regionally as "boxed," construction, is considered by many a type of frame construction, local builders always distinguish a boxed house from a frame house based on its single-wall construction and minimal amount of framing. As one local man de-

Bennett boxed house, Little Cataloochee (Photo courtesy of Great Smoky Mountains National Park)

scribed it: "Well, you take a boxed house—take the boxed, they ain't got framing in it. They just built the whole plate around and nail the boards down here up. And just slat it over. See, a frame house, it got two-by-fours in it, put the weatherboarding on the outside like this and ceiling on the inside. Boxed house ain't got it."

Although boxed construction was probably known in the region before 1900, it grew considerably more popular after the widespread advent of timbering. Milled lumber became cheaper and more available, and more people, having entered "public work," had cash to spend. A boxed house took considerably less time to construct than a log house, an important advantage for those drawn into the cash economy. This feature of boxed construction allowed rural communities to maintain cooperative building practices, despite the new constraints on available time. Furthermore, traditional house forms were usually maintained, though boxed construction heightened the trend toward rooms that were smaller but more numerous.

While boxed construction was frequently used in the hastily built timber camps, it also became the favored form of construction in many rural communities in the Smoky Mountains during the first decades of the twentieth century. Today their flimsiness and relative impermanence would seem to indicate that there was a vast decline in housing standards during this period of time. In fact, the majority of boxed houses built during the early twentieth century no longer survive, belying their commonness on the landscape. However, at the time many people saw boxed houses as "nice and new," a step up from a log dwelling. At worst, they were seen as equivalent to log houses; as indicators of economic status, boxed and log dwellings were both judged negatively in relation to painted frame houses.

Even the new painted frame houses built after the turn of the century were not solely representative of rural prosperity. Many were a product of yet another strategy for survival in the new economic order. Men associated with the timber industry, drummers (travelling salesmen), and tourists all were flooding into the mountains and needed to find housing. For those who could afford the cash outlay, the construction of ten-to-twelve-room boardinghouses provided a way to profit from this trend. Boardinghouses were largely the domain of women. They were a godsend for widows, but even when they were owned by married couples, the business was usually considered the woman's and the cash earned was hers to spend. Although offering a new form of independence for women, this occupa-

Frame house built large enough to accommodate boarders, Cataloochee, N.C. (Photo courtesy of Great Smoky Mountains National Park)

tion emphasized domesticity, a domain not necessarily highly valued by some women in the mountains. Many older women of the region today claim that they hated to be cooped up in the house and were proud of the fact that they could work "like a man" at agricultural tasks. The selling of domesticity and domestic space was a difficult transition for some women. Such was true for the sister-in-law of a Maggie Valley woman who later lived in the same house:

[Hattie] was a person, she didn't do housework too much. She was interested in hard work, feeding cattle; she was raised to do that, you know, to take care of a bunch of cattle and hogs and chickens. That's what they all done over there [in Cataloochee]. This house, it's got eleven rooms, two large halls, front porch, plenty of house. And I reckon they built this house big enough 'til they could keep boarders. 'Cause they did keep boarders.

She managed [this house] and outside too. But these drummers' wives, they lived in Canton, it seemed most of them did, well, they got to coming here and they loved Hattie, she was a wonderful person, but they seen she couldn't do all things and keep house too. So she didn't have no furniture in this house, just enough for them I reckon. So they told her that she needed furniture and told her what to get, the outfit for the room. Burlon [her husband], he went to Knoxville and he got a set for every room.

While for some folks in the Smoky Mountains entering the cash economy meant building a boxed dwelling or a new frame boardinghouse, for others it meant losing the family home altogether. In some cases whole families moved from timber camp to timber camp, wherever the men could find jobs. Women found that they could sell their domestic skills in these camps, cooking for crews or boarding single men in company-owned houses. If privacy was hard to come by in the single-pen dwelling or in the boardinghouse, where every bedroom might be rented out to strangers, it was even more difficult for women of the timber camp who no longer owned the space in which they performed their domestic activities.

Ultimately, it was the decline of community work patterns, brought about by dislocation and the changing economy, that ended traditional building practices. Boxed construction provided a necessary transition, allowing for community-built houses that could be constructed quickly, but ultimately its adoption marked the beginning of the end of traditional building. By the third decade of the century, fewer and fewer houses were being built with an open hearth, which had once been the center of family life. As stone chimneys became less common, new house forms were adopted. Boxed houses began to be built with front rather than side gables (somewhat resembling a shotgun house, a type not traditional in the Smokies). Although cooperative building and log construction experienced a brief revival during the Depression, it was short-lived. Even boxed construction dwindled by mid-century, especially as rural electrification made single-wall construction impractical. Today, our understanding of traditional building in the Smokies must rely largely on the structures that survive as artifacts of the past and on the memories of older people who knew firsthand what these structures meant and how they were used.

A neglected aspect of the study of Appalachian folk architecture is the examination of the building practices of the Cherokee, particularly in the post-Removal era. While the log cabin is seen as representative of Southern Appalachian folk tradition, log construction is seldom associated with the Cherokee. However, the Cherokee were the first to use horizontal log construction in the Great Smokies region and possibly preserved the tradition longer than their non-Indian neighbors.

Contact with people of European descent was established long before white settlers came to the Great Smokies. Sometime in the eighteenth century, the Cherokee adopted European-derived log construction for their dwellings. The Cherokee habitations described by naturalist William Bartram in 1776 were not constructed in the traditional manner of waddle-and-daub, but of "logs or trunks of trees, stripped of their bark, notched at their ends, fixed one upon another." Round ceremonial and civic structures continued to be built into the nineteenth century, but the domestic structures differed little from that of the non-Indian encroachers.

In the early nineteenth century, the variety of Cherokee housing closely resembled that of the non-Cherokee settlers in the same region. Prosperous river valley farmers began to leave log construction behind in favor of larger frame (or even brick) dwellings, while the more traditional mountain dwellers continued the log tradition. However, the Removal served to dislocate the more prosperous of the Cherokee, leaving behind those who lived in the Great Smoky Mountains. These, the most traditional of the band, continued to rely largely on log construction for the next century.

While the architecture of the Eastern Cherokee was physically undistinguished from that of their non-Cherokee neighbors, it is quite possible that patterns of spatial use within the homes might have been different. With the lack of any substantial research on this matter, the question remains open for future researchers. There is, however, surprisingly good evidence of the physical nature of Cherokee housing during the 1920s and 1930s. During these years the Bureau of Indian Affairs' Cherokee Indian Agency conducted "industrial surveys" that included descriptions of domestic structures.

Of the over two hundred Cherokee homes documented in the survey of 1922–23, approximately half were constructed of log. Of these log dwellings, about 50 percent were single-room structures. One was described as "just large enough for one bed, a small table and a chair or so." At least one of the one-room log houses was newly constructed. The larger log houses were mostly two-room dwellings. Photographic evidence suggests that most of these were single-pen dwellings that were either partitioned or had a rear kitchen. However, at least three were double-pen structures with exterior end chimneys. Only half a dozen of the exclusively log structures were listed as having more than two rooms. Another half dozen were constructed of a combination of log and frame.

Not all Eastern Cherokee lived in log structures during this period. About thirty-five lived in boxed structures (mostly two- or three-room dwellings) and sixty-six lived in frame structures (although the distinction between boxed and frame construction is not always clearly made). Frame homes were generally larger than log or boxed structures; most had three rooms or more. Photographs show them to be similar to those owned by non-Indians in the region. The largest frame house documented had nine rooms. The survey also listed a seven-room frame house with a bath.

As there are no comparable surveys from the same period of non-Indian housing, it is difficult to assess how Cherokee housing differed. It seems probable that log housing was more common overall and boxed structures less common than in non-Indian communities. However, the circumstances of individual communities varied greatly in the region. The comments in the survey do indicate that many male Cherokees, like their non-Cherokee neighbors, were seeking public work on road crews and in logging camps, and in some cases Cherokee women were cooking for the crews.

The industrial census of 1932 used a survey rather than a narrative format. While more types of information are asked for, the dwellings are not consistently described, and there are no photographs. While rooms and windows are counted, the method of construction is frequently omitted. One-room log houses are most frequently noted, however, and their number did not seem to decline with the passing decade. In fact, several log houses were labelled as new, indicating that the log tradition was continuing. It is possible that log construction experienced a revival during the Depression years, as it did in the non-Indian communities of the region. The construction of boxed houses (in this survey labelled "plank") also seemed to be on the rise. Housing conditions varied from the extremes of a single-room boxed house that sheltered eleven people to the "best home on the reservation," an eight-room whitewashed house with nineteen windows.

Neither industrial survey indicates that the practice of taking in

Cherokee basketmaker, Nancy George Bradley, working in front of a boxed house, Wright's Creek, 1940 (Photo courtesy of Great Smoky Mountains National Park)

boarders was as common as it was among the non-Cherokee in the Great Smokies. However, Moses Owl's wife, Mary (who was a Pueblo Indian), was listed in 1932 as taking into her five-room house summer boarders who visited on the reservation.

An unusual feature of the 1932 census was that it included a listing for "musical instruments." Victrolas and radios were included in this listing and the former were particularly popular among the Eastern Cherokee. Almost half the homes surveyed owned a Victrola. These machines were not owned only by the most affluent; they were also found in the smaller log houses. Other instruments were less common, although twenty-two organs, thirteen banjos, eleven guitars, eight violins, and three pianos were found. Of course, the accuracy of all the survey material must be questioned. The noted fiddler Manco Sneed, for example, was listed as owning a mandolin but not a fiddle.

By the 1950s, the number of log houses had declined significantly among the Eastern Cherokee. In Painttown, approximately 10 percent of the houses were of log or pole construction, while half were of "simple frame construction" (which may include boxed houses). The number of ranch-style houses and the use of concrete block construction was on the rise. Almost three quarters of the houses had electricity. However, more conservative townships such as Big Cove possibly had a higher rate of traditional housing. Big Cove also had a significantly higher number of household members per dwelling than Painttown.

Some traditional uses of space may have also been maintained by the Cherokee at mid-century. The simple frame houses that were built by the owner-occupant may have had a bedroom or two in addition to the main room, but sleeping occurred in all rooms except the kitchen. On the other hand, in the larger "bungalow type" houses (which constituted approximately a quarter of the houses in Painttown) "bedrooms, living room, kitchen, and often, dining room and bathroom are clearly distinguished from each other." In the owner-built houses, cardboard was often used to cover the walls. Carnation Milk cartons were particularly favored.

While nothing comparable to the industrial surveys exists for non-Indian dwellings in the region, the most systematic attempt at documenting mountain culture in the Great Smoky Mountains National Park in the 1930s was the survey of structures located within the park boundaries. Initially, the policy was to remove structures from the park area as quickly as possible. Depending on their condition, they were sold, given away, or, in many cases, burned by park personnel. The latter action, as park superintendent J. Ross Eakin noted in 1932, aroused "considerable ire among residents." The superintendent, however, was of the belief that "houses should be razed as soon as their occupants move out." Whether it was the superintendent or the National Park Service that had a change of heart is unknown, but within a few years a systematic "cabin survey" was undertaken. During the 1930s and early 1940s, Civilian Conservation Corps employee Charles Grossman inspected over seventeen hundred structures within the park area, "including dwellings, barns, corn cribs, apple houses, pig pens, bridges, six types of grist mills, smokehouses, and blacksmith shops," and made photographic records and maps locating these structures. Grossman's work stands as one of the first comprehensive surveys of folk architecture conducted in this country. The Historic American Buildings Survey during this period also produced measured drawings of six buildings within the park.

Due to these early efforts, we have a rare glimpse at the folk architecture of the Great Smoky Mountains region as it survived into the 1930s. Attempts were also made during this period to restore and stabilize at least some of the structures, so that they are preserved today. During the 1940s, with the CCC dismantled, it was lessees within Cades Cove who proved to have the traditional knowledge and capabilities to stabilize and repair log barns in that community.

Grossman dreamed of a "comprehensive program to preserve the architecture of the region in natural settings and to permit tracing the development of structures from the most primitive to pretentious frame house." However, in 1943 he also felt that "up to the present time personnel and funds have been lacking to carry on the program in a logical manner." The documentation and stabilization of structures and the plans drawn up by this date, did, in fact, provide the basis for future interpretation. If the mountain culture program was not fully realized, groups of buildings were preserved. Some are still in their original locations, while others were moved to enhance and facilitate interpretation.

Still, the surviving structures do not necessarily tell a fully accurate story of life in the Great Smokies. The photographic record left by Grossman and others is far more objective, because it records a range of buildings not chosen for preservation. Grossman himself advocated that at least one representative boxed house be preserved, but his advice was unheeded. Although vertical plank construction was probably the most common form of building existing at the time of the creation of the park, no examples were preserved. A few of Grossman's "pretentious frame" houses were preserved, but to a large extent it was nineteenth-century log construction that was favored for long-term preservation. Evidence of the recent industrial past also was not preserved. Although the logging industry transformed the lives of the majority who lived in the Great Smoky Mountains, the physical evidence of this change has largely disappeared.

BASKETRY

Quite probably the oldest continuous craft tradition in the Smoky Mountains is basketry. Archaeological evidence indicates that some form of baskets have been made in the region for approximately nine thousand years. Twilled rivercane basketry was introduced as early as A.D. 600, and cane remained the principal material used by the Cherokee for baskets into the early twentieth century. However, by the nineteenth century, the Cherokee were also making baskets of white oak, possibly as a result of European contact. More recently honeysuckle and maple were added to the raw materials in the Cherokee basketmaker's repertoire.

While today Cherokee basketry is to a large degree a tourist art, in fact commercialism has shaped the craft for almost two hundred years. Even before the Removal, baskets were used as a barter item with European-Americans, and Cherokee women continued to sell or trade baskets with non-Indians throughout the nineteenth century. To appeal to this market, aspects of European-derived forms and technology were incorporated into Cherokee basketry, most notably the inclusion of handles on many baskets. Despite the fact that Cherokee baskets early became a marketable item, basketmakers continued to make functional items for use in their own community. Frank Speck, who studied Eastern Cherokee basketry in 1913, noted that common forms included pack baskets, baskets used to catch fish, and a variety of baskets for processing and holding food.

The nineteenth-century Cherokee craftswoman had to travel far to sell her baskets. Even in the early decades of the twentieth century, basketmakers from Snowbird travelled long distances by foot to market their wares. Bessie Jumper, interviewed for the Fading Voices project, remembered the long trip to Andrews carrying bundles of baskets: "We went over the mountain. We'd leave here at five o'clock in the morning. It's a long way. When you get to the top of the mountain, then you go down a long way. I walked with my mother over there so many times." Baskets were either sold for cash or traded for food. "You could get a lot of food back then for five dollars or less. We got a lot of pinto beans for fifty cents. But we always got just what we could carry back." It would be seven or eight at night by the time they returned from their trip.

At Qualla, however, potential buyers were increasingly brought to the basketmaker. In 1909 the Qualla Boundary was linked by rail to the Southern Railroad bringing tourists wanting souvenirs. In the next decade new venues, such as the Cherokee Indian Fair, developed for marketing baskets. Although the handicrafts revival generally did not focus on Cherokee crafts, it indirectly helped create a market for these products, providing a seasonal source of income for a growing number of basketweavers. The creation of the Great Smoky Mountains National Park, of course, meant significant growth in the potential tourist market for baskets, although it was not until the post-war era that the increase of visitors was dramatically felt. In 1946 the Cherokee Indian Crafts Co-op was created, giving Cherokee craftspeople greater control over the production and sale of their products. Nine years later, the co-op became the Qualla

Arts and Crafts Mutual, Inc., a nonprofit organization. Today, the organization is an oasis among the cheap souvenir stands in the town of Cherokee, and baskets remain their best-selling craft.

With increased tourist demand, Cherokee baskets have changed in function. Fish baskets and corn processing baskets have given way to wastebaskets, purses and baskets whose primary purpose is display. Although color has long been used in some Cherokee baskets, the use of dyes, both natural and commercial, has significantly increased in this century. Novelty items, such as basket earrings, are now frequently sold, but the traditional doubleweave cane baskets still command the highest prices. Unfortunately, both rivercane basketweavers and the supply of rivercane are now growing scarce.

Despite the fact that the majority of Cherokee baskets are now made for sale to non-Indians, there is still a strong sense of continuity in this ancient art form. While some older basketweavers perfected their skills at Indian boarding schools (and consequently were exposed to the basket traditions of other Native Americans) and today formal basket classes are held in Cherokee, many Cherokee basketweavers learned the rudimentary skills in the traditional way. Most were exposed as children to basketweaving in their homes, learning the basics by hanging around, watching the basketmakers, and experimenting with scraps.

Of course, the desire to make baskets does not always take hold the first time around. Louise Goings, the daughter and granddaughter of basketmakers, recalled: "Mother always was a basketmaker, that's how she raised her eight children. So that's how I learned to make baskets and I must have started I guess between the years of eight and twelve, when, you know, I did a few baskets for some spending money. I guess it's why I did it then. And then I didn't get married til I was seventeen, so in my teen years I didn't deal with baskets, until after my husband came home. I must have been about twenty-three, twenty-four years old then I started making baskets again." Louise Goings's mother, Emma Taylor, a noted rivercane basketweaver, taught her five daughters to make baskets but has not yet passed on all her skills. A weaver of white oak baskets, Louise Goings still expresses the desire to learn rivercane weaving from her mother.

Although basketmaking was once predominantly a woman's craft, the role of men in the tradition is growing. Louise Goings remembers her mother cutting down her own trees, even with a baby on her back, but increasingly men are helping to supply the raw materials, such as blood root (for dye) and rivercane or white oak, which are now growing scarcer. Some Cherokee men make money by selling these materials to local basketmakers, while others aid the female basketmakers in their own families by helping to gather raw materials. In some cases, Cherokee woodcarvers

Louise Goings demon-
strating at the Smithson-
ian Folklife Festival
(Photo courtesy of Center
for Folklife Programs and
Cultural Studies, Smithsonian Institution)

(who tend to be males) carve handles for basketmakers. The sense of family tradition is so strong that Louise Goings has taken this trend a step further, teaching her son to be a basketmaker after he returned from the service. "If I would have suggested to him to make baskets when he was a teen going to school, he'd have probably said, 'Oh God, you gotta be kidding.' So when he came back, after he'd been here about a year or so, then I told him, I said, 'Well, Ed, I don't have any girls now, so I'm going to have to teach you how to make baskets.' And he didn't say no." Not only did he not resist, he showed an aptitude for the craft. In one of his first competitions, he beat out both his mother and grandmother. "We told him we was gonna run him off," Louise Goings kidded. However, she also stressed that a student's work reflects on the teacher. A young grandson is now in training. "That's all I have is just males. Have this one son and then I have two grandsons . . . But we haven't talked Butch [her husband, a woodcarver] into trying yet."

Cherokee basketmakers pass not only skills through their families but also aesthetic values. Preferences for color schemes, shapes, designs, and the size of splits all run in families. A basketmaker can often recognize the work of certain families in a craft shop and in some cases will know the work to be the product of an individual basketmaker. However, while aesthetic preferences may be passed down for generations, a basketmaker may also be open to new influences. Louise Goings collects basket books purchased at the mall to use as inspiration for new designs. Even though she considers her basketmaking largely "a hobby," she is also open to market influences. "I more or less prefer [baskets] the colors of the roots and barks, but if anybody specifies different colors, or like we think around Christmas time people like red and green, then that's what we use. And then at Easter time we make a lot of Easter baskets with different colors too."

While the influence of the marketplace is ever present, the degree of professionalization of the basketmaker varies. For some older women, basketweaving served as the primary source of income, but for many others it supplemented the seasonal nature of the tourist trade. Louise Goings's father "chiefed" in the summertime; her mother's income helped the family make it through the winter. Louise, who works for the school system, has her summers free and during this period pursues her hobby. Today, while basketmakers are more likely to get a fair price for their intensive labor than in earlier times, the work is less likely to be done for financial reasons. More than a commodity, baskets can also be tokens of affection among family members. Louise Goings's house is full of baskets, some she made for her husband on special occasions, some her mother or son made for her. She also keeps a photo album of her baskets, as if they were favorite relatives, some of whom have left home.

According to Louise Goings, the desire to learn and to be the best you can are the most important traits in a basketmaker. Patience is also a virtue. The rewards are not just monetary. Unlike her mother, who needed the financial returns from her basketry to raise eight children, Louise has the luxury of choosing to be a basketmaker. Perhaps for women of her generation, raised by parents who were beaten at school for speaking their own language and who therefore declined to teach their children Cherokee at home, what is important is the sense of connectedness that basketry offers. "In my own self, when I make baskets, I get this feeling, you know, this being Indian. And it gives me a good feeling about myself that I can, you know, show a part of culture that's been for years."

The sense of continuity is perhaps less strong for the non-Indian basketmakers of the Great Smoky Mountains region. European-derived basket techniques were introduced to the southern mountains two centuries ago. Basketmakers of European descent had to adapt their techniques to the raw materials at hand and quite probably were influenced by Native American traditions, just as Cherokee basketry was in turn influenced by European techniques. Although a variety of materials were at times used to make baskets, white oak was the material of choice.

According to Rachel Nash Law and Cynthia W. Taylor in *Appalachian White Oak Basketmaking*, three basic varieties of white oak baskets are found in central and Southern Appalachia: rib, split, and rod. The rib basket, with its thin splits woven on a foundation of curved ribs, is the form most frequently associated with the region and is sometimes known as the "Appalachian basket." Frances Louisa Goodrich found this to be the most common form in the Laurel Country of Madison County, North Carolina. Honeysuckle was also woven on oak ribs. While the rib basket was the most distinctive of the Appalachian baskets, the simpler split basket was more widespread. The weaving of splits was well known in both Native American and European basket traditions, and in the southern mountains this technique was used especially for the larger bushel baskets, hampers, and feed baskets. Rod baskets were derived from European wickerwork traditions. Lacking good basket willow, American basketmakers substituted hardwood, especially oak, whittled or shaved into long slender sticks. Rod baskets were more common in regions with a large concentration of people of German descent, such as the Shenandoah Valley, and were considerably rarer in the Smokies than the rib and split varieties.

Through the early twentieth century, European-American basketmakers in the Smokies bartered or sold their wares, as did their Cherokee counterparts. While basketry required few tools, not every individual in the rural community had the knowledge, skill, or patience to make baskets, and white oak basketry existed into this century as a small home-based industry. Unlike the Cherokee, the non-Indian basketmakers traditionally were both female and male, and often it was family units that produced the wares for sale. Making chairs from the same raw materials sometimes went hand-in-hand with basketry. Letha Hicks of the Big Bend community remembered, "See my Daddy, he made chairs. Mother, she'd make baskets. My Daddy, he'd sell them chairs for a dollar apiece, he made. I've bottomed a many a one. They . . . go in the woods and cut white oak and drag long pieces, you know, and they'd split it up and make splits and bottom chairs with them splits . . . Yeah, and she made them baskets out of white oak splits."

By the turn of the century, commercial baskets constructed of machine-made splits began to compete with the handmade baskets. However, just as the market for handmade utilitarian baskets was declining, the handicrafts revival was latching on to baskets as one of its promotable fireside industries. The crafts programs especially promoted the rib baskets and, as usual, while touting tradition they also introduced aesthetic change.

The creation of the Great Smoky Mountains National Park also had both negative and positive results for local basketmakers. Basketmakers

Mack McCarter making chairs on porch of shop (Photo courtesy of Great Smoky Mountains National Park)

such as Mack McCarter of Sevier County lost their homes to the park, as well as their source of raw materials, but found a new market in the tourists who began to flow through Gatlinburg. Although fewer and fewer people wanted baskets for practical purposes, many tourists found baskets to be appropriate souvenirs from their trip to the Smoky Mountains. McCarter and other basketmakers expanded their trade from rib and split baskets to other woven novelties. Still, while tourism expanded the commercial outlet for baskets, Cherokee and non-Indian basketmakers alike were meagerly paid for their labor-intensive craft.

Today, although tourists still seek out handmade baskets as souvenirs of the Smokies, non-Indian basketmakers in the region are less likely to be from basketmaking families or to have learned in a traditional manner. Indeed, the European-American basketmaking tradition seems more vital in other parts of the Upper South; rib basketry is still found in family tradition in some parts of central Tennessee and southcentral Kentucky and the split basket tradition is now most viable in the Blue Ridge of Virginia. Traditional non-Cherokee basketmakers have not completely disappeared in the Smokies. One older, Jackson County basketweaver continued into the 1980s to produce white oak baskets in her home. The craft had so taken over that she had set up a shaving horse in her living room and much of her floor was ankle deep in shavings. However, the older basketmakers are rapidly giving over to a newer generation of formally trained revivalists.

The irony of the situation involving crafts such as basketry is that the agents of preservation are also the agents of change. Those crafts whose value has changed from being predominantly functional to primarily aesthetic have survived best in the twentieth century. However, these are the crafts most vulnerable to market forces and to reinterpretation by outsiders. The more functional skills, such as the making of axe handles or the splitting of shingles and boards, have changed less. But as the need for these skills declines, they will disappear, except perhaps as a curiosity in a living history demonstration.

QUILTING

In the early twentieth century, the handwoven coverlet was the darling of missionaries and crafts revivalists and became known to outsiders as the textile craft of the mountains. In the late twentieth century, quilts have largely usurped this role. As with coverlets, the romanticized nonsense written about quilts greatly exceeds the serious research, and there is still much to know about quilting traditions in the Smokies, particularly in the nineteenth century.

Quilts and woven covers alike traditionally came in both plain and fancy varieties. A handwoven cover could be either a plain blanket or an intricate overshot coverlet. A quilt could be an elaborately pieced or appliquéd work or a more functional item, perhaps made only of squares or strips of recycled material. It is not easy to find out whether woven blankets and coverlets were more numerous than quilts and whether plain or fancy covers were more common. Textiles are not as enduring as some artifacts, and the plain covers were not as likely to be earmarked for preservation as the fancy ones.

At the end of the nineteenth century, the coming of the railroad made cheap cloth available in the mountains. Handweaving declined as more and more women were able to afford store-bought cloth. By the turn of the century, sewing machines had also become more common in the region. The effect these changes had on quilting is not altogether clear. On the one hand, women could afford cheap cloth to use in quiltmaking, but on the other, many could now afford to buy blankets to replace the quilts. There were probably more fabric scraps available for quilts as women who had sewing machines and no longer had to rely on handwoven fabric were likely to produce more clothes for their families. However, because some women now had more money, they could purchase fabric explicitly for quilts.

In the nineteenth century, it is unlikely that most fancy quilts were made from recycled materials. Folklorist and quilt historian Laurel Horton discovered that the fancy quilts made by middle-class quilters in the mid-nineteenth century in Macon County, North Carolina (just to the south of the Smoky Mountains), were made of materials purchased specifically for the quilt. Horton suggests the possibility that these formal, planned quilts, which resembled nineteenth-century quilts made in other parts of the country, were the rule rather than the exception. If this was true, then quilting may have been more common among middle-class than among poorer rural women.

To the extent that nineteenth-century quilts were made of recycled materials, they were probably not made of pretty scraps of calico but of plainer stuff. Tennessee quilt historian Merikay Waldvogel has documented the tradition of making linsey quilts in the South during the nineteenth century. Linsey, at that time a plainweave fabric made of a wool weft and a cotton warp (rather than wool and linen), was a coarse and stiff cloth that raveled easily, thus limiting the types of designs that could be used. Among the quilts documented by Waldvogel is a sixteen-patch quilt made in the late nineteenth century in Sevier County, Tennessee. This coarse quilt was used to hold down the feather comforter underneath so it would not fall off at night.

Even into the twentieth century, some families in the Smoky Mountains continued to make utilitarian quilts from recycled fabric. Letha Hicks remembered: "We bought meal and flour, it come in cloth bags then. [Mother]'d buy diamond dye and color them pokes and cut them up and piece them up in quilt tops. And then old cloth, she'd have us raveling it and then she'd take and make bats out of it, you know. She had cords to cord it. Get wool, she got a bunch of wool, she'd make bats to pad the quilts with. I've sit and raveled on them rags for many of a night. Get so sleepy!" The tradition of making quilts from flour sacks began in the nineteenth century and was maintained by rural people through the early decades of the twentieth. By the Depression years, flour companies, acknowledging this use, were printing instructions on removing dyes from the sacks, and some were even marketing flour sacks in pretty pastel colors. Undergarments were also sometimes made of flour sacks, a fact which led to countless humorous stories. In her study of Depression quilts, Merikay Waldvogel notes that a Sevier County woman remembers that her mother made men's underwear from the Red Cross flour sacks. When the ink would not come out, she centered the red cross across the backside of the shorts.

The nature of quilting in the Smoky Mountains varied considerably with the economic situation of the individual family. Some could purchase fabrics specifically for use in quilts, while others were forced to rely largely on recycled materials. Even the batting might either be purchased commercially or recycled. Families dislocated by the search for public work, and particularly women who of necessity sold their domestic skills for wages, were less likely to continue quilting. Still, a number of older women remember quiltings as one of the cooperative activities that was maintained in their rural communities during the early twentieth century.

During the early decades of this century, regional quilting traditions were affected by the growing number of women's magazines and newspapers carrying quilting columns and instructions and the national marketing of quilting patterns. This trend, which affected middle-class quilters first, culminated in a full-blown national quilting revival during the 1920s and 1930s. The revival, affected in part by the colonial revival, created new myths about the prevalence of quilting in early America, which in the mountains were overlaid with myths already present about handicrafts in Southern Appalachia. The revival also led to a homogenization of quilting across the country, and those in the mountains were similarly affected by the new nationwide preferences for pastel colors and the popularization of patterns such as Grandmother's Flower Garden, Dresden Plate, and Double Wedding Ring. A number of quilts from the Smoky Mountains region dating from the 1920s and 1930s used designs that were available from mail order catalogs or were printed in magazines such as *Progressive Farmer*. The Mountain Mist Company supplied quilt patterns with its commercial quilt batting.

By the 1960s and 1970s, a second nationwide quilt revival was in full swing, and quilts and quilt patterns from the first revival were redefined as traditional. Some older women such as Letha Hicks kept up an unbroken tradition: "[Mother] was all the time making quilts. I took up her habit; I make a lot of quilts." In 1984 when she was interviewed, Mrs. Hicks had a whole room of her small house devoted to quilting, with an old type of frame suspended from the ceiling. Younger women sometimes revived quilting traditions once found in their families, and others created tradition by making quilts for the express purpose of passing them down in the family.

To some degree, quilting can be set apart from most of the other craft traditions in the Smokies that have been affected by the various revivals. Unlike the majority of basketmakers, weavers, or woodcarvers, a substantial number of quilters do not sell their products. Of course, a number of quilters do sell some or most of their products, and a few, perhaps, squeeze out a living from quilting. Other quilters work cooperatively on quilts for charitable causes. But many more make quilts primarily for family members. Whether or not their families had a tradition of quilting, the new generation of quilters intend their quilts to become part of such a tradition.

Quilting exists in the Smoky Mountains pretty much as it does elsewhere in rural America. While many flock to the mountains to purchase authentic Appalachian quilts, that authenticity is primarily in the mind of the buyer. As Laurel Horton argues, those who go in search of true Appalachian quilts tend to find what they expect to find. In reality, quilts are traditional primarily because that is usually part of the quilter's intention. In creating her art, the quilter may choose to emphasize the importance of family or of a sense of place. The authenticity of the design, color, or material is largely beside the point.

Quilting also epitomizes that tension found in all folk arts between individual creativity and shared aesthetics. As with all traditional crafts, part of the maker's creativity involves working within the constraints of traditional aesthetic principles. But a quilter also makes the choice to work alone or within a group. While piecing is usually an individual act, the quilting itself may be collective, and some women still gather in clubs to have the social pleasures of quilting in the company of other women. Friendship or album quilts, in which each block is made by a different individual, exemplify this collectivity. Women may work together on a present for a coworker expecting a baby or someone else who is retiring. In some cases, families produce these quilts.

The Baxter family quilt is an example of such an item. Following a

Thanksgiving celebration in 1989, members of the extended Baxter family decided to create a sampler quilt representing the family. The following year at Thanksgiving an elaborate ritual of "casting lots" was devised, and one family member claimed ownership. Both the creation of the quilt and the ritual of defining ownership represent tradition in the making. The new owner called the quilt a "piece of family history."

As with most quilts made collectively, each block represents the individuality of the maker. Some blocks had images depicting occupations, hobbies, pets, homes, or achievements (including a block with quilted silver and gold records, representing the career of an award-winning song writer). Other blocks simply represent the aesthetic preference of the individual maker in choice of design or color. Collectively, however, the quilt symbolizes the family, as did the act of creating it. The project itself was chosen in part because of the association of quilting with the oldest member of the family. As David Baxter (the only male member of the family to make his own square) wrote: "My grandmother, Celia Elizabeth Williams Baxter (Granny), was once an excellent quilter, and many of her children and grandchildren own quilts that she made. The quilt project allowed us to participate in a tradition we associated with Granny." The actual quilting was done on a frame that had been made by her husband, who died in 1974.

The final product was made of thirty squares (plus an additional square made into a pillow). The diversity of designs was unified by a navy blue print fabric used for the stripping. The names of each contributor or contributing family were embroidered on each square, with parents' names in one color and children's in another. The layout itself symbolizes the structure of the family, with the older members of the family toward the center and subsequent generations on the outside. At the center was a square with the silk-screened image of a log cabin, the place where Celia Baxter's husband, James Scott Baxter, was born. The Willis Baxter Cabin still stands near Cosby, Tennessee, within the boundaries of the Great Smoky Mountains National Park. The hike to the homeplace is one of the focal points of the family's annual fall retreat (see chapter 8). Although the family is now spread over several states, with no members living in the Smokies, a strong sense of family and of place, two central values found in the region, are embodied in this quilt.

CHAPTER 5

Food, Drink, and Medicine

FOODS OF MEMORY

Foods and food traditions are often believed to be important components of regional identity. On the surface, however, there would seem to be little distinctive about Smoky Mountains foodways. Tourist establishments are hard-pressed to promote distinctive foods of the region and, if they try, fall back on traditional southern favorites or trout caught locally in mountain streams (or so the tourist hopes). Gift shops sell assortments of preserves, mountain honey, and sorghum (often not produced locally). Even at Cherokee, food is an almost invisible part of a culture that is packaged as a commodity for non-Indians.

If, unlike music and dance, foodways have played a minor role in the defining of Smoky Mountains culture to outsiders, that does not mean that foodways are an unimportant part of the region's folklife. Specific food preferences are generally similar to those in a much larger regional area. As in most of the South, corn and pork remain the cornerstones of the traditional diet. However, as elsewhere, the range of foods actually consumed has vastly changed in the past decades with the coming of chain supermarkets and restaurants. In the 1970s and 1980s, fast food restaurants made inroads in most counties in the Smoky Mountains region, often amidst considerable excitement among much of the local population. Still, what constitutes the locally significant foodways of the Smoky Mountains region is not so much a matter of what is consumed and how often, but of what meanings are attached to specific foods and what customs surround them.

Nostalgia is a theme often promoted to tourists in the Smoky Mountains region through crafts, music, and occasionally foods. However, for many of the people of the region, especially the older ones, memories of the past are important in ascribing meaning to certain foods. As cookstoves were not common in many rural mountain communities until after the turn of the century, there are still witnesses to this dramatic revolution in food preparation. Although the number of individuals who remember open hearth cookery is rapidly dwindling, those who do recall it do so with a powerful sense of longing.

Surely, most of the cooks who obtained their first cookstove must have viewed the acquisition with delight, or at least relief. Their burden was lightened. Cooks no longer had to stoop over the fire; they could stand up straight. More variety in cooking methods became available, since many rural women had not previously had any kind of oven except a dutch oven placed in the fire. Furthermore, the acquisition of the first stove frequently meant the construction of a separate room for a kitchen, giving cooks more room for food preparation. However, there seem to be mixed feelings about the effects of these kitchens. While creating more privacy for the cook, who no longer had to work in front of visitors, it also separated her from the hearth, which was the heart of the house. Most witnesses are also adamant that food just plain tasted better when it was cooked on the hearth. Some remember that their mothers or grandmothers continued to cook certain dishes on the hearth, either regularly or as special treats, even after they bought a cookstove. And while the children and grandchildren of these women would not wish to return to open-hearth cooking, their eyes or mouths water when they remember this form of food preparation.

Cornbread is the food item most frequently remembered that was cooked on the open hearth. In fact, it is perhaps the most important memory food in the Great Smoky Mountains region. The South's economics and agriculture resulted in the taste preference for cornbread. In the mid-nineteenth century, cheap wheat flour and commercial baking powder began to alter eating habits. The already-established preference for quick, hot breads at every meal resulted in the southern biscuit tradition. However, in communities less quickly drawn into the cash economy, cornbread held its dominance, although some mountain farmers grew wheat or purchased white flour. Breads made from white flour, either homemade biscuits or store-purchased "light bread," were more prestigious than cornbread. In *Dorie: Woman of the Mountains*, Dorie remembers of her childhood in the years soon after the turn of the century: "Cornbread was fine for the two other meals, but to eat cornbread for breakfast indicated poverty or laziness or both. Pa always said that while he was alive, we'd never have to eat cornbread for breakfast" (p. 18). However, it is the taste of cornbread that many remember when thinking about their childhoods.

Not necessarily just an accompaniment, cornbread can be a meal in itself. Served with (or crumbled in) milk or buttermilk, and sometimes with spring onions, it was once a common supper for rural folks who ate a larger noontime "dinner." This meal preference continues among some older individuals and is considered a treat by younger people who associate it with memories of parents or grandparents.

In a region where "plain" is considered a compliment, the humblest foods often have the most significance, reminding people of a time when many had little money but did have strong values. Another such food is soup beans. These are usually served with raw onions, also a distinct taste preference in the mountains, and, of course, cornbread. This trinity of beans, onions, and cornbread can be seen as the quintessential traditional meal of the region. While most frequently served at home, this meal is also found at some local restaurants. "Poor man's suppers" are still held in some communities at churches, schools, or community centers. Usually held as a fund-raising event, people pay for the privilege of eating beans, onions, and cornbread. Few complain.

If plainness has a certain value in the foodways of the region, it is not at the expense of hospitality. While myths of southern hospitality are often associated with a certain opulence, hospitality in the mountains, like plain food, was linked to economic necessities and traditional values. In the days when travel was difficult in much of the Smoky Mountains (still well within living memory), any degree of socializing demanded that visitors routinely be fed and put up for the night. Strangers travelling through the area would also be fed and housed for free. The tradition of feeding everyone was not restricted to the white population. The 1922–23 industrial survey conducted among the Cherokee noted that the wife of Nicodemus Bigmeat was "one of the old timers who feeds everyone who passes by."

The ethic of feeding all comers is still alive among many rural people. There are older people who would not hesitate to invite a total stranger in for a meal (and a few will still offer a room). This is no idle invitation. They expect the visitor to eat. And even in communities where strangers are no longer so readily trusted, there is a strong tradition of feeding acquaintances, friends, and kin. Much of the visiting and the feeding of visitors is still rather impromptu. For many rural people, it is considered far ruder to turn down an offered meal than it is to show up unexpectedly at mealtime.

The real mark of a traditional cook in the region seems to be the ability to turn out a meal for an unspecified number of people, often without warning. Formality is not a trait of these meals. The message of such an offering is "we are simple people but we are more than happy to share what we have." Despite the virtue of plainness, abundance is often apparent, more in variety than in the quantity of any single food. Particularly in the summer, a staggering assortment of vegetables may appear, and at other times a wealth of items may emerge from Tupperware containers in the refrigerator, jars in the basement, and bags in the freezer.

Traditionally, the appearance of abundance was aided by the fact that food cooked at midday was (and sometimes still is) left on the table, covered by a tablecloth, or on the stove for hours to serve latecomers for dinner or to serve again as supper. Not only did this keep people in readiness for any friends or family who might drop by; it also freed women from having to prepare another cooked meal in the evening. Frequently the food was not reheated, and some people still express a preference for eating foods in that manner. John Baxter remembers visiting his uncle and aunt in the Smokies. In this rather unusual case, his aunt was the breadwinner and his uncle the cook and housekeeper, but the patterns of cooking and serving food were traditional. "I always remember going to Uncle Bill's and he would cook in the middle of the day . . . So we would have cream corn and beans. Then when supper would come we would go back and dip from those things but he wouldn't heat it up. I remember just how good that tasted. And even today I don't like hot food, really. I don't guess he taught me to like cold food, but I can just always remember how good that cold corn and cold beans tasted as we'd eat that for supper."

The preference for certain foods and the open hospitality clearly reflect the value placed on the past. Although people remember poverty and hard times, they tend to focus on how good the food tasted, the abundance nature usually provided, and how generous people were. Alice Hawkins Haynes, born in 1899 on Fines Creek in Haywood County, North Carolina, wrote in her memoirs of her family's "pork sharing neighbors," recalling: "Community sharing also included any kind of grain or animal fodder. Milk, butter and eggs were commonly shared too. Before and after Sunday School or preaching, borrowing and swapping took place in the churchyard all the time. We always knew whose hens weren't laying and whose cow had gone dry. Often neighbors would loan a cow to other families to furnish them with milk and butter until their cow came fresh again." Although as a child she had only one pair of shoes, which would wear out before the year was up, Letha Hicks of Big Bend (also Haywood County) remembered the abundance of foods at holidays:

They'd start a baking a week or two before Christmas . . . the older girls, Heidi and Mary and Florence, and all of them, you know, they'd bake up and have plenty cooked.

And Mother, she'd make souse. They'd kill about two or three hogs and cook up a big bunch of hog meat and she'd make a big bunch of souse. She had them two-gallon crocks, she'd fill them full. People would come in and they wanted them some souse, they just take a knife and go slice them out a hunk, slice of souse and eat it.

And go into the cupboard, had stack cakes, big, high, and stacked. Cakes, pies, they just filled the cupboard full. Sometimes on the table, if they couldn't get it [in the cupboard]. And they had them coffee buckets . . . They'd fill that full of sweetbread.

The irony of all these fond memories is that they pertain to a time when well-intentioned outsiders were writing of a Southern Appalachia where malnourishment and hunger were rampant. In his chapter "The Land of Do Without," Horace Kephart painted a bleak picture of the diet of mountain people. "Even to families that are fairly well-to-do there will come periods of famine," he wrote. However, Duane Oliver, writing more recently of cooking on Hazel Creek, the mountain community Kephart knew best, concluded from his interviews with former residents that "except for some disaster, there was no excuse for anyone on Hazel Creek or anywhere in the Smokies to go hungry." It is hard to reconcile the vastly different portraits drawn of the nature of traditional diet in the mountains. However, it should be noted that while some people choose to remember the best of times, it was the worst of times that the chroniclers of the region were eager to document. As is true for all agricultural people, nature is not always a reliable source of food. (However, more went hungry when they left family farms for public work and were caught in the boom-and-bust economy of timbering or other local industries.) It may also be significant that there are vast cultural differences in the perception of what constitutes a good meal.

The importance of memory in giving significance to food is heightened by the fact that change has been so dramatic. Members of a generation who remember open-hearth cooking are now likely to have microwaves in their kitchens. Just as pork, cornbread, greens, and onions may still be favored, so too perhaps are the traditional forms of cooking—frying and boiling—that were possible on the open fire. But this has not kept traditional cooks from venturing out to try new foods and new techniques. Substantial changes in the foods themselves occurred during the early decades of this century. By 1930 milk had become preferred over buttermilk; citrus fruits were common; beef, cheese, and canned fish were more frequently a part of meals; and sugar began to rival molasses as a sweetener, while the use of honey and maple sugar declined. Today most chain supermarkets in the region give little evidence of any specific regional food preferences. If a "Smoky Mountains cuisine" does not exist as a distinct entity, however, food still plays an important role in defining the past.

GIFTS FROM NATURE

The abundance of nature in providing foods is a common theme when individuals in the Great Smoky Mountains remember the past. While today foods that come directly from nature, rather than being cultivated or purchased, represent a tiny proportion of what is consumed, they do play a continuing role in defining the significant food traditions of the region.

During the early twentieth century, a large number of edible fruits grew wild or semi-wild. From May to August, a succession of berries—wild strawberries, raspberries, blackberries, and huckleberries—were available for picking. Though berries do not grow in the abundance they once did, blackberries in particular still thrive, and those who are willing to risk the briars, chiggers, and poison ivy make these wild fruits into cobblers and preserves. Apples, grown in orchards or found in the wild, played an important role in the traditional diet. Drying or sulphuring were common methods of preservation in the early twentieth century, and dried apples could later be used in pies and stack cakes. By midcentury, the ledges under the rear windows of cars were often used to speed the process, though as fresh apples became commercially available year-round in supermarkets, drying became less frequent. Many people, however, still make applesauce or apple butter at home. By 1900 in communities such as Cataloochee, apples were being grown commercially, and they are still a cash crop in the Smoky Mountains region.

Chestnuts also were grown in orchards and found in the wild. Older people almost universally mourn the passing of the American chestnut tree and have fond memories of roasting chestnuts on the fire. Those who were industrious enough to gather large quantities could sell chestnuts commercially. Alice Hawkins Haynes remembers that a peddler would come through Fines Creek with a wagon in November. "He'd buy all the chestnuts he could, haul them to Waynesville and ship them to Asheville." The dried chestnuts were sold for five cents a pound. Cherokee cooks made even more extensive use of the chestnut than their non-Indian neighbors. Chestnuts were frequently added to cornmeal dough that was then boiled or baked. Hazelnuts, hickory nuts, walnuts, and persimmons also grew wild in the mountains and were available for those who took the trouble to gather them.

In the springtime, wild greens supplemented the diet. Bonnie Meyers, who grew up in Cades Cove, remembered that "along the creeks we would get crow's foot, bear lettuce, that came out like in March you know and that was good herb-like food, and like lettuce, you'd put a little dressing of some kind on it." Poke had to be parboiled several times and then fried in bacon fat before it was rendered edible. Other plants such as sorrel and young dandelion took only one boiling and then were dressed (or "killed") with hot bacon drippings. Among the most popular of the wild greens was spring cress, known as "creesy greens." Fresh creesy greens are still available in some markets in the spring, and canned creesy greens can be found in some stores.

While the consumption of wild greens has been common throughout much of the southern United States, the most quintessentially "mountain" of the items gathered from the wild are ramps, which only grow at elevations of three thousand feet or more. A wild leek, ramps are gathered in late April or early May in dark, moist areas. Onions in general are a regional favorite, and ramps are known for their particularly sweet taste. They were also consumed as a spring tonic and were traditionally served with sassafras tea. Ramps are still eaten raw or are parboiled and fried in grease, frequently with scrambled eggs.

Foods gathered in the wild are considered more special as they become harder to find and are consumed less often. Access to ramps in particular is limited, not only by the declining amount of habitat where they can grow, but also because of the creation of the national park, where digging plants is forbidden. Whereas once children were the most common gatherers of wild foods, now real skill and knowledge are needed to locate some plants. Gathering itself has become a sport.

So too has the sport aspect of hunting and fishing overtaken the importance of these activities as a means of food procurement. Wild game once constituted a sizeable part of the Cherokee diet and a not-insignificant proportion of the food consumed by their non-Indian neighbors. By 1900, however, hunting had taken on a relatively minor role in the procuring of food, though in times of hardship, the hunting of small game such as squirrels did put meat on the table. At the same time, however, hunting as a recreational sport grew, becoming one of the lures of the Smokies to outsiders even as the number and variety of game dwindled. Hunting became one of the traditional skills that was transformed into a marketable commodity as the region was invaded by visitors seeking the wilderness. A number of local men became hunting guides, selling their knowledge of the area's terrain and the habits of its fauna.

A similar transition applied to fishing. The Cherokee had relied extensively on their well-developed skills at fishing to supplement their diet. Fish were shot with blow guns, trapped with a combination of stone weirs and baskets, speared, and caught with cane poles. While mountaineers were stereotyped as being bait fishermen, they also used flies. One of the valued flies used in fishing during the late nineteenth century, by Cherokee and non-Indians alike, was the Cherokee floating deerhair fly. Aside from the use of the deerhair fly, wet-fly fishing was generally preferred over dry well into the twentieth century.

Even as mountain fishing was beginning to attract eager fishermen from elsewhere, farming and timbering were beginning to take a toll on the local trout population. In the final decades of the nineteenth century, the states began to stock local streams, introducing new species of trout to the Smokies. Meanwhile, local people began to profit from the growing craze for fishing by serving as guides, by boarding fishermen visiting the region, and by tying flies. However, even as fishing and hunting skills became marketable, these activities continued to provide recreation (and food) for the local population.

The traditions of procuring foods from the wild have been altered not only by the dwindling resources of nature but also by new rules of access. Game and fishing laws now strictly regulate these activities, and there is little property that is not regulated as public land or strictly defined as private. One cannot freely roam the mountains looking for the bounty of nature. In the Smokies, a profound change governing the taking of nature's gifts came with the creation of the national park. If park officials often tended to view the local population as less than law abiding, most of the conflict was over new rules. Early superintendents' reports abound with accounts of individuals fined for poaching, violating fishing regulations, or even digging ramps. In a region where independence and self-reliance were highly valued, this disagreement over the reaping of gifts from nature was emblematic of the central cultural conflict in the Smokies of the twentieth century: massive governmental intervention versus local tradition.

GARDENING AND FOOD PRESERVATION

Although the activity of gathering foods from the wild has been sharply curtailed in this century, gardening has remained a viable aspect of the culture. While the produce from home gardens represents a dwindling percentage of the food actually consumed, most rural people in the region who are physically capable have some type of garden. The importance of gardening, in fact, arises in part from two sets of values in the region that are often interpreted as contradictory: independence and self-reliance on the one hand and cooperation and sharing on the other.

While a high percentage of rural people in the Smoky Mountains region have gardens, few make much money growing food crops. Even the small farmers' markets that are common in some regions of the country are not found there as frequently. Still, a good many people grow more than their families can consume. The garden is a sign of abundance, of having enough to share with others. It is also a sign of independence, especially for older individuals. Many people garden into extreme old age and find it a difficult transition when health problems finally prevent them from doing so.

Gardens, of course, reflect traditional dietary preferences; a garden isn't a garden without corn, beans, onions, and usually both sweet and white potatoes. Still, items such as zucchini squash, "English" peas (and now sugar snaps), and hot peppers have made inroads into local gardens.

Methods of preservation have changed dramatically. For many rural people at the turn of the century, preservation of food was a vital means of feeding the family through the winter. However, methods of preservation were limited primarily to cold cellaring, pickling (mostly cabbage), and drying. Cooperative work that transformed labor into social events sometimes included food preservation. Many older women fondly remember "bean stringings." Dried beans took two forms: "leather britches"—dried green beans—and "shucky beans"—dried beans that would later be shucked.

By the 1920s and 1930s, canning was becoming more popular as glass mason jars were made available and rural people had the cash to pay for them. Some philanthropic organizations and agencies such as home extension offices provided instruction and facilities for canning. More recently, freezers have provided another means of preservation, though frozen food has the disadvantage of not being as easily given as gifts. Not only do people often grow more than they are going to eat, they also preserve more. The giving of home-canned goods extends traditional notions of hospitality and sharing.

Gardening and especially canning not only provide a means of independence and sharing with others, they are also a form of aesthetic expression. Visual pleasure is taken in a well-ordered garden and particularly in rows and rows of canned goods. "Aren't they pretty?" one woman asked as she proudly displayed her jars of food to a stranger. Obviously, some effort had gone not only into the appearance of the individual jar but to the combination of form and colors in the arrangement on the shelf.

Home canners are also willing to embrace new forms. Salsa is now a popular item, perhaps not surprisingly, since the commercial sale of salsa currently outranks the sale of ketchup nationwide. And, for home canners, this is a logical extension from the canning of tomatoes and the making of such items as chow chow or pepper relish. At a western North Carolina fair, a sizeable number of salsas were judged in the canning exhibition.

CHEROKEE FOODS

Much of what can be said generally about foodways in the Great Smoky Mountains region is true of Cherokees and non-Indians alike. By 1900 the food preferences of these two groups were quite similar, the product of years of mutual influence. Historian John Finger's description of the turn-of-the-century Cherokee diet, with only slight variations, would also be true of non-Indians in the region: "Tribal diets primarily featured a multitude of corn dishes, but chestnuts were also important, in their natural state and especially for bread. Other foods included a variety of berries, homegrown apples and peaches, bacon, and coffee. Some of the more well-to-do or acculturated Indians also used honey, molasses, and flour bread. Pork was the preferred meat." Indeed, the base of the southern diet, particularly the reliance on pork and corn, was the result of the marriage of European and Indian food habits that began as early as the founding of Jamestown. While the Cherokee accepted a number of European food traditions, they also contributed their expertise in gathering the wild plants of the region, in fishing and hunting, and in the cultivation of the local terrain. Most of the wild plants commonly consumed by the North Carolina Cherokee today, such as ramps, sochan, poke, creases, and wild berries, are also eaten by non-Indians in the region.

However, not all of what the Cherokee considered gifts of nature were enjoyed by non-Indians in the region. The Cherokees ate some varieties of toads and frogs, parboiled or cooked in stews. Another dish probably not appreciated by their non-Indian neighbors was a soup made of browned yellowjackets. (Although consumed by many cultures throughout the world, insects have never been accepted as a food by European-Americans.) In these few items, definitions of edibility divided the two cultural groups.

Differences also existed between Cherokees and non-Indians regarding some methods of food preparation and in the significance ascribed to certain foods. Corn, while traditionally essential to the diets of both groups, was for the Cherokee also a significant part of their cosmology. Sacred mythology described the origin of corn and provided instructions on how it was to be grown. The Green Corn dance, which celebrated the harvest, has been revived several times in this century. In Cherokee cosmology, corn was associated with women, who traditionally were the principal horticulturalists (men were responsible for providing meat, primarily wild game).

Cherokee corn itself was different. The Cherokee produced two types of corn, a flint corn and a larger corn for flour. Hybrid corn has largely replaced the former, though a few individuals still produce flour corn in their gardens. Efforts to revive cultivation of this corn have begun in recent years. In the early twentieth century, the Cherokee were also likely to grind the corn differently from how their neighbors did. While some used hand grinders or took corn to a local mill, the more traditional continued to use a large wooden pestle, four to five feet long, and mortar. The use of this *ko no na* survived among a few into the mid-twentieth century.

Today the aspect of corn preparation that most signals Cherokee ethnicity is the making of traditional bread, or "dumplings." Cornmeal is mixed with hot water, shaped into balls, wrapped in green corn blades, and boiled (or sometimes baked). Taking the union of pinto beans and cornmeal one step further than their neighbors, Cherokee cooks often mix

Cherokee woman grinding corn with *ko no na* (Photo courtesy of Great Smoky Mountains National Park)

cooked beans into cornmeal in the preparation of this bread. Chestnuts or pumpkin may also be added. Another regional corn favorite, hominy, is also given a distinctive Cherokee twist when it is prepared with pinto beans or walnuts.

If traditionally prepared breads such as bean bread are an important symbol of Cherokee ethnicity in their own community, another type of bread has become one of the few Indian foods marketed to non-Indians. As with much else in Cherokee, the making of fry bread is more a result of pan-Indianism (and a general ignorance of distinctions between one tribe and another among non-Indians) than it is a part of traditional Cherokee culture. Fry bread itself was a native response to the distribution of specific government rations—white flour and lard—among a number of Native American people, particularly in the western United States. Today, fry bread is a popular treat sold at the Cherokee Fall Festival and other local celebrations.

As was the case among white Appalachians, the traditional diet, frequently remembered with fondness by older people, was the subject of negative scrutiny by outside do-gooders. The boarding school, that agent of enforced acculturation, was used to introduce Cherokee children to new diets. In the 1920s, the Cherokee superintendent believed that Cherokee children were in fact better fed than their white neighbors because of the schools. Despite their efforts, officials had limited success in altering traditional food preferences. Callie Wachacha, interviewed for the Fading Voices project at Snowbird, was probably not alone in remembering that food from home was much better. After school vacations she would bring some of her grandmother's dumpling bread back with her to boarding school. Although she kept it at the head of her bed, it sometimes got swiped. "I never reported it when my food got gone. I just thought somebody else was hungry, too."

By mid-twentieth century, Cherokees were more likely to be criticized, not for adherence to traditional diets, but for their use of commercial products, such as hot dogs, soft drinks, and cake mixes. However, as with their non-Cherokee neighbors, health problems are perhaps more associated with the growing sedentary nature of their life-style than with a diet traditionally heavy in fats and starch (and now sugars). Traditional views of ideal weight among both Cherokees and non-Indians differ from those currently popular. Cherokee babies were deliberately fattened up; chubby babies were thought to be healthy babies. Non-Indians also associated a certain amount of fat with health, and older people are more likely to express concern than congratulations over someone losing weight ("falling off").

BEVERAGES

Regarding at least one traditional beverage preference, people from the Smoky Mountains were well ahead of their times. They are true connoisseurs of water. Many who moved away to towns or cities during the early twentieth century remember vividly discovering how bad water could taste and how relieved they were when they returned to the fresh, clear water of the mountains. People could discuss long and hard the merits of a particular spring. Although water in the Smokies, as elsewhere, has suffered from pollution, people from the region still tend to be sensitive to the taste of water.

The other common beverages at the turn of the century were milk, or more commonly buttermilk, and coffee. Even rural people who purchased almost no other foodstuffs did buy coffee. Most considered it a necessity. "Dozen eggs about worth a pound of coffee. That was something Mother and Pap couldn't do without, was their coffee. Mother would take a headache, just nearly kill her. Daddy would get ill if he couldn't get his coffee," remembered one woman who grew up in the Smokies. Beans were roasted at home and ground daily in hand grinders or grinders mounted on the side of the house. (Today, however, most older people in the region would find the mania for freshly roasted and ground coffee a little silly.)

A number of herbal teas were also consumed, both by Cherokees and non-Indians, though often for medicinal purposes rather than for quenching thirst. Today the Smoky Mountains region shares the southern mania for iced tea (simply called tea, as it is elsewhere in the South), drunk in all seasons of the year. Inhabitants also resemble other southerners in their passion for soft drinks (still called "dope" or "sodey dope" by some old-timers), and, like others in that part of the country, are far more likely to drink it in the morning than Americans elsewhere.

Of course the most controversial beverage of the mountains was corn whiskey, particularly illegally produced "moonshine." Many are still sensitive to the stereotypes of "hillbillies" drinking homemade whiskey out of a jug. Apologists would argue that the production of whiskey was part of a Scotch-Irish heritage and also of the economic reality of the frontier. Of course, whiskey was made throughout the South (although Southern Appalachia suffered the brunt of the stereotyping). However, it is also true that there are more social strictures against drinking in most of the South, including the Smokies, than there are in much of the rest of the country.

The making of corn whiskey and of brandy from apples, peaches, and grapes, was not uncommon and was not necessarily illegal during much of the nineteenth century. Few profited from this production, and small-time makers were likely to share with their neighbors, as they would other surpluses of agricultural production. While there was little tradition of social drinking, whiskey and brandies were extensively used for medicinal purposes and as tonics.

In the late nineteenth century, governmental restrictions and taxes on the production of alcohol grew. So too did religious condemnation of

R. O. Wilson (left) of Jackson County, North Carolina, and Hamper McBee of Monteagle, Tennessee, demonstrating the making of corn whiskey on the National Mall (Photo by Melissa Johnson, courtesy of Center for Folklife Programs and Cultural Studies, Smithsonian Institution)

drinking. In the early twentieth century, while more and more people were disapproving of the consumption of alcohol, even for medicinal purposes, the sale of alcohol became more profitable. Taxation on alcohol actually made the sale of homemade whiskey more profitable for those who were willing to take the risks, and some interpreted the conflict as one more effort by the government to interfere with the independence of the individual. As more and more people were drawn into public work, moonshining became one way for people to enter the cash economy. And some who had become dependent on the cash economy turned to moonshining when local paid work dried up.

National prohibition in the 1920s increased the demand for homemade whiskey and widened its market. Even after alcohol was made legal again, the lack of work during the Depression years forced many, non-Indians and Cherokees alike, into moonshining. As one man remembered for the Fading Voices project: "Everybody was needy; half of them didn't have shoes. I finally got to where I just didn't care. Young and stout and couldn't get jobs. I'd been all around South Carolina—just hitch-hiking everywhere trying to find a job. Finally, I came back home in the fall. We'd made a crop; I'd left it with the old lady. And I started making liquor. I had to have some money." "Bootlegging," the marketing of illegal alcohol, was generally a separate profession. As the man quoted above remembered, "Finally, I got me an old car, but I never did boot-leg much. You couldn't do that and make whiskey. You'd get caught."

In subsequent decades the production of local whiskey declined, though it did not disappear altogether. The knowledge of how to make whiskey still remains, as does some sensitivity about making that knowledge public. One western North Carolina man was willing to make the "beer" for a demonstration at a local heritage festival but initially was reluctant to demonstrate whiskey-making in public. He also did not wish to go to the store and buy the large quantities of sugar and corn meal required, for fear of raising suspicions (though the whiskey was made legally under permit).

The profession of bootlegging has not altogether disappeared, though the profits are not in selling whiskey that is made illegally. With the strange patchwork of local liquor laws in the region, some individuals continue to make a profit by illegally bringing alcohol over state, county, and municipal lines and reselling it.

FOLK MEDICINE

The Smokies region is rich in herbal lore, largely because of the Cherokee, who have preserved knowledge of the medicinal properties of many indigenous plants. They have passed some of this information on to their non-Indian neighbors, who brought with them medicinal lore from their own cultures.

In the early years of the twentieth century, knowledge of folk medicinal practices was still widespread among many rural people. Just as the wild produced many foods that could be consumed, so too did nature provide medicine. "So many plants and flowers could be used for sickness. Slowly, I learned what was good for the afflictions of man. We gathered cockleburrs to be boiled into a cough syrup for winter colds. Tansy was a fern-like plant used as tea for upset stomachs and headaches. Boneset and catnip were brewed into tea for fretful babies and nervous disorders. Sassafras was a good blood builder. Spignet root was kidney medicine. Crushed ragweed was rubbed on skin blistery from poison ivy and oak" (*Dorie*, p. 25). Even decades later, in the 1930s and 1940s, traditional remedies were still used. Bonnie Meyers remembers: "We had . . . homemade cough syrups, my mother would make, use cherry bark, and make cough syrup. She'd put rock candy in and a little touch of whiskey, you know, for cough. And poultices for . . . like you had a sore or something on your foot, they'd put poultices on it made out of peach limbs, they'd scrape that young bark underneath, you know, put a poultice on it."

Spring tonics were particularly common in the mountains. Most were believed to purify, thin, or tone the blood, according to a folk hematology suggesting that many illnesses were due to blood that was too high or low, thick or thin. To the extent that most hematic herbs do have some therapeutic characteristics (usually acting as diuretics, stimulants, purgatives, or fever reducers), tonics were effective to some extent. (Though in recent years some members of the medical establishment have warned that sassafras, a particularly popular hematic herb in the mountains, may be carcinogenic.)

Many of the items used as spring tonics, such as ramps, poke, and burdock, were the same plants that were consumed in spring before gardens starting producing. Considering the winter's monotonous diet of dried and preserved foods, it was no wonder that these fresh greens had a tonic effect. A popular nonherbal tonic often inflicted upon children was sulphur and molasses. Tobacco juice, kerosene, and, of course, whiskey were also used in home healing. The ever-present onions and lard played a role as well; massive quantities of onion would be cooked in lard to produce poultices.

One of the best-known plants with medicinal properties in the Smokies was *Panax quinquefolium*, American ginseng. The Cherokee used ginseng for headaches, cramps, and "female troubles." Ginseng was also used in the mountains as a tonic, to reduce fatigue and to retard the aging process. Some shared the belief found in many Asian cultures that it was an aphrodisiac. The form of the gnarled root, which often took humanoid shapes, was believed to affect its healing power. The use of ginseng in the mountains was limited, however, because of its more powerful ability to bring in cash or to be used in barter. In the early nineteenth century, as they began to lose their traditional sources of livelihood, some Cherokees sold ginseng to local traders. By the late nineteenth century, much of the ginseng dug in Southern Appalachia was ending up in Asian markets, and the plant was becoming scarce in some parts of the mountains.

Ginseng was not the only wild plant that brought in cash for some mountain families. Letha Hicks remembered: "We'd get out through the summer and dig ginseng, spignet, wild ginger, and sassafras bark. And my daddy would take it plumb on into Meadow Fork, to the store. He'd buy Mother a pair of shoes and he'd get us a pair of shoes and enough cloth to make us about two dresses and that would have to do us for a year." While ginseng brought about eight or ten dollars a pound, wild ginger brought only thirty-five cents. According to Hicks, "Sassafras was about the best-price herb there was except ginseng."

Although ginseng is much more difficult to locate now than it was a century ago, the art of locating and digging it is still passed down in some families. Responsible gatherers know not to take it all or to plant the berries, so that it will continue to grow in years to come. Many are secretive about where they find it. Some use ginseng tea for its "tonic" effect (one woman reported that it was great for getting housework done), but the primary motivation, as it was in 1900, is still economic. Prices can fluctuate quite a bit from year to year, but ginseng still offers a good return for those who have the time to look and know how to find it.

Not all folk medical belief in the Smokies was strictly herbal or natural. Especially for the Cherokee, healing was an integrated part of a larger belief system, which focused especially on the relationship of humans to the larger plant and animal world. A particular emphasis was placed on the maintenance of equilibrium or harmony. In one Cherokee myth, disease was interpreted as the animals' revenge for human overpopulation. Taking pity on humans, the plant world offered a cure for each disease, though it was up to the conjurors to discover which plant cured what disease.

During the early nineteenth century, the introduction of Christianity altered Cherokee beliefs. However, the Cherokee often found ways to reconcile traditional and Christian beliefs and were most likely to accept those aspects of Christianity that were compatible with beliefs they already held. The traditional belief system was maintained through practices that superficially appeared to be recreational (ballplay and dancing) and through medical practices. While the introduction of the Sequoyah syllabary permitted the Bible and hymns to be written in the Cherokee language, it also preserved and codified sacred medicinal formulas. Although knowledge of the efficacy of hundreds of plants was part of the healing system, so too were specific rituals and ceremonies.

In many cases, in the nineteenth century the traditional Cherokee healer also preached the gospel. This may still be the case in a few instances. In her study of the Snowbird Cherokee, Sharlotte Neely mentions that one Indian doctor was a Christian minister as well. She also writes of another Baptist minister who included in his sermon a reference to the myth of the origin of disease and medicine. "Instead of counterposing Cherokee mythology and Christian doctrine, the minister considered the two compatible. In the minister's reinterpretation of the myth, only Jesus can heal illness, accomplishing His purpose through physicians or 'conjure men,' whose duty it is to locate the plant or herb which will cure a particular disease" (*Snowbird Cherokees*, p. 64). Neither is modern medicine necessarily seen in opposition to traditional healing. While some may turn to a traditional healer if they are initially dissatisfied with modern medicine, the two approaches are often used in combination.

Today, knowledge of the specific healing properties of certain plants is preserved by some conservative Cherokees. The number of healers who still practice the accompanying ceremonies is far smaller, though the actual number is impossible to know. Many aspects of healing are not made public. To the extent that healing still exists in the context of traditional ritual and belief, it is practiced privately and not for onlookers either inside or outside the community.

6

Verbal Lore

S P E E C H

Among the most stereotyped aspects of southern mountain culture is speech. As with most stereotypes of Appalachia, it is double-edged. The language of the mountains is portrayed both negatively, as ignorant and uneducated, and romantically, as ancient and poetic. The issue of whether there is such a thing as Appalachian speech is made problematic by the fact that many of its characteristics are similar to those found elsewhere in the Upper South; at the same time, there can be considerable subregional variation within Southern Appalachia, and even within the Smoky Mountains region itself.

The complexity goes beyond subregional variation, however. Within a single community, differences can exist according to age, educational level, social standing or aspirations and pure personal predilection. These variations often exist even within a single family. Finally, there is the fact that every individual has the ability to vary his or her manner of speaking, according to both the situation and the subject matter. In the Smokies this is most apparent among those Eastern Cherokee who are bilingual, but every individual has the ability to switch style of speech if not actual language. Whether it is done consciously or unconsciously, speech can be used as a subtle part of regional identity.

Despite the stereotypical manner in which mountain speech is presented, especially in written dialect, Southern Appalachian speech is generally subtler than some other southern dialects. A northerner is far more likely to understand and be understood in the Smoky Mountains region than in the Deep South; there is simply not such a strong line between northern and southern speech styles. Unlike in the more southern states, northerners are not generally told that they talk too fast or are incomprehensible.

For the outsider, most difficulties in comprehension lie in those words or phrases that mean something different in the Smokies (and perhaps elsewhere in the southern mountains) than they do in most of the rest of the country. For instance, the nomenclature pertaining to flora and fauna can be confusing; thus rhododendron is known locally as "laurel," while mountain laurel is known as "ivy." A "boomer" is a type of squirrel. For older people, especially, not only is dinner the noontime meal, but "evening" can be any time after noon (but before supper). As in African-American speech, the term "bad" does not necessarily have negative connotations. In the southern mountains it can signify personal predilections; as one woman said, "My dad was bad for wanting vegetables for breakfast." One potentially embarrassing situation is a nonnative's misunderstanding of the term "don't care to," which regionally means "don't mind." If someone tells you that they "don't care to help you at all," they are probably being friendly.

Among the most distinctive regional pronunciations is the transformation of the final "a" to a long "e," especially in proper names. Barbara may become "Barbry," Sylva (the seat of Jackson County, North Carolina) is pronounced "Sylvy" by some, and the historical character Tom Dula becomes the "Tom Dooley" of song. Horace Kephart claimed that in mountain dialect "all vowels may be interchanged with others." While today this would be quite an overstatement (and probably was even in Kephart's time), as with many southerners, words such as "pin" and "pen" are seen as homonyms and may even be taught as such in local schools. (In a more scholarly vein, Appalachian studies scholar Cratis Williams wrote of mountain speech that "both front and back vowels and diphthongs are pulled toward the middle of the mouth as if all were being reduced to schwa. . . .") Substitution of consonants, wrote Kephart, was not so common but did exist. One of the still relatively common pronunciations, typical of the consonant changes in Appalachian speech and still used by some older folks, is "chimly" or "chimbly" for chimney.

The speech of the Smoky Mountains has been portrayed and studied for over a century. Local color writers were the first to attempt to capture Appalachian speech. Among these writers was Mary Noailles Murfree, who, under the name Charles Egbert Craddock, published a number of stories and novels in the 1880s that were set in Cades Cove. Several decades later, Horace Kephart devoted a chapter of *Our Southern Highlanders* to the "mountain dialect." As he did in the book generally, Kephart both decried stereotypes and gave the public what they wanted to hear. He starts his chapter by noting the outrage local people feel when confronted with a portrayal of their dialect in "an orthography that is as odd to them as it is to us" and by commenting that a neighbor in the Smokies confronted him with the fact that "you educated folks don't spell your own words the way you say them." However, while stating that the "curse of dialect writing is elision" he apparently felt it was necessary to capture the "excessively clipped" nature of highlands speech. Although much of his portrayal of mountain speech falls short of the mark, he does make a few useful observations. While patterns of regional speech have changed considerably since then, people in the region would not find anything particularly unusual in some of the "quaint idioms" he lists (though they might well object to the label): "Sam went to Andrews or to Murphy, one." ("One" is an abbreviation of "one or the other.") "Come in and set."

The first scholarly study of the speech of the Smoky Mountains was conducted by Joseph Hall. One of the few trained scholars studying the culture after the park removals, Hall, a doctoral student in literature at Columbia University, was appointed by the National Park Service in 1938 as a student technician and was assigned to conduct a study of the speech dialect of the Great Smokies. Later he obtained the status of "collaborator" for the park service and for several decades continued his study of the Smokies. Although his primary interest was linguistic, Hall, in his effort to document the spoken language, also recorded folk history, ballads, and descriptions of the folklife of the region. In his scholarly publications, Hall criticized the distortions of mountain speech made by popular writers, including Kephart. He did not find the speech of the Smoky Mountains to be distinct from that of most of America, though he found "close affinities with the speech of the rest of the South." In his popular writings on the Smokies, however, Hall paints a more romantic picture of the "quaint survivals" of Smoky Mountains speech.

The idea of the antiquity of southern mountain speech is so entrenched that it is still common to hear references to the "Elizabethan" or "Shakespearean" speech of the mountains. While there may be noticeably conservative aspects of the speech of the mountains, no living language is static. All languages change; so do they all retain some antiquated forms. Still, old stereotypes are slow to die. While recognizing the dynamic nature of Appalachian speech, Cratis Williams, a preeminent Appalachian studies scholar, turned the old stereotype on its head by insisting that mountain speech was *older* than Elizabethan English. The speech of Southern Appalachia, Williams argued, descended from the dialect spoken along the Scottish-English border just before the time of the emigration of lowland Scots to northern Ireland. No longer speaking Scottish, these lowland Scots spoke a form of English that was far older than the dialect of southern England. It was this dialect, according to Williams's theory, that was taken first to northern Ireland and subsequently to the new world.

While his ideas on the Scotch-Irish origins of mountain speech may be controversial, Williams's greatest contribution to our understanding of the language of Southern Appalachia was his insistence that it was more than phonetics, morphology, and survival forms. The speech of the mountains could be understood only in a cultural context; it expressed "basic views of life, attitudes, ways of looking at things." Among these regional views is the attitude that speech is not just instrumental; it is valued in and of itself. The routine exchange of conversation is so important that it might be considered rude to get right to the point.

Particularly among older rural people in the Smoky Mountains region, routine visiting is a vital part of social life. "Visiting" doesn't have to involve any particular activity other than the leisurely exchange of conversation. This conversation often proceeds along fairly conventional lines: the health of friends and relatives, the weather. Even these subjects can be commented on in conventionalized forms. Speaking of a month of rainy weather, one woman told me: "If it didn't rain of a day, it rained that night . . . It's liable to be dry a right smart piece." A short visit can be an almost impossible feat, and even after hours have passed, a visitor's attempts to leave are often met by "stay awhile," "don't leave." To a large extent, the hospitality and invitations to visit are still extended even to strangers. Many older people to this day insist that they "don't know a stranger." One woman, in her nineties and living alone, insisted on inviting a stranger in, even though, as she said, "I don't know you from Adam's house cat."

As the above example demonstrates, speech is not only valued for its role in social interaction but is also seen as an opportunity for play. Cratis Williams called mountain speech "metaphor-studded and decorated with abundant similes." Particularly for some older people, the delight in saying something in a poetic or interesting manner overrides interest in straightforward talk. Why walk when you can "take shank's mare"? Noting her mother's habit of cooking for anyone who stopped by, one woman recalled, "Mama said she'd cooked for lawyers and judges and doctors and preachers and bootleggers and I don't know what all . . . she just said bootleggers . . . but she didn't know any."

While traditional speech might be generally metaphoric in nature, abstract ideas are often expressed through concrete examples. Poet and novelist Jim Wayne Miller, a native of western North Carolina, notes:

Well, the most characteristic thing—the people's way of talking and way of making points—is to tell little stories that will illustrate their point. And it results in going the long way around sometimes instead of expressing a thing abstractly. A typical way of beginning, if a subject is under discussion, would be to say, "Well I'm by that the way so-and-so was when this-and-that happened." And then an anecdote will come out of it. And it's the making of abstract meanings through the telling of very particular incidents and events. And I think that's central to the tradition, and sometimes people have to tell the story in order to make their point.

Miller uses his own family's narratives in his prose works. Unlike the Appalachian literature of a century ago, written by nonnatives to express the "otherness" of the people of the southern mountains, Miller's work and that of other writers from the region use local speech patterns and narratives to express a regional identity.

While speech is potentially always capable of expressing social values as well as regional and individual identity, issues regarding language are especially complicated among the Eastern Cherokee. Linguistically, the Cherokee language belongs to the Iroquoian family. Before the Removal, different dialects were spoken among the various town groupings of the Cherokee Nation. These dialectal differences still remain among Cherokee speakers today; the majority of Eastern Cherokees who still retain the language speak the Kituah dialect, once associated with the Middle and Out towns, but among the Snowbird Indians, the Atali dialect, akin to what is still spoken among some Oklahoma Cherokee, is used.

Before the Removal, retention of the Cherokee language was important, even as the Nation acquired the trappings of European-American culture. Sequoyah's invention of a Cherokee syllabary permitted the language to be written (and printed) in its own distinctive form. The syllabary is still used for the writing of Cherokee. The spoken use of Cherokee remained strong among the Eastern Band into the early decades of the twentieth century. However, since mid-century, it has declined considerably.

The primary agents of the demise of spoken Cherokee were the federal boarding schools. Older Cherokee speakers came of age during a period when Indian children were punished, even beaten, for speaking their native language. Many of this generation felt that it was unwise to teach their own children to speak Cherokee at home, though they might continue to use the language themselves.

A survey in the 1950s found that in the conservative township of Big Cove, close to a third of the households used Cherokee as the preferred language of communication at home. However, the percentage of households in Painttown where Cherokee was regularly used was only half what it was in Big Cove. Use of the language was found to be concentrated among the most conservative and those who had the highest percentage of Indian inheritance. Among the conservatives, Cherokee was used both because of its symbolic importance of "being Indian" and because many older speakers were more fluent in Cherokee than English. In households where Cherokee was spoken sometimes, it was used to facilitate communication with those who could not or would not speak English, in moments of anger, and when speakers wanted to exclude non-Cherokee speakers (especially children) from the conversation.

In the past couple of decades, schools, which were once the agent of decline, have become the agent for the preservation of the Cherokee language. As the generation who for the most part had not learned Cherokee at home grew up and had children of their own, the loss of the language was acutely felt. At the same time, there was a growing awareness of the heritage of the Cherokee and of Native Americans in general. The Cherokee language is now taught in the school system at Qualla and adult language classes are also held. Although in recent years increasing attention has been paid to the teaching of the Cherokee language, there are still difficulties in developing textbooks for such teaching, especially since many of the teachers and aides in the school system do not themselves speak Cherokee.

Learning in school is different, of course, from acquiring language at home, and required language classes often come at a time when students are least interested in learning about their own culture. As Louise Goings, who works in the school system, admits, "We're trying to, you know, do culture things with them at school, and they hate it. Even our language, they say, 'Oh, I wish we didn't have that old Cherokee language class.'" However, the instruction is taking hold with some. "There's several students I know that speak to my mama now, that had the Cherokee course, and they speak to her in Cherokee. So I guess some of them's picking it up and speaking." Probably most children who learn Cherokee in the schools will never become fluent. With the vast majority of Eastern Cherokee at Qualla now English speakers, fluency is not required for communication. However, it is now a point of pride for many to be able to speak at least a little Cherokee.

Fluency in the Cherokee language is more frequently found among the Snowbird Cherokees in Graham County than it is at Qualla. Almost three-quarters of Snowbird residents over the age of eighteen are fluent. Several churches use Cherokee routinely, and it is spoken at community club meetings. While Cherokee is now taught in the Snowbird schools, a much higher percentage of children and young adults than at Qualla learned Cherokee at home. At Snowbird, fluency continues to be an important marker of ethnic identity.

For non-Indians, the legacy of Cherokee is primarily found in place names. Especially on the North Carolina side of the Smokies, Cherokee names are given to ranges and peaks, rivers and creeks, and the communities found nearby. Tuckaseegee, Nantahala, Cullowhee, and Santeetlah come readily off the tongues of non-Indians in the region, though some transformations have taken place. The range Yalaka becomes the community Alarka or even " 'Larky" (with the traditional transformation of the final "a"). Cataloochee is Cataloch to some former residents.

NARRATIVE

In the past decade or two, the storytelling revival has been in such full force that storytelling is thought by many to consist of a performance by a specialized artist on stage before a relatively passive audience. However, most storytelling, in the Smokies and elsewhere, takes place in the course of everyday life, as a part of regular conversation. In fact, as has been pointed out, people in the southern mountains are perhaps more likely to infuse their everyday talk with stories than are people from other regions of the country.

Despite the fact that it is fairly ubiquitous throughout much of rural America, storytelling, like quilting, has become emblematic of the culture of the southern mountains. The popular view that storytelling is somehow unique in the southern mountains is reinforced by the tendency scholars have to fix on those forms that are most distinctive rather than those that are most common. "Jack tales" are a case in point. Although their existence in oral tradition is now exceedingly rare (and may be almost nonexistent in the Smokies), they are frequently thought of as "the" folk tales of the southern mountains.

Jack tales are a form of märchen, complex fictional stories of European origin. Most Americans would call these stories "fairy tales" (though fairies don't usually appear in them) and are familiar with only one story involving Jack, "Jack and the Beanstalk." However, soon after the southern mountains were found to be the repository of old British ballads, this European storytelling tradition was also found to be alive in the region. The telling of Jack tales appears to have strong connections to the ballad-singing tradition. Like ballads, they were performed at home and were maintained through strong family traditions. Generally, traditional Jack tale tellers also shared the deadpan, nonemotional performance style of ballad singers.

Not surprisingly, Appalachian Jack tales were first discovered in the same fertile ground where Cecil Sharp found the richest ballad tradition: Madison County, North Carolina. In 1923, Isabel Gordon Carter recorded "Jack, Will and Tom" tales from Jane Hicks Gentry of Hot Springs, who, in the previous decade, had sung ballads for Sharp. (Gentry was the great-aunt of current well-known ballad singer Doug Wallin.) A couple of decades later the Library of Congress collected songs and tales from Gentry's daughter, Maud Gentry Long. Jack tales were also discovered in the 1920s in Cades Cove, Tennessee, by folklorist Mellinger Henry. One suspects, however, that the telling of Jack tales was never quite as widespread as the singing of Child ballads. The fact is that almost all of the traditional Jack tale tellers documented in the North Carolina and Tennessee mountains were descendants of the same man, David Hicks. The Jack tale tellers of the Smoky Mountains region were part of the same Hicks/Harmon/Ward family network who produced the Jack tale tellers of the Beech Mountain area of northwest North Carolina. It is this latter group north of the Smoky Mountains who are now best known, because they actively preserved the tradition into the late twentieth century. So while the ballad singing and Jack tale telling traditions were probably once closely intertwined, in recent decades Sodom-Laurel in Madison County became known as the repository of the ballad tradition, while Beech Mountain became the community primarily associated with Jack tales. In both cases, however, it was individual families, not communities as a whole, who kept the traditions alive, aided and abetted perhaps by the scholarly and popular attention they received.

These days, the true traditional storytellers of the Smoky Mountains region are those who, as most people do, construct stories from their own personal experience. Their stories are traditional in style and context, though not necessarily in content. The ability to construct stories from personal experience is almost universal; some scholars believe that the development of long-term memory in children is linked to the ability to construct a narrative of events. We make sense of our lives through narrative, but we also entertain and communicate values.

Many of the best storytellers of the Smokies are individuals who have never been on a stage and have only "performed" for family, friends and visitors in their homes. Older people in particular "study on" the changes they have witnessed in their lifetimes, talking of these changes not abstractly but in terms of specific events. Letha Hicks of the Big Bend community along the Pigeon River in the Smokies remembered from her childhood how hogs, which were allowed to run free, had to be hunted down:

I catched a big old boar once. [We] had two dogs and one of them was running around and barking and the other was eating on that old boar's ears. Had one ear eat off and I run in, caught that old boar by the leg. He looked little to me, down in there. And my Daddy, he was behind me and I had that, took both my hands to reach around his leg, had one leg up. My Daddy he run in and grabbed the other leg. And we throwed him, laid the rope to him.

Old Wonder [the dog] . . . that hog had cut him plumb to the heart on both sides. Just nearly killed him, but he was still fighting that hog until, you know, we got him throwed . . .

They hauled the old hog in and they had to go plumb to Big Creek. It wasn't our hog. It belonged to Lonzo McCabe. That ear had a hole cut in it, you know, you had to mark it . . .

Daddy and them put it in a log pen, but [the hog] worked on it you know.

Put him in there, said he'd weakened him down so he couldn't get out. Next morning, that hog had tore that pen down and was gone! Yeah, it didn't weaken him enough for what he didn't tear that gosh damn log pen and got away. Well, we got a part of him three or four years later! [laughs] We swapped Lonzo a shoat for his half of it.

Personal experience stories don't always adhere to the truth, particularly in the Smoky Mountains region. Linked to a stylistic appreciation of exaggeration and a humor tradition that values pulling someone's leg, the narratives can take off on flights of fancy. Everyone is potentially a storyteller, but the noted storytellers are often those who don't let the facts stand in the way of a good tale. The deadpan manner in which stories are often told can make it difficult to judge whether or not someone is pulling your leg. The line between fact and fiction can be difficult to discern. A family story that Jim Wayne Miller used in his fiction was one his grandfather had told him about a mysterious migration of squirrels. "And later on when I was in college I came across [a *Newsweek* magazine account of] some scientists who were studying that very phenomenon. And at the time I couldn't have been sure that it wasn't just a tall tale he was telling me."

Personal experience narratives are transformed not only into tall tales but into legends. Eyewitnesses to events pass on the accounts to others who in turn tell the story. In the past, events worthy of becoming legends were often those that also became grist for the mill of local ballad writers. Murders and other tragedies were especially likely to be recounted again and again. Personal experience narratives also became family stories. Civil War narratives are still found among some older folks, and in the Smokies one can collect stories from both sides. Often these stories involve bushwhackers or marauding soldiers (Yankees or Rebels) who arrive to strip a family of their possessions. Luckily the family treasures have usually been buried before the soldiers' arrival.

Supernatural stories are also told, though they are not as common as they once were. Often stories of supernatural occurrences are told as personal experience narratives and then get passed on to other tellers. Doug Wallin remembered one particular storyteller:

He was pretty old at that time when he was a telling these big things. They said he was a pretty good banjo player, back when he was young. Got his arm cut off, I believe it was his left, at the sawmill, running an edger saw that trimmed the edge of lumber. Got it cut off. And he could tell some big stories.

I don't know if it was true or not. He said three times in his life he saw this little old woman, just after night, about that high. Said she'd always get away from him or disappear. Said one night, he was, I believe that was here back up on the mountain, he'd been to a frolic or a party with his banjo. (And, of course, it was before he got his hand cut off.) So he was coming along, just a narrow path, he was picking that tune "Jesse James," he said with his thumb and finger.

Said he looked out and saw this little old woman a-coming and he said to himself, "Old girl, I'm not going to give you the path this time." Said that she came right up to him and rubbed against the banjo so hard when she passed him she made the strings ring out. Man, he could tell some big ones.

Other stories with supernatural themes have humorous or unexpected endings. Doug Wallin remembered another prolific storyteller's tale:

He could tell you some stories. Said one night (I was telling about these revival meetings, people would go after night to, didn't have much lights or nothing), said people got to telling coming from that meeting, seeing a man with no head on. Said there was a bridge where they seen him, right above a man's house. Said several told about seeing him.

Said one night, said he was a going along, it was dark, and said he come along there and he looked all at once on this man with no head, loomed up at him. Said he jerked his old pistol and shot him a time or two and he fell.

That old man, he went home and got to study. He was worried to death that he had killed somebody. Said he got up the next morning so worried he couldn't eat breakfast and his daddy noticed he was sick or something. Told him he wasn't feeling so good or something. Moped around there for an hour or two.

Said after a while one of the old neighbor women, he showed exactly how that old woman come, [she] was one-eyed. She come up to talk with his mother, said they talked a little while, said that old woman, said [using high falsetto], "Do you know, somebody killed that man's calf down there at the ridge last night." Said his feelings eased off that he knew he hadn't killed somebody . . . Man, he could tell some good ones.

Just as common, perhaps, are personal experience stories that describe testing supernatural occurrences or tricking others into believing in supernatural phenomena. Zena Bennett told of a time when men were helping her father cure tobacco, a process that involved staying up all night to run heat under the plants:

I guess I was six or seven years old . . . Our cemetery was around that way and people got to telling around that they had seen things up at the cemetery. They don't tell tales like they used to, but used to, they'd tell ghost tales. That was all in the past.

But Mama sent me to take their suppers to them. Well, I went up there and I was going to come around by the graveyard and see if I could see a haint. And so I sit down and Dad said, "You better be going home. It's going to get dark." I said, "Well, I'm going, right in a few minutes."

I went down below there and set down until it got plumb right dark . . . And I never saw nothing.

Now my older sister, people would tell old ghost tales and tell tales that way, and she was scared. But she was scared all her life and I was right the opposite. I wanted to see something.

Storytelling about supernatural events often allows the teller and the audience to discuss whether such events are true. Many tellers, such as Doug Wallin and Zena Bennett, disavowed any personal belief in the supernatural (or at least in ghosts) but enjoyed telling stories about unexplained events or people's willingness to believe in supernatural occurrences. Many of these stories were set in a time when electric lights were not found in the mountains and, as in the stories above, people often travelled along mountain paths and roads in the pitch dark. Stories of mysterious lights are common. Doug Wallin told one story of the Brown Mountain lights, noting that while some said that it was train lights people saw, others described seeing lights before there were trains in the region. A woman from the other end of the Smokies who told similar stories about mountain lights explained their appearance in the context of religious belief, the "signs and wonders" of the Bible.

While the Cherokee, like their non-Indian neighbors, spin the majority of their stories from personal experience, they have their own distinct narrative traditions. James Mooney characterized Cherokee narratives as belonging to four categories: sacred myths, animal stories, local legends, and historical traditions. The sacred myths were frequently genesis stories, dealing with the creation of the world and the sources of knowledge. Even a century ago, Mooney thought that the sacred myths were "broken down" and that the tradition was dying. The majority of the stories Mooney included in *The Myths of the Cherokee* were collected from a single individual, Swimmer. Although Cherokee myths are not common in oral traditions (and, in fact, knowledge of much mythology was always limited to a few), as in many traditions that are pronounced "dying," individuals who can carry on seem to keep emerging. Walker Calhoun tells narratives that address the origins of many of the traditional songs he learned from Will West Long. In many Cherokee myths, the origin of tradition is found in sacrifice. As previously discussed, traditional healers are also familiar with myths associated with origins of disease and medicine.

Cherokee animal stories often deal with why individual animals have certain peculiarities—for instance, why a possum does not have hair on its tail. Mooney noted that by the late nineteenth century, these stories had largely lost their sacred character and were told for entertainment. The Fading Voices project conducted in Snowbird revealed that some of these stories are still found in oral tradition (though among the younger Cherokees, these folktales are more likely to be learned as part of the school curriculum). Solomon Bird, interviewed for Fading Voices, remembered when people would gather around the fireplace at night to hear tales of a time when animals could talk: "Some animals were very tricky and the worst liars . . . the wolf was a mean one. He caught anything that moved for his meal. So this time rabbit got caught, and he had to get wise very quickly." After recounting the tale of how the rabbit escaped from the wolf, he recalled another where rabbit outmaneuvered wildcat. "Whatever he wanted to do, it happened because he was tricky. He knew what to say and do."

Many of the animal tales, especially stories of the trickster rabbit, have marked similarities with African-American tradition. Even Mooney considered the possibility of exchange between the two traditions, though he could only consider the possibility that African-Americans adopted some Cherokee stories and not vice versa. While some similarities may be coincidental, it is quite possible that exchange took place in both directions (and intermingled as well with European-American storytelling).

Another tradition that Mooney notes (and possibly, given his love of Irish folklore, felt some personal identification with) involved stories of "Little People" who lived in the mountains. While generally kind-hearted, they also did not like to be disturbed. Traces of them might be found in footsteps or in sounds of the music they loved to play. Bessie Jumper, interviewed for Fading Voices, recalled a number of stories, told both from personal experience and from the experience of others, about the Little People. "There are trails all over the road and under the house. Sometimes you can hear them rattling on the pipe line. I believe these are the Little People walking all over the place. They say they're good Little People. You're not supposed to tell if you know for sure they are the Little People. They'll shorten your life if you tell."

Among the most enduring legends that address the historical experience of the Eastern Cherokee is that of Tsali, the hero-martyr of the Cherokee Removal. As with most legends, variants of the story abound, but in most versions, Tsali, an old man, along with a small group of other Cherokees escape federal soldiers, killing one or two (usually in defense of a woman). Subsequently, Tsali turns himself in, and with his death, General Winfield Scott agrees to stop pursuing the remaining fugitive Cherokees. In some variants, Tsali is portrayed as the embodiment of traditional values, though in the one presented to tourists in the outdoor drama *Unto These Hills*, Tsali is a Christian. Either way, Tsali represents both the Cherokee and Christian emphasis on martyrdom as the source of renewal. According to one interpreter of this legend, Catherine L. Albanese, the story of Tsali is important because it provides a new myth of origins for the Eastern Cherokee. Although the ways in which different North Carolina Cherokee groups eluded removal varied considerably, the theme of flight to the woods and the martyrdom of Tsali provided a unifying narrative.

HUMOR

Traditions of humor in the Smoky Mountains are closely intertwined with storytelling and local speech patterns. The playfulness with language has always had its humorous side. For instance, a woman from a family of thirteen children noted that there were twelve girls and "every one of them had a brother apiece." Much of the regional humor occurs in the context of storytelling, and much delight is taken in getting someone to believe something that is not true. This pulling of a listener's leg can also take place in the context of more ordinary conversation. Musician Jack Wallin, brother of the ballad singer Doug Wallin, delighted in the fact that he had convinced a certain young folklorist when she called on the phone that Doug had just recently died. Years later he still "told it on her" with some pride and humor.

A vein of mischievousness seems to run through many who live in the region. One older woman, Anna Collett, told a long story of getting the best of her sister when they were both children. With a twinkle in her eye, she said, "Wasn't that mean! Oh, that was really mean!" Another of her stories of mischief was about scaring her grandmother with a dead rattlesnake:

And the next morning was Saturday, and they always had church on Saturday morning, and Mama and Daddy and Grandma went to church, left us children there. I took the snake out and coiled it up right where she had to step. Stuck its head up under a rock. And I thought how funny it would be, you know, to let her step on that snake . . . And Daddy said for me to help her to get in the house, you know, when he got her out of the buggy. I got her by the arm and was leading her in the house and she stepped on that snake. And I hollered "snake" and it scared her and, boy, she went falling backwards, and I hollered at Mama to come help me hold Grandma up . . . Now you talk about begging, not to tell on me for scaring her. My Daddy would have tanned my hide!

Mrs. Collett was not expressing any ill will toward her grandmother: "I just loved her to death. She was the sweetest thing in the world. And I was all the time doing, teasing her . . . never mean to her, just to get to laugh at her."

Of course, the same range of humor exists in the Smokies that is found elsewhere in the United States: topical jokes, racist jokes, obscene jokes, and "knock-knocks" can all be found. But a certain brand of humor has been linked to regional values. Jim Wayne Miller notes:

There's a kind of humor in Southern Appalachia that is a leveling humor . . . You can tell stories and anecdotes that prick the balloon of any kind of pomposity. That is, they level people down. Anyone who tries to get, sit a little higher than someone else, you'll tell something on them that brings them down to base level.

And this not only works on other people, but people have a self-deprecating humor. They'll tell stories on themselves. And the end result seems to be: We are all common. "Just as common as an old shoe," which is an expression, you see. And that's the desired state to be. And I think it's a view of who you are. It's a view of what it is to be human that comes out of that kind of humor.

While leveling humor is usually focused on friends, family, and neighbors, it can also target public figures. One local singer tells a story of a country musician who dies and goes to heaven. St. Peter meets him and shows him around. The singer is delighted to see his heroes Ernest Tubb, Lester Flatt, and others. Then he spots a gentleman with sideburns playing the mandolin. "Why, did Bill Monroe pass before me?" he asks. "No," says St. Peter, "that's God. He just likes to think he's Bill Monroe."

Sometimes humor that appears to be self-deprecating is also an inversion of stereotypes. In some cases, the teller is cast in the role of trickster, playing up to certain stereotypes in order to get the best of an outsider. In other cases, as with the humor of other regional or ethnic groups, stories that involve stereotypes when told by outsiders become humorous when told within the group. Folklorist Bill Lightfoot notes that a story told in Ohio to ridicule Appalachian migrants is also told among Appalachians. In this story, a man dies, goes to heaven, and is shown around by St. Peter. Although the place is a paradise, he spots a group of people who are chained and asks why this is the case. "St. Peter replied, 'That's a bunch of hillbillies, and every Friday at 5:00 p.m., they want to head home for the weekend.'" As Lightfoot notes, this story ridicules migrant Appalachians who feel constantly compelled to go home, but it can also be used (though probably not with the term hillbilly) to express the view that the mountains are preferable to heaven itself. This story is also told in western North Carolina, though usually Carolinians ("tarheels") are specified, with the story conveying their strong attachment to home.

One form of humor that might appear to rely on stereotypical notions if told by people from outside are the "so far back" stories. Joseph Hall collected one version from a man in Del Rio, in Cocke County, Tennessee, who stated that he lived so far back that "in the mountains they use possums to carry the mail in. Then I pipe the sunshine in and the moonshine out." A Madison County man who had an especially treacherous driveway told me, "We live so far back, we get Grand Ole Opry on Tuesday nights." (The radio show is broadcast on Saturday nights.)

Rural Americans have always had a brand of humor that dealt with urbanites straying into their midst. Traditionally, the visitors are outwitted by the rural folk. Unlike in some other parts of the South, the quintessential outsider in the Smokies region (particularly western North Carolina) is not from the north but from further south. For over a century and a half, people from the lower South have fled to the mountains during the heat of the summer. In recent decades much of the influx has consisted of retired Floridians, many of whom can afford to build a summer home in the mountains. While traditionally the best place to build a house was along the bottomland, Floridians prefer to have a view. They build at the tops of hills and mountains, as one woman commented dryly, "So they can look down on the rest of us." A lesser complaint about Floridians, though one that fuels considerable local lore, concerns their driving habits. According to local stereotype, the typical Floridian is an aging retiree, used to driving on flat roads, piloting a Cadillac or Lincoln along mountain roads. Their driving is either too slow or is erratic. One western North Carolina native remembers when Florida license plates were red. "Treat those license plates like a stick of dynamite," instructed his driver's education teacher.

Much of the humor about Floridians has an edge to it. Whether the humor actually defuses the tensions that typically exist between summer people and permanent residents or exacerbates it is hard to say. Much of the tension exists because these outsiders do not respect the egalitarian ideals of the region and "look down" on local people. They want to enjoy the scenery of the mountains but do not respect the country ways of its people. "Floridiots," the permanent residents in turn mutter under their breath.

PART THREE

Tourism and the National Park

Parklore

One of the primary catalysts of change in the Great Smoky Mountains region was the creation of the national park. Today the National Park Service is the major interpreter of the traditional culture of the region. The park, however, not only offers its unique interpretation of Smoky Mountains folklife but also generates its own folklife. Employees of the park service have their own occupational folklore, and the interaction of rangers, tourists, local people, and wildlife have given birth to new forms of folklore.

PARK INTERPRETATION OF LOCAL CULTURE

In creating national parks in the eastern United States, the park service not only had to contend with the removal of the population who lived on and owned the land but also had to decide how to interpret the culture or cultures they disrupted. Should the land simply be allowed to revert to wilderness, or should the lives of the former inhabitants be told as part of the story of the park?

In the Great Smoky Mountains National Park, initial efforts to preserve cultural artifacts were partially motivated by the need to appease the population that was being dislocated. Churches and cemeteries were, for the time being, to be preserved for the use of the communities that had been eliminated. However, during the 1930s, the park service adopted the position, at least theoretically, that "mountain culture" should be preserved in the Great Smokies. Ironically, as local people sold out or lost their property to eminent domain and as legal suits over condemnation dragged on, it was the supposed uniqueness of this culture that was stressed. In one memorandum from park personnel in 1937, the significance of the Smoky Mountains culture was said to lie in the fact that "there has survived a manner of living, an entire cultural complex, which almost everywhere else within the boundaries of the United States has disappeared entirely. The Smokies might be conceived as a cultral [sic] island, to a great extent, isolated from the outside world, where we are able to see the survival in our contemporaries of language, social customs, unique processes, that go back to the 19th century and beyond." In 1939, the secretary of interior's annual report stated that "attention has been given to the unique opportunity presented in the Great Smoky Mountains National Park to preserve frontier conditions of a century ago, which have vanished elsewhere."

Despite the official policy that the preservation of mountain culture should come second only to preservation of the natural environment of the park, only a modest amount of systematic documentation or preservation of traditional culture was actually accomplished. Considering the fact that the 1930s were the heyday of federally sponsored documentation of traditional culture, it seems unfortunate that the National Park Service was unable to provide trained specialists for the study of the "unique" culture of the region. A series of outside experts discussed and drew up plans for the "mountain culture program," but the day-to-day work of actual documentation and preservation fell primarily on a few dedicated individuals assigned to other duties, most of whom were on the payroll of the Emergency Conservation Work (ECW) or the subsequent Civilian Conservation Corps (CCC).

Most of what was accomplished during this decade was the result of the efforts of H. C. Wilburn and Charles Grossman, along with the support of park naturalist Arthur Stupka. In 1935, initial plans were underway to build a museum or museums for the park, and committees were appointed in both Tennessee and North Carolina to oversee the gathering of items for the museum collection. Wilburn was lent to the North Carolina committee to assist their efforts at collection. All gifts were donations, as no money was appropriated for this project. Grossman, who was assigned to conduct a cabin survey, also collected items for the museum, as did the Tennessee committee. Space to house the collections was not provided by the park, and the collections were moved from one site to another until 1942 when room was found in the administration building.

Initial museum plans were submitted by Alden B. Stevens, a curator for the National Park Service, in November of 1935. Two museums were proposed: one, stressing archeology and culture, would be located near Smokemont, North Carolina, and the other, to be near Gatlinburg, would emphasize natural history. The Smokemont complex was also to contain a field for Cherokee ball games as well as an amphitheater for Cherokee dances that might "also be used by local people for folk festivals, 'sings' and other activities staged in connection with the educational and entertainment program of the park."

Apparently little, if any, action was taken, and three years later, Wilburn, Grossman, and Stupka submitted their own report on a proposed mountain culture program. Their proposed "culture" museum did include a section on the historic Cherokee culture, but otherwise the plan de-emphasized the Cherokee component. The main contribution of this report was the attention to "field exhibits" of original structures (some moved, others *in situ*) to be created at Cades Cove, Cataloochee, Sugarlands, Greenbrier, and Deep Creek, and the authors' almost tentative proposal of a plan to make "the exhibits live." This proposal suggested that local people might be engaged to produce marketable articles of craftsmanship. Further, they suggested that "the persons employed in this connection might be permitted to live in the cabins included in the field exhibits, and so carry on their activities under natural and realistic conditions. Thus they would serve as custodians of the buildings so occupied and also continue the cultivation of such fields as are designated to be kept open in these areas." The following year, Wilburn sent a memo to the superintendent calling his attention to an article on the "living" folk museums of Norway and Sweden and suggesting that this was more or less what they had in mind.

The crafts and music revivalists were also influential in the development of proposals for the preservation of mountain life. Wilburn corresponded with both Lucy Morgan of the Penland School and Olive Dame Campbell of the John C. Campbell Folk School. After a trip with Grossman to visit the folk school in 1936, Wilburn wrote to Campbell that he understood that it was the school's practice to put on "entertainment programs in the way of folk dancing, ballad singing, dulcimer and whatnot," and that he and Grossman were particularly impressed by the performance of John Jacob Niles. He went on to inquire if it "would be permissible for some of us park folks to attend certain of your programs." Mrs. Campbell also served as one of the vice-chairs of the western North Carolina committee selected to collect artifacts for the proposed museum.

Even earlier, Bascom Lamar Lunsford had been consulted by other park personnel. In 1935, H. C. Bryant, assistant director of the National Park Service, wrote that "several conferences with Mr. Lunsford of North Carolina have stirred interest and we are anxious to utilize and promote folk arts in connection with the educational program." It is evident from the weekly reports of museum curator Stevens that the suggestion that the proposed facilities at Smokemont be used for "sings" and presentations of mountain music and culture was Lunsford's. According to Stevens, Lunsford believed that mountain people "could easily be persuaded to use the park and to contribute much to its educational program if approached properly."

Although it is regrettable that the proposals to "preserve" mountain culture in the Great Smoky Mountains were not based to any substantial degree on actual research about the individuals being displaced by the park, evidently it was expedient for the park service to reach for the models already developed by Lunsford, Campbell, and the other exponents of the folk revival. Wilburn, Grossman and Stupka, in fact, suggested that the proposed Mountain Crafts Trading Post could be run by the Southern Highland Handicraft Guild.

If the American counterpart to the European folk museum had yet to emerge, the 1938 report seemed to be an early development of the "living history" concept. The statement that "it is believed that a story such as we have to tell would become so much more interesting if made to live through the activities of real people" is very much in its spirit. However, the plan was not without its stumbling blocks. Certainly some people must have noticed the irony of a plan to repopulate portions of the park on the heels of the removal, and it would surely have seemed remarkable to those removed had they known of it. It is also evident that some park personnel (if not Wilburn or Grossman) were more comfortable with "mountain culture" in the abstract (or as purveyed by the folk revivalists) than with real mountain people.

Such a view was held by Dr. Hans Huth, who, three years after Wilburn et al. submitted their report, prepared yet another report on the preservation of mountain culture. Visiting the Smokies as part of a survey of American folk studies undertaken by the Branch of Historic Sites of the National Park Service, Huth believed there was "little hope of still finding much of the past in the present and retaining it." However, he endorsed the plan drawn up by Wilburn, Grossman, and Stupka, and in fact took it to an extreme probably not imagined by those men: "According to this project, carefully selected settlers, some of them skilled craftsmen as well as farmers, would live and work in the park area wherever it would be deemed necessary and possible to rededicate a farm, for example, to actual life." The choosing of "desirable and adoptable people" for this work would be accomplished through an elaborate screening process. Huth imagined that there might be some difficulty in locating these individuals, since, he stated, many of the local people had criminal records. He even suggested the possibility of using girls from a local college in Asheville. The chosen few would be closely supervised in a manner that would "correspond to the procedure employed by the Bureau of Indian Affairs in dealing with Indians," though the supervision would be "even closer," as only "certifiable work can be put on the market." In terms of controlling the product, Huth endorsed in explicit terms the attitude of the crafts revival for, as he stated, craftsmen in the region had "lost the faculty of creating a worthy piece." Huth's scheme, however, went beyond producing sellable items. The "enterprise should be regarded as an experimental form similar to biological laboratories."

Though Huth's brave-new-world-approach was never implemented, it did highlight important issues about the preservation of culture that have yet to be resolved. Can culture, particularly those aspects that are intangible, truly be preserved, and at what cost? Several months after Huth's report was submitted, a special committee meeting was called to discuss interpretive and museum aspects of the plan for the Great Smoky Mountains National Park. One expert stressed that a people's whole culture should be emphasized, not simply aspects such as folk literature, arts, or handicrafts, and stated that the "broader anthropological view of the mountaineers—as if they were the tribesman in the northern Riff of Africa or the Seri Indian of Lower California—should be accepted as a basic concept." However, another believed that "certain aspects of material culture can be perpetuated but the other integral elements of a culture cannot be." In regard to resettling individuals back in the park, one expert emphasized that there were "many undesirable characteristics of the mountaineers' culture" that should not be preserved and said he was opposed to the idea of "establishing mountaineers in typically primitive conditions and then subjecting the group to the scrutiny of visitors." Yet another felt that they could not expect that "individuals will be content to live in crude, rigorous surroundings following the hard way of producing their handcraft solely for the intangible reward of being a scientific guinea pig, particularly when their neighbors can have cars, radios and new dresses."

Even as park officials were hitting this impasse, many of those who had been involved with the proposed mountain culture program were getting discouraged by the lack of progress. However, some recognition of the value of the cultural landscape was finally being made into official policy. By 1940 it had become policy to maintain the meadowlands in Cades Cove rather than let them revert to wilderness, and in 1943 the National Park Service decided to issue special use permits where it was desirable to perpetuate or restore man-made conditions. However, during the early 1940s, American involvement in the war squelched any hope that the museum plans would see the light of day in the immediate future. Park attendance plummeted, personnel left as the CCC was abolished or as they were called up to war, and no one felt that funding was likely during a national emergency. Still, museum plans continued to be drawn up during the 1940s, and a temporary pioneer history museum was finally opened at Oconaluftee in 1948. During the 1950s, selected buildings were relocated to Oconaluftee, and the pioneer farmstead was opened in 1953.

By the time cultural interpretation became a reality in the Great Smoky Mountains, the intent was to re-create rather than to preserve mountain culture, although even in the late 1950s, park personnel were still writing of the survival of a "unique cultural complex." However, mountain culture was mostly presented as something in the past, rather than as a living breathing thing. In a 1958 report, H. W. Lix wrote that "the Great Smoky Mountains National Park is guilty of hastening the rapid loss of the Highlander's character. But the Park has also gone a long way towards preserving a small section of our pioneer past for the present and all future generations to see and enjoy." This mixed blessing (in terms of cultural preservation) was heightened by the emphasis on the supposed uniqueness and pioneer nature of Smoky Mountains culture. Actual people and the realities of their lives in the early twentieth century often became obscured as interpretation was shaped by stereotypes and half-truths. The trauma of dislocation was too often ignored while the park service invested in the myth that Smoky Mountains folk culture was a unique remnant of the past.

The people removed from the park played only a small role in the development of cultural interpretation. A few found jobs within the park. Others were interviewed by those associated with the park service, such as linguist Joseph Hall. The tenants who stayed on within the park boundaries helped maintain the historic structures and in a few cases found themselves in the position of becoming museum displays. The most famous of these were the Walker sisters of Little Greenbrier who resisted relocation and were given a lease to their land. Their persistence in maintaining a traditional life-style attracted tourists and the sisters made a modest income from poems and souvenirs peddled to the visitors. Finally, by the 1950s the surviving sisters, who were getting on in years, could no longer accommodate the onslaught of tourists, and they asked the park service to remove the sign to their house.

Today, the preserved buildings in the Great Smoky Mountains National Park have more of the emotional impact of ancient ruins than the intellectual experience of interpreted historic sites. Most of the cultural interpretation takes place at the Cable Mill complex at Cades Cove and the Mountain Farm Museum at Oconaluftee. Although printed guides provide some historical information about other structures, visitors are largely left to draw their own conclusions. Because of the lack of staff for interpretation and the fear of vandalism, these buildings are empty shells. And the nature of interpretation today is shaped as much by park policy in the hiring and training of interpreters as it is by a coherent program of research and education.

RANGER LORE

Not all the cultural interpretation created by the National Park Service staff focuses on the folk culture of the Smokies. While official programs may focus on people of the past, informally it is the legions of tourists who come through the Great Smoky Mountains yearly who are most "interpreted" by park rangers. Among themselves, park rangers try to make sense of a strange tribe: Americans away from home.

All occupational groups create their own folklore, which may include an esoteric language, initiation rites to test those new to their profession, and, most importantly, strategies for coping with the stresses of their particular occupation. Those whose job it is to deal constantly with the public have their own specific set of problems. The lore of interpretive park rangers is in some ways similar to the "problem patron" lore of librarians. Often idealistic, with a genuine interest in imparting knowledge and helping others, park rangers sometimes find that the public is not as grateful, cooperative, or intelligent as might be hoped. Furthermore, rangers are subject to the stress felt by all who must serve tourists, people who sometimes feel less constrained by codes of proper behavior when they are away from their home community and who feel entitled to have a good time.

Officially, there are no "tourists" in the national park. They are "visitors." However, on a bad day, to a park ranger they may be "tourons" ("What do you get when you cross a tourist and a moron?"). Of course, a ranger would not dream of calling people tourons to their faces, but they may talk of tourons to other rangers. All national parks have "tourons," but individual parks have their own particular cast of characters. In the Smokies the quintessential tourists ("probably from Ohio or Michigan or Florida") are "Maud and Henry." Maud and Henry are not mean; they are simply (like a lot of tourists in ranger lore) befuddled. "Maud and Henry came up to the desk [at the Sugarlands Visitor Center] each with a map open and one said, 'So this is Sugarcreek? Our friends told us to be sure and stop at Sugarcreek Center. What do we do here?' " While Maud and Henry appear in oral lore, their antics are also recorded in Maud and Henry books. In these spiral-bound books, rangers, as well as staff or volunteers from the Natural History Association, record dated entries of amusing, strange, or troubling encounters with visitors.

The short narrative above, from a Maud and Henry book, typifies a few of the characteristics of this tourist couple. First, they can't ever get place names right and therefore ask for directions to Codes Cave (Cades Cove) or Kingman's Doom (Clingman's Dome). Maud and Henry also don't quite know what to do in a national park. "Is all there is to see around here mountains?" Hearing that they might see wild animals on the Cades Cove loop road, they inquire about whether they will see giraffes. Maud and Henry also worry about where the deer go when it rains.

The proximity of the park to Gatlinburg and Cherokee also contributes to anecdotes in the Maud and Henry book. A tourist expects a park ranger to tell him which hotels in Gatlinburg have waterbeds or cable television. Or, hearing that there is an Indian reservation on the North

Carolina side of the park, someone asks, "Will the Indians hurt you?" Another asks if you can drive in Cherokee, "or is it just walking?" One tourist comes wandering into the park in search of Appalachians; when a ranger tries to point out that some of the people who work at the visitor center are from the immediate area, the tourist is clearly not pleased that they don't measure up to hillbilly stereotypes.

Rangers' stories about visitors range from truthful anecdotes, often fragmentary in nature, about real encounters, to longer, embroidered narratives about stereotypical tourists. There can be many variations on a single theme. Either the tourist, attracted by outlet stores or amusements in Pigeon Forge or Gatlinburg, is surprised to hear that there is a national park "somewhere around here," or a tourist wanders into a visitor center within the park boundaries seeking directions to the Great Smoky Mountains National Park. This narrative cycle is found in the other national parks as well. As one seasonal ranger commented, "I have heard that narrative about 'I hear there's a national park around here.' I've heard that one here and I've also heard it at Mammoth Cave. It's also one that I've heard from folks at Yosemite, because you've got that corridor through Yosemite." The fact that many seasonal guides bounce around from park to park insures that a certain amount of ranger lore is found across the National Park Service.

While ranger lore is often about the trials of coping with visitors to the park, it may also pertain to other stressful aspects of the job. Young idealistic rangers find themselves working in a system that is authoritarian, hierarchical, and stratified. And while rangers in interpretation may be concerned primarily with environmental and cultural issues, they find much emphasis in the park service on maintenance and law enforcement. Referring to the amount of traffic going through the Smokies, some joke that they are working for the "National Parking Service." Tensions sometimes exist between groups in different divisions such as the rangers and maintenance personnel (who are perceived by the former as being better paid and having better hours) as well as between the different types of rangers. As one ranger in interpretation stated, "It's a 'them and us' kind of thing . . . There's an occupational thing that's been passed around for years that the only real rangers in any National Park . . . are the law enforcement officers. The rest of us are just allowed to play ranger."

As with most occupational lore, ranger lore is esoteric, largely shared and understood by others in the occupation. While helping members of the occupation to cope with stress through humor and to adjust their idealism to the realities of the job, such lore is not an indication that park rangers are a disgruntled lot. Despite low wages and what for many is a gypsy life-style, park rangers cheerfully serve the public. In fact, the park rangers in the Smokies are among a select few, because it is considered among the most desirable parks in the system.

The peripatetic life of the seasonal ranger also affects the nature of cultural interpretation in the Great Smoky Mountains National Park. Because these rangers bounce around to different national parks, they sometimes find that they must prepare interpretive programs "cold turkey," with only two weeks of training and another week to prepare their own programs. Orientation tends to stress "critical issues," usually dealing with controlling the public's behavior rather than with cultural history. Furthermore, while some rangers have backgrounds in history or the social sciences, the average ranger is more likely to have a background in the natural sciences. This system therefore creates a situation in which the people responsible for interpreting the local culture may have just arrived in the Smokies themselves, may not have had any training in cultural history, and may be given an extremely short period of time to develop programming. "Classic hit-and-run research," one ranger characterizes it. The archives at Sugarlands provides excellent resources for primary research on the culture of the Great Smoky Mountains, but most rangers simply don't have the time to get in and root around. Instead, the same few published sources are often examined during the development of historical programs.

Oral lore plays a surprisingly large role in the development of interpretation—not the oral traditions of people of the region, though an enterprising ranger might squeeze out the time to interview an "old timer" or two, but the oral traditions of the interpreters themselves. Guide lore is part of the interpretation at most historical sites and museums. Information, sometimes of questionable veracity, gets incorporated into an interpreter's spiel, and then gets passed informally from one interpreter to another. However, while inaccurate information sometimes gets passed along this way, in the national park this informal information is often as crucial as the formal training in developing interpretation. With so little time to develop programs, newcomers mine the seasoned guides' programs for useable information, seeking advice and feedback in developing their own programs.

Bear Lore

Park rangers often find that although some visitors may be interested in the former residents of the Smokies or in the current flora and fauna, what many really want to know is "Where do we see the bears?" Bears are the totemic animal of the national parks, especially the Smokies. For visitors, the Great Smoky Mountains black bear is a symbol of the wilderness but at the same time an unthreatening presence. Raised on anthropo-morphized images of bears, such as the kindly and wise Smoky and the humorous trickster Yogi, many visitors want to have direct encounters with bears and ignore the potential hazards.

Bear lore of course existed in the region long before the national park came into being. In Cherokee mythology, bears take on anthropomorphic characteristics (and in some cases are transformed humans) and are gener-ally benevolent figures. European-Americans in the Smokies tended to see the bear in a more adversarial role, although some individual bears also were viewed as tricksters. Horace Kephart wrote of "Old Reelfoot," who left behind a peculiar track by twisting his hind feet and "whose cunning had defied our best hunters for five or six years." Kephart was in fact so fascinated with bear hunting in the Smokies that he devoted a chapter of *Our Southern Highlanders* to his exploits with local bear hunters. Several decades later, linguist Joseph Hall collected bear hunting stories from former residents of the Smokies. Most of these stories concerned

Hunters with bear and turkey, 1935 (Photo cour-tesy of Great Smoky Moun-tains National Park)

close calls—"dangers safely passed"—but some were also exaggerated "bear tales."

With the creation of the national park, bears became protected animals rather than adversaries, much to the consternation of the lessees who continued to live and farm on the land they formerly owned. It was illegal to shoot a bear, even if the bear was in the chicken house. Nationally, the development of national parks, along with auto-tourism, brought bears into the awareness of the American public. Roadside attractions across America featured bears that could be fed, and, as the national parks brought in tourists while prohibiting hunting, bears were not reluctant to make exhibitions of themselves.

The Great Smoky Mountains National Park does not feature live animal exhibitions and has long officially discouraged "overstuffed tourist bears." Problem bears are removed from high traffic areas, and the park service discourages direct interaction between visitors and bears. However, bear lore affects even the park service. The early superintendents' reports include comments on the activities of some of the well-known bear characters in the park, such as "Old Tom," "Sadie," and "Diane the Dimwit," and sometimes bear cartoons clipped from other sources are included in the reports. Bear narratives are occasionally related:

On June 25, Dr. Burlen Thompson of Bryson City and party were camped at the Bryson Place on Deep Creek and experienced an unusual incident with a bear. They had gone up the creek a short distance from their camp, leaving their personal possessions in their tent. Upon their return they found that a bear had visited the tent taking Dr. Thompson's pants, all the bread, meat, butter, frying pan and all the Camel cigarettes and leaving the Lucky Strike cigarettes. Dr. Thompson fortunately had a second pair of pants which relieved his embarrassment. The only item returned was the frying pan, which was found approximately a mile from the camp. The bear to date has not shown up on the highway wearing Dr. Thompson's pants.

This narrative from the early 1940s, probably also circulated in oral form, is typical of many bear stories. Although such stories frequently feature a bear destroying property, the animal (such as this one who has a preference for cigarette brands and might be inclined to stroll down the road wearing stolen pants) is also portrayed humorously as a trickster.

Among the park personnel and those who came frequently to the park, certain bears became known for their individualized tactics of destruction and food acquisition. Jeff Rennicke, in his book, *The Smoky Mountain Black Bear*, listed a number of these colorful characters, such as "Old Volkswagen," who, having once discovered a bucket of chicken in a VW, took to attacking cars of this make, and Sheba, who charged backpackers so they would drop their packs, which she could then pick through. There

Young bear inspecting a car in the park, 1957 (Photo courtesy of Great Smoky Mountains National Park)

are also numerous generic stories of humorous encounters between bears and visitors at campgrounds.

Bears are also prominent in families' memories of trips to the Smokies. Norma and Atwood Sizemore visit the Smokies often, and, with their son, Randy, remember one particular incident that happened decades earlier. As is typical of family narratives, the story is pieced together collectively. Norma started the story: "Years ago when Randy and Stan were little boys we made a trip to the mountains and we packed our lunch and took it with us and we went up on the mountain. And the bears were so thick that they were just everywhere." After her son remembers an incident of bears chasing a rolling watermelon, Norma continues:

This man next to us had a watermelon on the table and this mother bear with two little cubs come after that watermelon. And [the man] had a hat. Do you remember him having that hat? [Randy: "No, I don't."] He had a hat and he kept trying to shoo that bear with that hat. He'd say, "Shoo! Shoo! Shoo!" [laughs] And that bear came right on and got that watermelon. [Atwood: "And Charles stood back with a pop bottle in his hand like he might fight him."] But that bear carried that melon right up to the top of that mountain. Right back up that mountain he went.

Got almost to the top and dropped it. And it went, "Ploink, ploink, ploink, ploink!" It just cracked into a million pieces. [Randy: "It was breaking and rolling and they just chased it back down the hill."] . . . That was one of the best trips for seeing bears we'd ever had.

Unlike the bears of western lore, those in the Smokies are generally not feared. In fact, the ranger lore about encounters between visitors and bears often stresses that the visitors do not have enough respect for bears. One ranger told a narrative about visitors placing their children inside a hog enclosure with a bear who had inadvertently become trapped. "It's like they assume that because this is a national park, nothing's going to happen to them," she mused. Less dangerous antics with bears are also recounted, and rangers roll their eyes at visitors who seem to think that bears perform at regular intervals at set places within the park. Although officially the park service does not have a sense of humor about bears, one suspects that rangers take particular enjoyment from stories in which the trickster bear outwits the tourist.

TOURISM AT THE GATES

Park rangers are not the only ones who cope with "tourons" (or that particular breed of touron from Florida, "Florons"). Many people living near the Great Smoky Mountains National Park make a living from the tourist trade. In the past half-century, the development of tourist attrac-

Tourist shop featuring live and not-so-live bears in Pigeon Forge (Photo by Hillary Glatt)

Gatlinburg before neon,
1935 (Photo courtesy of
Great Smoky Mountains
National Park)

tions has flourished around the boundaries of the Great Smoky Mountains National Park, particularly at the two major entrances into the park at Gatlinburg and Cherokee. Initially, the National Park Service fought heartily against tourist development along its borders. It appropriated land to create a buffer zone, denied leases of land to local people who wished to build tourist accommodations, and tried to prevent "the hotdog stand, the soft drink stand, the gaudy filling station, the stand selling celluloid dolls and the bill boards from marring the natural beauty of our gates." Not only did the park service lose the battle, it lost it in a big way. Gatlinburg and Cherokee became quintessential tourist traps.

Although the park service seemed particularly concerned about "irresponsible" mountain people profiting from the presence of the park, the greatest profits have typically not been made by local people. True, a few local people did prosper with the development of tourism at Gatlinburg and Cherokee, but even in those cases it tended to be the more affluent who stood to gain. The argument has been made that at Cherokee, it was the "white Indians" (individuals of only partial Cherokee descent who tend to identify with European-American cultural values) who profited the most from tourism. To the extent that the rest of the population benefitted, it was through their employment in the tourist trade. While tourism has offered jobs that might otherwise be scarce in the region, critics have pointed out that the work consists mostly of seasonal, minimum-wage, dead-end jobs that are vulnerable to the whims of the national economy.

Critics have also suggested that tourism in the Smokies offers "degraded" portrayals of local culture. Surprisingly, this probably applies more to depictions of white Appalachian culture, which can take the form of hillbilly stereotypes, than of Cherokee culture. (For instance, at tourist sites Cherokee Indians are not portrayed as lazy drunkards, while white Appalachians routinely are.) Some critics further imply that the workers at tourist sites have themselves internalized these stereotypes or are in other ways being degraded. Such an assumption does not give much credit to the intelligence of people from the region.

Tourism in the Smokies has created new occupations. Among the strangest, and most criticized, is the occupation of "chiefing." Ever since Cherokee began to develop as a tourist town, Cherokee men have dressed up in Plains Indian war bonnets to make money having their pictures taken with tourists. Many people who work in tourism are pragmatic

Cherokee, North Carolina, beginning to feel the effects of auto-tourism, 1940 (Photo courtesy of Great Smoky Mountains National Park)

about the need to give visitors what they expect to see. A story that may be apocryphal is told of the Cherokee "chief" who, devising his own experiment, switched back and forth between the war bonnet and traditional Cherokee garb. He soon found that there was no profit to be made in looking authentically Cherokee. Perhaps as the American public becomes more knowledgeable about Native American traditions (if indeed they ever do), the occupation of "chiefing" will fall by the wayside. Some younger Cherokee already criticize the practice as degrading to their heritage, though they may well embrace other forms of pan-Indianism. Still, someday "chiefing" may be recognized as a unique occupation with its own occupational folklore.

Tourists are offered the choice of a more "authentic" cultural experience. The National Park Service accomplishes this for European-American culture, though it offers relatively little interpretation of Cherokee culture. In Cherokee, a tourist tired of the cheap souvenir can go to the Qualla Arts and Crafts Mutual or the Oconaluftee Indian Village. Although the co-op has been criticized for its selling of nontraditional or non-Cherokee crafts, and the "village," a living history museum, has been accused of including historical inaccuracies, these places do offer an alternative portrayal of Cherokee culture. Some Cherokees feel that the museum plays a valuable role in teaching not only tourists but Cherokee children about their heritage. Working at Oconaluftee can serve as an apprenticeship in traditional culture for young people in Cherokee.

The social and economic problems of being dependent on tourism are quite real. Too often, however, critics do not give local people credit for intelligence, pragmatism, or humor in dealing with their situations. Like park rangers, these people study and categorize visitors to the region, laughing at the "tourons" behind their backs. In Cherokee, especially, contact with tourists is inevitable. In a 1975 article for the *Cherokee One Feather* (reprinted in *Now and Then*), the unidentified author divides tourists into two groups: the cheapies who complain about prices and think that Indians live off the federal government, and those who claim Indian heritage and try to "out-Indian the Indian." Like others who deal with tourists, the Cherokee have developed coping strategies. "They have learned to answer the most inane questions imaginable with frankness. They can tactfully and usually, humorously turn aside the most rude or ignorant comment." If all else fails, they can try the famed Indian impassivity. As the author suggests, "It may be that Indians are the most impassive when they are trying their best not to laugh in your face!"

8

Displacement and Sense of Place in the National Park

The human history of the Great Smoky Mountains is a history of displacement. Despite this fact, or perhaps because of it, people from the mountains feel a strong sense of place. Some left and never returned. But a remarkable number of those removed, and their descendants, celebrate their continued sense of connection with this place. However, while the sense of place inspires celebration, it also fuels political conflict when the desires of those with traditional ties to the Smokies conflict with the agenda of the National Park Service.

HOMECOMING: CATALOOCHEE AND LITTLE CATALOOCHEE

On a warm Sunday morning in 1992, some six hundred people gather together to celebrate their tie with a community that has been uninhabited for over half a century. They make the trip even though it means traveling a long winding road, a good bit of which is unpaved, up to the Cataloochee Valley on a rainy morning. Park personnel are directing traffic, and it is clear that if the reunion continues to grow, parking is going to be a problem.

The majority of those in attendance are descendants of the families who lived in Cataloochee Township. A dwindling number actually lived in Cataloochee; the youngest of those born in the valley is now in his upper fifties. The Palmer and Caldwell families, once prominent in Big Cataloochee, are particularly well represented. Although Little Cataloochee has its own reunion, a number of individuals from that community also attend the reunion at Big Cataloochee.

Outsiders appear to be relatively few in number. Family friends and those who have married into Cataloochee families probably make up the largest number of nondescendants. A few politicians and aspiring politicians, as well as some journalists, make the scene. While stories about the

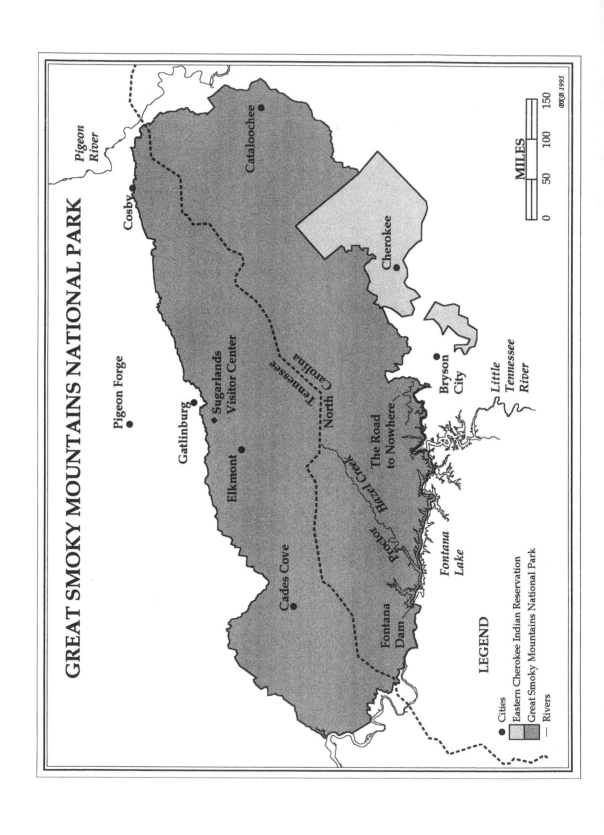

GREAT SMOKY MOUNTAINS NATIONAL PARK

Pigeon River

Cosby

Cataloochee

Pigeon Forge

Gatlinburg

Sugarlands
Visitor Center

Elkmont

Cherokee

Cades Cove

Tennessee
North Carolina

Hazel Creek

Proctor

The Road
to Nowhere

Bryson
City

Fontana
Dam

Fontana
Lake

Little
Tennessee
River

LEGEND

- Cities

Eastern Cherokee Indian Reservation

Great Smoky Mountains National Park

— Rivers

MILES

0   50   100   150

©KB 1995

reunion may appear in local papers, the park does not publicize it, and tourists are few. The park personnel on the North Carolina side seem rather protective of the event and have expressed relief that it has not been transformed into something like the Old Timers' Day at Cades Cove.

A church service at the Palmer Chapel begins the reunion. Not everyone attends the service; many visit outside or arrive only in time for the meal. While one attendee expresses concern that many no longer attend the service, the little Palmer Chapel is packed to capacity and can hold only a fraction of those who come to the reunion. Only part of the service is actually religious in nature. Hymn singing by the congregation begins and ends the service. The singing is unaccompanied, and although some hymnbooks are available, the majority of those present still know all the verses of "Amazing Grace" and "Revive Us Again." A visiting minister gives a relatively brief sermon toward the end of the service.

The nonreligious aspects of the service include the introduction of special guests such as the visiting politicians (speechifying is kept to a minimum) and the reading of announcements and a treasurer's report. The emotional core of the event is the recognition of those who are in

Palmer Chapel during the Cataloochee homecoming, 1992 (Photo by author)

attendance and those who are not. All who were born in Cataloochee are asked to stand, and the youngest and oldest are identified. Then the names of the families who once lived in the valley are read, and those who are members of these families are asked to stand. Of course, many can trace their ancestry to more than one Cataloochee family. Finally, the names of those individuals from Cataloochee who have died in the past year are read, and the church bell is rung for each one.

Cataloochee homecoming, 1992 (Photo by author)

The service is followed by a dinner on the grounds of gargantuan proportions. With what appears to be very little external organization, the participants spread out the food on tablecloths they have brought, and drinks, plates, and utensils are provided to those who need them. Fried chicken, ham, deviled eggs, potato salad, beans, biscuits, cakes, and many other standards of southern potlucks are spread among more than fifty tables. Most eat while sitting on lawn chairs that individual families have brought with them, though some spread blankets on the wet ground or take refuge in the chapel.

Other than the service and loosely organized meal, the reunion is unstructured. It has the loose, slightly chaotic quality of traditional social events in the rural South. Unlike the more recent "heritage" events, with their created traditions, no one dresses in costume, plays music, or demonstrates crafts. Children dabble in the creek, but there are no organized games. People gather and talk; many take pictures or videotape the event. Some go off to visit homesites in the valley. A good bit of verbal genealogy takes place, with ample opportunity for the favorite southern game, "Who are you (related to)?" The park service presence is relatively unobtrusive. A small exhibit featuring pictures of a former reunion and a slide/tape show currently under production is set up next to the chapel. It sparks the interest of some former residents who gather to identify images and voices.

The event bears a resemblance both to church homecomings and to family reunions. It unites two important themes in mountain culture—a sense of place and a sense of family. It is an act of renewal, not just remembrance. While people may visit with family members they otherwise see infrequently, they also strengthen the bond with those they see often. One young woman says that the event is important to her because she takes her granny every year.

The reunion at Little Cataloochee is only a fraction of the size of the Big Cataloochee event, which is just as well, since there is almost no place to park, and the road, which is usually not open to vehicular traffic, is difficult to traverse. On the sunny reunion day in 1993 a car breaks down on the road, delaying the arrival of many participants. When they do arrive, the elderly must be helped up the small hill on which the Little Cataloochee Baptist church sits. Still, more than enough show up to fill the beautiful late-nineteenth-century church.

The Little Cataloochee reunion makes the events at Big Cataloochee seem formal. The "service" has no preacher, or politicians either. It begins with a prayer and the singing, appropriately enough, of "Old Country Church." A few other favorite songs are chosen from the songbook and are informally led. At Little Cataloochee attendance is small enough for individuals to stand and identify members of their group of family and friends, explaining their relationship to the community. As at Big Cataloochee, the church bells are rung for those who have died. As the meeting closes, those in attendance are urged to keep the reunion going, to bring younger members of the family.

Grave decoration is an important part of this reunion. Many bring flowers, both fresh and artificial, to place on the graves in the church's cemetery, which the park service now cleans ahead of time. (In the past, cleaning the cemetery was part of the activity at the reunion.) Some bring enough to decorate graves of families not represented and urge others to do likewise. After the dinner, which is attended by over a hundred people and a couple of deer, members of the Hannah family go down to the family cemetery, located near the Hannah Cabin, the only surviving domestic structure in Little Cataloochee. Others hike up Coggins Branch to the remains of the stone apple house on what was once the Cook place. Others simply continue visiting, awaiting the mid-afternoon mass exodus, since almost everyone's car is blocked in by someone else's.

The reunions at Cataloochee and Little Cataloochee (and the other homecomings throughout the park) initially represented a means of coming to terms with dislocation, though not everyone's reaction was the same. Martha White Bennett of Little Cataloochee, for instance, felt too much sadness to be able to return after she was dislocated, and she never set eyes on the community again. She is buried at her home community of Liberty, just outside the park, rather than with her husband (who died several decades before the park's creation) at Little Cataloochee. Many others, however, have made frequent pilgrimages to old homes or homesites.

Homecomings in the park began soon after the removal. In 1940, Joseph Hall wrote:

> Great numbers return for the homecomings held in each cove or other districts where a settlement once existed. This yearly event draws many people from distant places. The good attendance bears witness to their affection for their former homes. In Cades Cove I was told by the local fire-guard that a certain family returned frequently, as often as every two or three weeks in the summertime, and sat on the site of their former mountain-side home drinking water from the nearby spring and eating wild strawberries which run rampant over the place.

For many, such as the family described by Hall, the dwelling itself no longer existed. The park service destroyed many of these houses, with some of the dislocated being given salvage rights. Many houses were simply burned for firewood. In truth, however, emotion was invested not so much in the structure as in the larger place. The home was often preserved better through family stories than through the structure itself.

In 1941 a park superintendent's report noted that the Cataloochee homecoming was attended by 678 persons, travelling in 109 cars. On the same summer day, 600 individuals held a reunion at Smokemont. The following year the gas rationing of World War II took its toll on the homecomings, and only 244 people attended in Cataloochee. They came in 21 cars and 2 pick-ups, as well as on 17 horses. The determination to continue the event despite transportation problems proved just as strong the next year when 224 people arrived in 13 cars and 8 trucks, with 22 on horseback.

In 1950, Robert H. Woody, a professor at Duke who was born in Cataloochee, wrote of the homecoming in *South Atlantic Quarterly*. His description indicates that the event has changed little in the past forty years. However, his essay focuses more on the changes that had been wrought on the community he knew as a child. Woody was not pleased with the "progress" at Cataloochee, particularly when it meant the demise of the community. "Homecoming on Cataloochee strikes a contrast between happy memories and the drab present. The Palmers and the Caldwells, the Messers and the Bennetts have departed . . . Only when those with the happy memories are gone will the present Cataloochee seem better than the old." While Robert Woody wrote in 1950 that the "time approaches when these reunions must cease," he underestimated the meaning of the communities even to those who never lived there. As the Palmer Chapel bell tolls every year for the passing of former residents, fewer and fewer of those who attend the homecoming at Cataloochee were ever residents. The homecoming becomes more about family history than individual memory. However, the event is in no danger of ceasing. In fact, the park service must struggle to accommodate the growing number of cars that climb the winding road to Cataloochee each homecoming.

Today, the sense of remoteness and isolation is strong at Cataloochee. The casual tourist is not likely to stumble upon this former community; not only is the road to Cataloochee long, it is not linked to either of the main entrances to the park. The current isolation, however, to some degree belies Cataloochee's history. Although its relative remoteness delayed permanent white settlement until the 1830s, construction of the Cataloochee Turnpike began the next decade. Cataloochee was located on the first major wagon road through the Smokies and hence was linked to markets in both North Carolina and Tennessee. By the 1850s, Cataloochee had grown enough that younger members of the Palmer, Hannah, Caldwell, and Bennett families moved to the other side of Noland Mountain and settled along the Little Cataloochee Creek.

By the early twentieth century, apples had become a major cash crop in Cataloochee, although cattle, honey, molasses, and tobacco were also produced for the market economy. A relatively prosperous community, Cataloochee was one of the largest settlements in the area that ultimately became the Great Smoky Mountains National Park. In 1900, there were approximately two hundred buildings in the township. After the turn of the century, several families in Cataloochee and Little Cataloochee built large frame houses or greatly expanded existing homes. While these dwellings reflected the growing prosperity of some residents of the valley, they were also the product of a new market for which the people of Cataloochee could provide. Some of the houses were built to take in boarders, who were sometimes school teachers and drummers but were mostly the many people who came to Cataloochee to fish. Several families also stocked trout streams and charged for fishing. So, even before the creation of the park, the natural resources and recreational opportunities of the Cataloochee Valley were attracting visitors. The difference after the creation of the park, as Robert Woody notes, was that there was no one left in Cataloochee to give the vacationers lodging or to sell them fresh milk or eggs.

A few "field exhibits" of original buildings are preserved at Cataloochee. Rather than reflecting the pioneer life-styles such as those interpreted at Cades Cove and Oconaluftee, much of the architecture here speaks of early-twentieth-century prosperity and the need to accommodate the growing number of tourists. Today, however, the sense of isolation is so complete that the buildings seem strange in this context. They defy the stereotypes of life in Appalachia, and the lack of interpretation makes them more puzzling than edifying. For those who attend the homecoming, however, the few remaining buildings at Cataloochee are a touchstone for the continuing sense of place.

OLD TIMERS' DAY: CADES COVE

For visitors to the Great Smoky Mountains National Park, Cades Cove is the most compelling reminder that the mountains were once inhabited. Though historic buildings still remain elsewhere in the park, they are generally less visited than those at Cades Cove. History is only part of the area's appeal; the view of the meadows surrounded by mountains is stunning. Many visitors, however, do not realize that these meadows do not represent the natural state of things and are as much a product of human culture as the log structures that dot the landscape. The cove's popularity also reflects the fact that the loop road through the area accommodates the auto-tourist. While some structures are not visible from the road, many of the cove's attractions can be seen by people who never leave the confines of their cars or Winnebagos. The auto route also makes certain forms of wildlife accessible to visitors.

Still, the message of Cades Cove is one of history, not wilderness. Its theme so differs from most of the rest of the park that it is often incorrectly assumed that Cades Cove was the only community inside the park's boundaries before the removal. While many of the buildings are original, Cades Cove was not a mountain community miraculously preserved within the park. Just as much of the "wilderness" of the Smokies was reconstructed, not preserved, so too has been its sense of history. Cades Cove is a highly edited landscape. Buildings were moved so as to be more accessible to the auto-tourist, and certain structures were imported from elsewhere in the park. Just as important are the buildings that are missing—the early-twentieth-century structures and others that did not fit the image of folk culture as the park service wished to display it. In springtime, flowers mark the locations of former homes that have been removed from the landscape.

Tourists come today seeking a sense of America's past. The Cades Cove they see bears little resemblance to the Cades Cove of living memory. Bonnie Meyers, who now works in the visitors center, grew up in a two-story frame house as did many of her neighbors. "Most of them frame houses that I knew . . . We never noticed these cabins, growing up, paid them no mind . . . All those [frame] houses were torn down. They left the cabins, you know, more pioneerish . . . [Visitors] can't believe that people used to be here and you had schools and stores and churches and stuff like that." The large school buildings, the boardinghouses and tourist cabins, the cannery, and other twentieth-century structures all went the way of the frame dwellings (the lone exception is the frame Becky Cable house). Hence, people assume that the people of Cades Cove lived like pioneers until the park was created. "Lot of people think that we never did go out to town, you know, and people here just lived and died and never went to the city. But, cars were in here in 1915, the first car came in. My mother was fourteen years old."

The visitor to Cades Cove is more likely to take away images of a generalized past in the mountains than knowledge of the real individuals who once inhabited the community. Cades Cove is the most studied of all the former communities within the park, and it produced its fair share of remembrances and histories by former residents and their descendants. The most scholarly example of the latter is Durwood Dunn's *Cades Cove: The Life and Death of a Southern Appalachian Community: 1818–1937.* The Cades Cove described by Dunn in this revisionist history is a community which, while physically remote, was not isolated from the rest of the world. Although the residents of the cove had a strong sense of community and patterns of communal work, the economic development of the community was also shaped by commercial agriculture and tenancy. As elsewhere in the mountains, isolation was more acute in the post-Civil War era than in the prosperous decades before the war, but it was never complete. Ultimately, Dunn argues, if Cades Cove has any meaning, it is that "the people followed regional and national patterns of development" (p. 256). At least they did until they became victims of eminent domain.

What the visitor usually does not hear during a visit to Cades Cove is the story of the impact of park removals on the former residents. Although one can visit a log house built by John Oliver, one of the cove's first white inhabitants, one does not learn about the bitter fight against removal fought by a later John Oliver, his great-grandson. One of the more prominent and progressive members of the community, Oliver was expected by the park supporters to go along with their plans. However, Oliver did not passively relinquish his 337 ½ acres. Instead he fought through the courts for years, finally exhausting his legal remedies. In 1937 he left the cove. In a rare acknowledgment of the park removals, a park service interpreter included Oliver in a dramatic portrayal of mountain people in an evening program at a park campground in 1993. The college-educated Oliver was depicted as an ignorant hillbilly trying to block the path of progress.

As elsewhere in the park, homecomings and reunions at Cades Cove provide ties to the old community. As Bonnie Meyers states, "They have homecoming at the Missionary Baptist Church. And then lots of people go to the Oliver reunion and the Sparks reunion, people that aren't by that name. But they still get to see a lot of their people, former friends." People from far away also wander into the Visitors Center at Cable Mill in hopes of establishing ties to the community: "Lot of people come in, they're Sparkses from Oklahoma or Gregorys from Spokane. And we just wonder, 'Is this some of our people?' We try to give them a book to read, you know, or send them to the county courthouse and look up some record. People just want to tie into it."

There is no single-community reunion like the one in Cataloochee, or at least not one started by former residents. There is Old Timers' Day, started about two decades ago by well-meaning park personnel to bring former residents back to Cades Cove. Old Timers' Day is now held twice a year at Cable Mill at the far end of the cove. Starting early in the morning, a massive traffic jam begins to form, much to the dismay of the walkers and bicyclists for whom the road is usually reserved on Saturday mornings. By mid-morning, traffic has slowed to a crawl, if it is moving at all. While some "old timers" may indeed return to Cades Cove on this day, this event is quite different from the other homecomings and family reunions held in the park.

Many of those drawn to Old Timers' Day are musicians or aficionados of old time or bluegrass music. In fact, the event's atmosphere is much like that of a bluegrass festival, minus the central stage. Musicians and

dancers simply show up, then group and regroup throughout the day. There is little evidence of any scheduled activity and, with the exception of a large number of horse-drawn mowers in the fall, few demonstrations. Park service personnel are available to provide security and some interpretation, but they do not play a prominent role. Music and dance are clearly the central attraction, but there are no stages and no microphones. Some team cloggers do bring their own wooden floors to dance on.

Hymn singing at Old Timers' Day, Fall 1992 (Photo by author)

Strictly speaking, the historicity of much of the music and dance can be questioned. When families were removed from Cades Cove, bluegrass music had not been invented and team clogging was in its infancy. Dulcimers were not known in Cades Cove, and mandolins were probably rare. The old-time fiddlers and the old timers who break into impromptu flatfoot dancing are representative of Smoky Mountains traditions in the prepark era. Former resident Carl Whitehead continued to show up and dance until he was in his nineties; he fell and broke his hip at an Old Timers' Day in 1992. However, the strong Primitive Baptist element in Cades Cove would most likely have discouraged fiddling and dancing within the community. The small groups of hymn singers, often drowned out by the other music, are perhaps better representatives of the musical

Dancing at Old Timers'
Day, Fall 1992 (Photo by
author)

traditions of the cove. Also true to the tradition of music and dance in the mountains is the emphasis on participation rather than performance.

Old Timers' Day has been hugely successful in bringing visitors to the park. If it grows any larger there will be serious problems for the park service regarding traffic enforcement and environmental impact. However, Old Timers' Day is no longer about the specific families who once lived in the cove or even about the folk traditions that once existed there. As Bonnie Meyers (who is glad she has those days off from working at the Visitors Center) assesses it: "Well, it seems like it's kind of strayed. There's just so many people, it's not really old timers anymore. They play music that we'd never even heard of and instruments we'd never heard of here in the Cove. But people like it, so I guess it'll continue."

At Cades Cove, visitors seem to be in search of a generic (and perhaps mythic) American past. The past at Cataloochee seems more specific, tied to particular individuals and families. Old Timers' Day is more about a collective sense of tradition (the historical accuracy of which is essentially beside the point), while the Cataloochee homecoming is about a sense of family and place.

R O A D   T O   N O W H E R E :   H A Z E L   C R E E K

Mowing demonstration
at Old Timers' Day, Fall
1992 (Photo by author)

If the former residents of Cataloochee find their old community isolated within the apparent wilderness of a national park, the case of Hazel Creek, also on the North Carolina side of the park, is even more extreme. Here, limited access has made it far more difficult for former residents to come to terms with dislocation through the act of homecoming.

Hazel Creek was the "back of beyond" to which Horace Kephart retreated soon after arriving in western North Carolina. It had been settled approximately seventy years before Kephart's arrival. A number of the earliest settlers on the creek arrived from Cades Cove. Despite the area's remoteness, by Kephart's time industrialization was rapidly encroaching. Small-scale timbering and copper mining operations had already been set up and the W. M. Ritter Lumber Company had begun to survey the forests near Hazel Creek.

By 1910, timbering had begun in earnest in this part of the Smoky

Mountains. With the arrival of the Ritter Company on Hazel Creek, Proctor developed into a boom town that housed over a thousand people and included a depot, barber shop, boardinghouses, a movie theater, and pool hall. The lumber company employed a number of local people, some finding public work for the first time, but also attracted a number of workers from elsewhere in the region. As the park service would a decade later, Ritter bought into myths about the local culture. An article in the company's magazine, *The Hardwood Bark*, exclaimed: "It has been said that the purest type of American is to be found in the Southern mountains, and our native neighbors around Hazel Creek are splendid specimens of the type." Not only did the company describe the local people as if they were trees, it also tended to see the population as a resource, along with the forests, to be exploited. The timbering by the big companies in any given area was short-lived, and the ready jobs did not last. As timber companies pulled out, they left behind dramatically altered landscapes and communities.

While radically transforming the life and landscape of Hazel Creek, the era of the Ritter Company was relatively short. In 1928 Ritter left Hazel Creek, taking with it the railroad, many of the businesses, and much of the itinerant (and some of the permanent) population. The people remaining struggled to keep the community alive, especially as the Great Depression set in.

For financial reasons, the original boundaries of the Great Smoky Mountains National Park did not include the area around Hazel Creek, north of the Little Tennessee River in Swain County, North Carolina. Therefore, the residents were not removed in the 1930s. However, their time would soon come. After the United States entered World War II, the long-planned dam at Fontana was speeded into production. Under pressure from the federal government, Alcoa gave the Tennessee Valley Authority its land along the Little Tennessee in exchange for needed electricity to produce aluminum for the war effort. Jobs once again became plentiful as the local population found work building what would become the highest dam in the eastern United States. The newly constructed Fontana Lake would inundate a number of communities located near the river, and though it would not flood the upper reaches of Hazel Creek, it would take North Carolina Highway 288, the only road that provided access to the communities and towns along the north shore of the new lake. Since building a new road during war time was not considered expedient, it was determined that the families who lived along the north shore would have to be removed. The TVA's solution was to give the forty-four thousand acres to the Great Smoky Mountains National Park, a plan that one park historian wrote was "received with great joy on all sides."

The joy was not shared by the residents of the north shore. Construction of the dam was well underway by the time the plan was announced, and many lobbied, to no effect, to have a new road constructed to their communities. The north shore communities were the last to be removed, partially because acquisition of this land began later and also because the TVA itself was not eager to lose its source of labor. The majority of the relocation, however, was completed in 1944. As in the creation of the park, a few land owners fought the land acquisition in court. Both the federal district court and the U.S. circuit court of appeals ruled that the TVA did not have a constitutional right to condemn the north shore property. However, in 1946, two years after the dam was finished, the Supreme Court overturned these decisions and ruled in favor of the TVA.

The Tennessee Valley Authority's approach to the removal of families was different from that of the National Park Service. A 1953 report on the TVA's relocation policy specifically cites the inadequate assistance provided to families in the creation of the Great Smoky Mountains National Park as one of the factors in developing their policy. The TVA was authorized to advise families displaced by construction projects and to work with federal, state, and local agencies in providing assistance. The TVA also developed a policy of acquiring the minimum amount of property necessary. Fontana was the exception.

Despite the TVA's good intentions, neglect was too often replaced by paternalism. Some of the relocation reports simply reflect the standard stereotypes about the people of the region, with little understanding of the specific communities. In the case of Fontana Dam, the TVA denied that a sense of community actually existed. The Proctor report, which covered all of the north shore communities, displayed a particular lack of effort; the majority of the narrative is a straight quotation from another publication, *Tar Heels*, and was laced with stereotypical images.

The construction of Fontana Dam ultimately resulted in the removal of 1,311 families. Of these, 711 were transients, and the TVA felt little need to give them aid in relocating; the other 600 had been residents of the area before construction of the dam began. Of these "original families," 163 were removed from the land given to the national park. Although these families received considerably more material assistance in relocating than those removed from the Smokies a decade earlier, the taking of the north shore left a residue of bitterness even greater than that from the other park removals. These people were not given the opportunity to lease their land back from the government, and even the act of homecoming was made virtually impossible by the inundation of Highway 288.

The only solace offered to the families removed from the north shore was that as part of the agreement the National Park Service was to make "all diligent efforts" after the war to secure funds to build a high grade park road along the north shore. However, the funds were long in coming. The two-and-a-half-mile section from Bryson City to the park boundary was built in 1959, and the road was begun within the park boundaries. However, ten years later only about six miles had been finished.

The north shore road was to have been part of a planned route that would encircle the park. However, by the late 1960s, environmentalists were vehemently opposed to the north shore road and construction was halted. The aborted "road to nowhere" would eventually become a symbol for some former residents of the bad faith of the government and the elitism of environmentalists who wished the area declared a wilderness, despite the human meaning that the place held for the former residents.

The first reunion of former residents of Hazel Creek was not held until 1976. The location of the reunion was not the former community itself but the Deep Creek campground near Bryson City. While some individuals had tried to maintain some of the cemeteries at Hazel Creek, others were in disrepair, and no decorations had been held in over thirty years. As an outcome of the first reunion, a decoration of four cemeteries at Hazel Creek was held in 1978. The park service accommodated the former residents and their families by helping to provide transportation to the cemeteries and stepping up efforts to maintain them. The former residents banded into a formal group, first called the Cemetery Association and later changed to the North Shore Historical Association. While many of their interests were historical, they also lobbied to complete the road to Hazel Creek.

During the 1980s, as the issue continued to fester, the political debate over access to Hazel Creek became increasingly heated. Swain County had never been compensated for its loss of a road and tax base and was willing to settle for cash. Meanwhile, the former residents of Hazel Creek became fearful that the environmentalists would not only block the construction of the road but would also halt the limited boat and vehicular access to Hazel Creek and even perhaps find the visits to the cemeteries by former residents to be environmentally damaging. Out of frustration or bitterness, some became virulently antienvironmental. While they were willing to settle for an unpaved, rather than a paved, road, they were unwilling to accept a compromise that did not include vehicular access to the cemeteries. Conservative Senator Jesse Helms became their champion in Congress.

As in the creation of the park itself, the issue of the greater good is not easily resolved. Despite Horace Kephart's fascination with the "highlander," he felt strongly that the park was necessary as a protection against the encroachment of industrialization on the wilderness, even if it brought a different type of encroachment, good roads. However, for many of the park promoters, good roads were exactly the point, and it was chambers of commerce and automobile clubs who actively promoted the creation of the park. Ironically, roads are now seen as a threat to the park. Whatever the initial arguments for the park, it was the residents who paid the greatest price, and for their sacrifice, they were not always treated with fairness, honesty, or respect.

The antienvironmentalism of some former residents of the Smokies grew from their astonishment that human concerns were taking second place to concern for the creatures of the woods. As Professor Woody wrote, "[T]he birds and beasts of the forest needed a home. In short, the people were to be moved and improved; the land returned to the bear, the fox, the wild turkey, not to mention the copperhead and the rattler." Louisa Walker, the poet of the Walker sisters of Little Greenbrier, expressed the situation in more vernacular terms:

> For us poor mountain people
> They don't have a care
> But must a home for
> The wolf lion and the bear

To a people who for generations had seen the wilderness as both resource and adversary, it must have seemed that the natural order of things was being destroyed. This sense of natural order, of man over animal, was confirmed for many by their religious beliefs. Louisa Walker found comfort that they still had a "title" in heaven.

> When we reach the portles
> of glory so fair
> The Wolf cannot enter
> Neather the lion or bear

> And no Park Commissioner
> Will ever dar
> To desturbe or molest
> Or take our home from us there

The former residents of Hazel Creek are particularly unmoved by environmental arguments. The initial sacrifice of those who lived at Hazel Creek was not made for preservation of the wilderness but for the war effort. In exchange, they were promised access to their former homesites and cemeteries when the national emergency was over. This promise was not fulfilled, adding to the bitterness of removal. And while Hazel Creek is now in one of the more remote reaches of the park, the community that many former residents remember was a booming timber town. Unlike the situation at Cades Cove and Cataloochee, former residents could not find solace in the fact that others cared to preserve some portion of their history. For this reason, the remaining tangible evidence of human habitation—the cemeteries—take on even greater meaning.

SUMMER VISITATION AND COMMUNITY: ELKMONT

At Elkmont, situated on the East Prong of the Little River in Tennessee, the park removals are more recent history. The "cabin holders" at Elkmont were not farmers tied to the land but former owners (or descendants of former owners) of summer homes that were part of two social clubs. The conflict over the continued tenancy of the Elkmonters has resulted in one of the most publicized disputes over land use in the Great Smoky Mountains National Park.

The recreational use of the Great Smokies by well-to-do urbanites developed hand-in-hand with the industrialization of the region. The development of rail access to the Smokies region in the late nineteenth century enhanced both tourism and the industrial potential of the region, but the remote reaches of the Smokies were largely inaccessible until after the turn of the century. Among the several large timber companies that moved into the Smokies after 1900 was the Little River Timber Company. Intent on cutting hardwoods and hemlocks at the higher elevations of the mountains, this company built its own standard-gauge railroad line into the mountains. Connecting to the Knoxville & Augusta Railroad at Walland (in Blount County, Tennessee), the line pushed through the narrow Little River Gorge and up the East Prong of the Little River in Sevier County. The town of Elkmont was built as the base for operations along the East Prong.

The Little River Company soon realized that its railroad provided more than an efficient means to extract timber from the mountains. An observation car was added to the lumber train for passengers who wished to view the scenery along the Little River, and by 1909 daily passenger service was available from Knoxville to Elkmont. The Little River Lumber Company also promoted the development of cutover land. In 1910 it deeded fifty acres above the town of Elkmont to the Appalachian Club, a Knoxville-based social club composed largely of businessmen. In 1919 the club was reconstituted and formally incorporated as the New Appalachian Club, with its headquarters in Knoxville and its principal clubhouse at Elkmont. Below the town of Elkmont, the lumber company sold land to real estate speculators who in 1912 built the Wonderland Hotel. The land adjacent to the hotel was subdivided into thousands of tiny lots, and hundreds were sold to gullible people across the United States. Despite the grand plans for the Wonderland Park development, the majority of the tracts were unsuitable for building. Many owners never visited their land and would not learn until decades later that their land in the Great Smoky Mountains was virtually worthless. The Wonderland Park Company was short-lived. Internal disputes led the company to sell the hotel and the immediately adjacent lands and buildings to a group of Knoxvillians who formed a private club, similar in nature to the Appalachian Club.

For almost a decade and a half, recreational and industrial use of the East Prong of the Little River existed cheek by jowl. On either side of the timber town of Elkmont, which consisted largely of simple boxed structures, lay rustic cabins, owned by members of the Appalachian and Wonderland clubs. Both clubs also ran hotels that were available to paying guests as well as to members. By the mid-1920s, however, the accessible timber above the East Prong had been removed, and the lumber company began to retreat. In 1925, the train to Elkmont was discontinued, and by the following year a gravel road had been built following the old rail line through the Little River Gorge.

Club life continued after the retreat of the timber company. In fact, after the transportation problems were solved, the absence of noise and disrupting logging operations probably seemed an improvement. Although the cabins of the Appalachian Club were generally small and rustic, the life-style hardly involved "roughing it." Meals were served by waiters at the clubhouse, and nurses cared for small children. Well-attired families promenaded on boardwalks. Annual entertainments included costume parties and performances. By 1933, Elkmont had sixty-five summer homes "owned by the very best citizens of Knoxville, some from Memphis, some from Athens, some from Nashville, and some from Kentucky, and other places."

As elsewhere inside the park boundaries, private land ownership came to an end with the creation of the Great Smoky Mountains National Park. Although many members of the Appalachian and Wonderland clubs would develop an adversarial relationship with the park service, many early members were proponents of the park. A member of the Wonderland Club, Tennessee Governor Austin Peay spearheaded the purchase of the first large tract for the park even before its authorization by Congress. The majority of those present at the initial meeting of the Great Smoky Mountains Conservation Association in 1923 were Appalachian Club members. Members of these clubs also had strong ties to the Knoxville Chamber of Commerce and the Knoxville Automobile Club, both institutions that supported the creation of the park.

Although the conservation association was initially interested in having good roads built into the Smokies, it soon directed its attention to the creation of a national park. Some members split with the association when its focus changed. Notable among this group was attorney James B. Wright, who supported a national forest but not a park, since the latter entailed removals and condemnations of land. Wright was retained by some members of the Appalachian Club who opposed condemnation of land (though Wright portrayed himself as champion of the poor farmers who were being dislocated, not the well-to-do who owned summer homes). A number of other Appalachian Club members, however, remained supporters of the park. Perhaps some believed that their land would be excluded from the removals. A Knoxville Automobile Club map published in 1927 shows the proposed park boundaries as excluding the Elkmont communities, which was quite a feat of cartography, as Elkmont lay well within the proposed park.

There is a popular perception even today that the members of the Wonderland and Appalachian clubs were given special privilege in the granting of lifetime leases. This is not wholly true, although it is probable that the Elkmonters posed a far more fearsome political lobby than the average Smoky Mountains farmer. In 1932 Congress consented to a plan in which landowners could be offered long-term leases. The majority of the developed properties at the Appalachian and Wonderland clubs were acquired for half the appraised value plus a lifetime lease.

Full-time residents who farmed the land in the park were also offered leases, but their situation had far different results. Leaseholders were no longer free to use the natural resources that surrounded their homes. Perhaps the biggest hardship, however, was the loss of neighbors. The rural communities that had made life viable in the mountains no longer existed for those who wished to stick it out in a life that now was full of federal regulations.

On the other hand, club life at Elkmont continued in a context that was only slightly altered. The town itself, already declining after the withdrawal of the Little River Timber Company, disappeared. It became first a Civilian Conservation Corps camp and later a campground for visitors. The club members probably benefitted from the cessation of commercial development at Elkmont. In fact they could profit commercially. Elkmont was not only in many ways their private reserve, but, as park superintendent Eakin was forced to acknowledge in 1934, the lessees at the Appalachian and Wonderland clubs were subletting their cabins and the "Wonderland and Appalachian Clubs are permitted to entertain paying guests, and are, in fact, hotels."

Some legally astute club members at Elkmont also attempted to maximize the length of their lifetime leases. Before relinquishing their land, these members signed over whole or partial interest to their children so the leases would extend over their lifetimes. However, the majority (though not all) of the Appalachian Club's lifetime leases were renegotiated in the early 1950s. Finding their electric needs unmet by the meager supply from the small hydroelectric plant, the majority of the club members agreed to twenty-year leases in exchange for the provision of electricity by the Sevier County Electric System. As 1972, the date for which these leases would expire, approached, members of the Appalachian and Wonderland clubs formed the Elkmont Preservation Committee in order to negotiate a new agreement with the Department of Interior. Despite opposition from park officials and environmentalists, a new agreement was reached.

One of the arguments made for the continuation of leases in the new agreement was based on the National Park Service's responsibility for interpreting the mountain culture of the Great Smoky Mountains. The preservation committee argued that the Wonderland Hotel, as one of the few remaining examples of a mountain resort hotel, was an "important example of one aspect of 'Turn of the Century' mountain culture and, therefore, is most worthy of preservation and interpretation to the visiting public by means of its continuing use and operations." Under the terms of the agreement, the preservation committee would be responsible for the proper maintenance and operation of the hotel. However, several years later an environmental review, while validating the agreement, called for several amendments. These included deletion of reference to the historic significance of the Wonderland Hotel. According to the review, a "determination has been made by the Park Historian, Regional Historian and Regional Historical Architect, that no historical significance is attached to this area." The review amendments also stipulated that within two years after they are vacated, "all structures and buildings will be removed by the National Park Service."

The issue of the historical significance of the surviving structures at Elkmont has become central to the ongoing conflict. Former park ranger John Morrell suggested that references to historical significance in the 1972 agreement "appear calculated to maintain the status quo of the Appalachian and Wonderland Clubs in perpetuity." In 1992, as the new twenty-year leases were due to expire, Elkmonters again turned to historic preservation as a way of maintaining their community. This time around, preservation law was more explicit and the concept of significance broadly expanded. Federal law mandated a review of significance before the park service could remove the structures.

While park officials continue to be reluctant to acknowledge the historicity of the Elkmont buildings, by most contemporary standards Elkmont is significant. Historically, it is important because of its association with the development of tourism in the Smokies and, perhaps ironically, with those involved in creating the park. Architecturally, the self-consciously rustic style of the cabins is less typical of the regional vernacular than of a vernacular style that developed in other summer resort communities. The structures at Elkmont are especially notable for their survival. Tourist facilities are particularly vulnerable to the pressures of remodeling and rebuilding, especially in an area as popular as the Smokies. Few buildings representative of this era of Smoky Mountains history survive in the area immediately adjacent to the park. And within the park, the selective editing of the landscape by the park service has eliminated buildings associated with timber and tourism in favor of those representative of folk culture.

While the park service may find it necessary to accede on the issue of significance, the Elkmonters may find that it does them little good. As other park residents discovered sixty years ago, the park may choose to preserve culture, but it is the tangible artifact that is saved, not the intangible sense of home or community attached to it. The Elkmonters may argue correctly that it is their continued sense of community that has preserved Elkmont and renders it significant, but while this "context" may be used as an argument for the value of the structures, the federal government has yet to develop regulations that preserve such an intangible aspect of culture. The buildings may be preserved, as at Cades Cove and Cataloochee, but the true significance lies with the community and culture that have been removed.

The sentiment expressed by one Elkmonter, whose cottage has been in the family for eighty years, is perhaps typical of many: "The cottage is imbued with experiences and memories of five generations . . . The cottage has served us in many ways but, most important, it serves as the hinge for the continued cohesion of our geographically scattered family." While the sense of loss over a place associated with family memories and a continued sense of community is real and deep, the Elkmonters do not generally have public sentiment on their side. Many, including some descendants of families earlier removed from the park, see a history of special privilege and do not feel sympathy for those who are losing a vacation home. The *Knoxville News-Sentinel* editorialized in October of 1992: "But fairness demands that the original intent of the leases be followed. It's time to let Elkmont—like the pioneers' homestead—fade away, cease being a source of resentment and become simply another rich, poignant chapter in the history of the wonderful Smokies."

If there is public concern for any preservation at Elkmont, it pertains to the Wonderland Hotel. During its final season, in 1992, a number of older people made pilgrimages to the old hotel to remember day excursions, family vacations, and particularly the big dances that once took place there. Some were bold enough to urge strangers sitting on the porch or in the lobby to write their congressmen and demand that the building be preserved.

The Wonderland is one of the few remaining early-twentieth-century resort hotels surviving in the Smoky Mountains. Since the hotel was leased, not owned, and since its future has been uncertain, the building has not been extensively renovated or modernized. However, as it was the only hotel in the park, it continued to attract visitors. In fact, because it lacked modern conveniences like telephones and televisions (and even adequate reading light) in the rooms, people congregated around the fire in the lobby or on the wide porches. Here they discovered a sense of camaraderie and communality that is missing from most modern resorts.

Some of the buildings at Elkmont may be preserved. The cabins may be rented by the park service and the Wonderland may be turned into a museum. However, as elsewhere in the park, something intangible is lost, even as the park service turns individual and family histories into a communal and democratic past.

Family Retreat: Cosby and Gatlinburg

The bitterness caused by the park removals resulted in new rituals to assuage the sense of loss and spawned political conflicts that continued for more than half a century after the park's creation. But not all left the Smokies with bitterness in their hearts. Celia Williams Baxter was born in Sevier County in 1904, the youngest of twelve children. Before her birth, her family had lived on Webb's Creek; the site of the homeplace and the family cemetery are now within the park's boundaries. Mrs. Baxter grew up in the community of Rocky Grove, just at the edge of what would become the boundaries of the park.

In 1923 Celia Williams married James Scott Baxter, whom she had met when he attended her Primitive Baptist church (he was a member of the Christian church across the road). He had grown up near Cosby. His homeplace, built around 1889, is still standing inside the park's boundaries. For a few years the couple lived up the road from the Baxter homeplace, until they sold out to the park. As Mrs. Baxter remembered, "We was glad to get out. Didn't get much for it. We didn't have many acres." For the Baxters, financial imperatives were at the time more important than the attachment to place. "He just wanted to get out somewhere where he could make a living. Because we just had a little rocky farm. Rocks—a few little smooth places where you could raise a little garden—but the rest of it was just rocks." The Baxters moved to the Keavy com-

Celia Baxter and her
daughter, Betty Gill, at
family retreat, 1994
(Photo by David Baxter)

munity of Laurel County, Kentucky, where they raised a family of eleven children. James Scott Baxter died in 1974.

On the surface, it seems unlikely that the Baxter family would maintain a sense of attachment to the Smokies. Celia Baxter, the oldest member of the family, is unsentimental about their move away from the Smokies. None of her direct descendants live in the Smoky Mountains region. Yet, every year, her children, grandchildren and great-grandchildren gather in the Smokies in October to celebrate, first of all, their sense of family, and secondarily, the family's roots in this particular place.

Unlike some of the reunions and homecomings in the park that have their roots in the park removal, the Baxter family's retreat is of more recent origin. After moving to Kentucky, the Baxters made only occasional visits to the Smokies, mostly to visit Scott Baxter's brother, Bill and his wife, Leah. Although infrequent, these trips are remembered vividly by the Baxters' children. Kenneth Baxter remembers travelling first on a Greyhound bus, sometime in the 1940s, and later in his father's first vehicle, a '49 Chevy pick-up truck. But, as his younger brother John recalled, "It was an infrequent trip to the mountains. I guess that road just seemed so long. And maybe it was that my dad just never really ventured far from home."

Now about a decade old, the family retreat started as a birthday trip to the Smokies for one of Celia Baxter's granddaughters, Charlotte Baird, a gift from her husband, Ray. Several relatives were invited to join them. The next year the Bairds extended an invitation to all the family for a fall

retreat, and the extended Baxter clan has gathered at the end of October ever since. It is not the type of reunion where people stumble upon relatives they have never met. "Granny" Baxter, her direct descendants, their spouses, and the occasional family friend take part. Still, it is not a small group; approximately sixty fill two chalets rented in the Gatlinburg area. Family members make it a priority in their lives, with many taking off from work or school. Most live in Kentucky or Tennessee, but others come from Ohio and sometimes Oklahoma or Hawaii.

Baxter homeplace in the Great Smoky Mountains National Park (Photo by David Baxter)

The retreat starts Thursday night and lasts until Sunday afternoon. As in most family reunions, eating is important. "We only just eat one meal," Kenneth Baxter jokes. "It starts on Thursday evening and it quits Sunday about noon." The family is proud to point out that the food is always homemade. Reminiscing, telling stories, and just visiting are also key elements. An important link to family traditions is the singing of hymns. Celia Baxter grew up in the minor-key a cappella tradition of the Primitive Baptists; her husband taught shape-note singing schools in Laurel County, Kentucky. A Sunday morning worship service ties the family to its spiritual traditions.

John Baxter at family re-
treat, 1994 (Photo by
David Baxter)

The retreat is largely about a strong sense of family: "Just being a Baxter," John Baxter says. The family could, and probably would, if necessary, meet somewhere else. But meeting in the Smokies adds more than a beautiful backdrop or the opportunity to hike in the mountains or shop in Gatlinburg. It adds a sense of place. Although no one but Celia Baxter has ever lived in the Smokies, there is still a tie. And, like other families, they seek out physical evidence of this sense of connection. Some family members, such as Nell Nelson (one of Celia Baxter's daughters) and her daughter, Jennifer Nelson, specialize in "graveyard hopping," locating cemeteries where family members are buried. "Sometimes that is the only place we have to go back and get in touch with some of our ancestors. Since both my parents were from the Smoky Mountains area—and their parents are buried there—it was just a natural that at some point I go back and start looking."

On Saturday morning, most of the family members take the hike up to Papa Baxter's homeplace, located in the park, a short hike up Maddron Bald Trail near Cosby. Kenneth Baxter remembers that even when he was a child, the visit to the log dwelling was a part of visiting in the Smokies: "They'd explain the cabin where he grew up, that was kind of impressive.

They'd show where the pig pen would have been. Where the garden was. You know, it was all relatively teeny . . . even in my eyes." Past the cabin is the hedgerow that Papa Baxter planted for Granny when they were first married, although their house is now gone. Sometimes the family gets a ranger to open the gate so a vehicle can drive Celia Baxter up to the cabin.

After visiting the homeplace, a few members of the family take the much more arduous hike up to the "upper place," where Granny Baxter's family lived before she was born. An old chimney and the foundation of an apple cellar are all that remain. Nearby is a family cemetery. About fifteen years ago, Celia Baxter made that hike herself. "She was going to go up there. There wasn't going to be anything that would hinder her from going up there . . . It was just like her heart's desire to once more— one more time, see that gravestone. Her brother Philip's gravestone," said her daughter-in-law, Lee Baxter. More recently Celia Baxter, then in her mid-eighties, made the hike again. This time the family carried a lawn chair, so she could rest along the way.

Celia Baxter's youngest son, John, thinks that the tradition of the retreat will pass on to other generations. And, while he thinks the reunion could be held somewhere else, there is something special about the connection to the Smokies:

We still probably would all go [somewhere else]. And yet, when we get that close, in terms of miles, to the log cabin and to the apple cellar . . . the hedgerow, the graveyard, we want to just go back up there and stand there and look and think, you know, "My Daddy, he lived right here. And he walked and played right here. And people that have been kin to people that I know—this has been part of their home." I know when we go up there and look at Philip's grave, and to think that I've got an uncle that died . . . before the 1900s. That I've got an uncle—and here I'm living in 1994, me almost forty-eight years old—and my uncle lived a hundred years ago and died that far back. That just stretches . . . a generation a hundred years. And that's almost an unreal concept. It just gives you an eerie feeling to be up on the side of a mountain that's now grown up and you can't hardly find your way in and find your way out. And you think, "This is the home of people that also were kin to me, but so long ago."

Displays of Culture

If we go off too long in search of authentic culture, especially at public events and institutions, we are apt to end up like the befuddled tourist, unable to find a real Appalachian. True, we can trace the history of individual genres of folklife and the ways in which they have changed during the past century, but it would be wrong to think that real culture exists independent of popular perceptions and scholarly representations.

Recent Appalachian studies scholarship has emphasized the extent to which Southern Appalachian culture has been selectively defined by outsiders who have their own political and individual agendas. This viewpoint, while valuable, runs the risks of reinforcing another stereotype: the Appalachian as passive victim. However, Appalachians have agendas of their own and they make use of public representations of their own culture in many ways.

Humor, as already discussed, can be one way to manipulate stereotypes. By stereotyping a stereotype, acting out a role that both meets and exaggerates public expectation, an individual plays a trickster, gets the last laugh. This was done for commercial gain in the early days of the development of country music when traditional music, regional humor, and the traditions of vaudeville and the medicine show married to produce a new form of performance. Many of the enduring "hillbilly" images came not from the local color and missionary writings of the nineteenth century but from hillbilly musicians' humorous satires of earlier stereotypes. Many of these performers were people from the region who honestly took delight in their own creations. While the mass media continue to feed more serious stereotypes of mountain culture, at least some of the audience for hillbilly or country humor comes from the region itself.

Touristic portrayals of culture are not always imposed from without. People make a living manipulating popular perceptions of their culture. Tourism, it has also been argued, can create a cultural buffer; touristic attractions give the tourists something to do, something to buy, while keeping them out of the hair of people trying to get on with their everyday lives. While many touristic portrayals of culture involve feeding back to the public their preconceived ideas, tourism can also act as a self-documentation. Tourism can enable some residents of the region to have a say in how their own culture is represented.

Even the audience for scholarly representations of southern mountain culture have not all come from without. Ballad singers own copies of Cecil Sharp's work; Cherokee Indians are familiar with Mooney's scholarship. These and other works, as well as public presentations, become the raw materials for an internal process of selecting what is perceived as traditional. The concept of tradition is a result of an active process of ascribing significance. Team clogging is seen as traditional dance not just by tourists but by plenty of people in the Smoky Mountains region. These people are not necessarily deluded; the relatively young age of the form may really be of little significance. While the folklorist may be amused at the heritage festival that prohibits soft drinks because they are "modern" but prominently features precision clogging and bluegrass, the majority of festival participants care little about folklorists' perceptions of authenticity.

If it is correct to describe Southern Appalachian and Native American cultures as having been "appropriated" by outsiders (and this is indeed a popular argument), then we may also suggest that cultural representations produced by the outsiders have the potential of being re-appropriated, manipulated, and selectively chosen for individual and collective economic and cultural reasons. Nowhere is this so apparent as in public displays of culture. If authentic culture could be neatly separated from public display, then one might expect to find events that cater solely to the local population and others that cater to tourists. This is seldom actually the case.

COSBY RAMP FESTIVAL

The Smoky Mountains region is festival crazy. Between April and November, there is a festival almost every weekend in the Smoky Mountains and sometimes two or three. Chambers of commerce and service organizations are frequently the sponsors of these events and many, if not all, focus on some aspect of traditional culture (or that which is perceived to be traditional culture). Since at least 1928 when the Asheville chamber sponsored Bascom Lamar Lunsford's first festival of dance and music as part of their Rhododendron Festival (the Mountain Dance and Folk Festival is now touted as the oldest folk festival in America), business interests have found public displays of local culture to be a profitable way to market the region.

Music and dance are central to most of these heritage-oriented festivals, but foods (and local food products) are a noticeable sub-theme, despite the fact that the region has been none too successful in marketing the concept of a distinct Smoky Mountains cuisine. Festivals that are built around a food theme actually appear to be more traditional and indigenous than other festivals, perhaps because they do not smack of the self-consciousness of folk festivals. Although the festival itself seems to be traditional, most are in fact of fairly recent origin and usually feature foods that are important to the local economy, such as apples, or to tourism, such as trout.

Noticeable exceptions are the ramp festivals, which take place in early May on both sides of the Smokies (one in Waynesville, North Carolina; the other in Cosby, Tennessee). These wild leeks play almost no role in the local economy; they are seldom sold (except at the festivals) or served in commercial establishments. Most people outside the region don't know what ramps are, and, at least according to local belief, would not like them if they did. In a way, though, this is exactly why they are important. While some foods may be used to market an ethnic or regional group

Menu at the Cosby ramp festival, 1993 (Photo by author)

cross-culturally, the foods that are most significant within a culture are those that require a unique knowledge to procure, prepare, or consume or that insiders alone have the stomach to eat.

Ramps are only found above a certain elevation, so that simply locating them takes a specialized knowledge. Most of the lore about ramps, however, deals not with their procurement but with their odor, or rather the odor they produce in humans who consume them. The plant's strong smell encourages various pranks, such as children putting ramps in school radiators. However, most of the verbal lore about ramps tends to center around sexual innuendoes. In a humorous twist on foods that are purported to be aphrodisiacs, the most common jokes focus on the fact that a person (usually a man) "won't get any" if he's been eating ramps. T-shirts sold at the Cosby festival proclaim that ramp eaters are "stinkin' lovers." The attendant message, however, is that ramps are worth it.

So why hold a festival purporting to celebrate a wild plant that makes you stink? The Cosby ramp festival, now over forty years old, is sponsored by the local Ruritan Club. Profits go to community projects. It's not an overly slick event. A hand-painted sign and picture of a ramp (which rather resembles the foliage of the lily-of-the-valley) point the way to a private campground with a spectacular view of the mountains.

Cooking ramps at the
Cosby festival, 1993
(Photo by author)

Is the festival really about ramps? Well, yes and no. Clearly, a lot of people are there to eat ramps. Volunteers chop huge quantities of ramps to be fried up in scrambled eggs, which turns the eggs a lively color of green. The more stouthearted can eat raw ramps that accompany a barbecued chicken dinner. Ramps are also sold in small plastic bags at a rather hefty price. In 1993 local sources must have been running low; the woman selling the ramps admitted that they were dug in North Carolina. Since ramps are not easily obtainable anymore, this is probably the one opportunity a year many have to consume ramps. Most of those who eat the plant are from the immediate region; among the local people the festival attracts a few Cherokees, whose culture originated the consumption of ramps. The festival also offers the traditional accompaniment, sassafras tea, and a rather spectacular assortment of homemade baked goods.

Ramps offer a humorous theme for the festival; they are treated with mock seriousness in a characteristically deadpan manner. A resolution presented to the Tennessee House of Representatives designating Ramp Festival Day in 1993 states that the "legendary root, distinguished by

Dessert sales at the Cosby ramp festival, 1993 (Photo by author)

odoriferous qualities, is purported to supply unyielding powers believed to have furthered the chivalrous and intrepid deeds of those who have chosen the mountains for their home." Typically, ramp humor tends to be of the sort that is superficially self-deprecating and subtly self-aggrandizing. Despite the fact that they (supposedly) make you stink, eating ramps is a manly thing to do. Maybe not caring that you stink is macho. However, the official ramp promoters shy away from any explicit reference to the sexual innuendoes that are at the heart of ramp humor.

The Cosby ramp festival is, however, also serious business. Its purpose is to raise money for the service organization and to bring business to Cosby and Cocke County, one of the less visited parts of the Smokies. While tourists may be attracted to the novelty of a ramp festival, they need to be offered something more than wild leeks. So the Cosby festival offers what most festivals offer: music and, of course, clogging. "Clog dancing is such an integral part of our mountain heritage that no festival would be complete without it!" exclaims the 1993 program. Two groups are featured, both precision teams. The older group is fresh from performing at Pigeon Forge and is scheduled to appear at Dollywood. The 1993 music includes gospel, a country quartet, and a rising country star. In the early years the organizers were able to attract some big names: in 1957 Roy Acuff played "Great Speckled Bird"; Minnie Pearl, Eddie Arnold, and Dinah Shore were also featured during the festival's first decade. The attendance peaked in 1959, when Tennessee Ernie Ford attracted a crowd of forty to sixty thousand.

As do many local festivals, the Cosby ramp festival includes a beauty contest. While "Maid of Ramps" might seem a rather humorous title to aspire to, the contest is taken seriously by the girls who participate. Beauty contests probably do little to promote tourist interest, but they do encourage regional attendance by people who come out to support friends and family members. Not all participants are from Cocke County; girls in 1993 came from as far away as Knoxville.

While celebrating a food that is little known outside the region and is purported to be enjoyed only by real mountain people, the ramp festival otherwise serves up fairly standard heritage fare. And, though ramps may seem to be an antisocial food, the goals of the organizers are to raise money and to bring more attention and visitors to Cocke County. The inclusion of clogging and country music is not simply a calculated move to give tourists what they think they will find; most people from the mountains have the same expectations. Although the situation may appear to contain contradictions, local participants see no conflict. Few people there would tell you that eating ramps is culturally authentic and that precision clogging is not (though older people may well know that precision clogging is younger than they are). Such an activity represents what the culture has become, what outsiders and those who live there alike have come to think of as symbolic of the region.

CHEROKEE FALL FESTIVAL

The contradictions in the Cherokee Fall Festival are even more complex. The festival takes place in early October, when the town of Cherokee has had a few weeks to recover from the height of the summer tourist season and is gearing up for the onslaught of leaf lookers. Unlike much of what takes place at Cherokee, the festival is not directed solely at tourists, though it attracts its share of outsiders, including non-Indians from the immediate region and non-Cherokee Indians from elsewhere.

The Cherokee Fall Festival was once the Cherokee Fair. In recent decades the name was changed to equate the event with traditional Cherokee autumnal celebrations. Some members of the Eastern Band have long worried that the event was not "Indian enough." In 1975 Gilliam Jackson, a Cherokee school teacher from Snowbird, wrote: "When we do have traditional food—such as at the Fall Festival—it is a real event and the preparation may take a day or two. But even the Festival, when we

Early agricultural exhibit at the Cherokee Fair (Photo courtesy of Lunsford scrapbook, Photographic Archives, Mars Hill College)

traditionally give thanks to all our blessings, has become commercialized and in some cases a mere imitation of Anglo ways. For example, the pageant for the selection of Miss Cherokee is too much like the Miss America pageant. Most people do not seem to know what the Festival is really for, except to make money, which is indeed its primary reason for existence nowadays." The perception that the festival is falling away from tradition makes sense only when it is viewed in comparison to the traditional Cherokee events of the distant past. In the context of the history of this particular event, however, the concern for tradition is stronger now than it was in earlier decades.

The Cherokee Fair was started in 1914, under the auspices of the Bureau of Indian Affairs Cherokee Indian Agency. Part of the motivation was economic: to bring visitors to the pre-park Cherokee reservation and to provide a market for traditional Cherokee crafts. However, the agency's main goal was actually to make the Cherokees less Indian. While traditional basketry and beadwork were displayed, the emphasis was on "progressive farming." "Better baby" contests were created; the purpose of this show, wrote the superintendent the first year of the festival, was to "instruct the mothers in caring for their young children." In a story on the fair a dozen years after its inception, the *Asheville Times* wrote: "Superintendent Henderson states that since the beginning of this enterprise the aim and purpose has been to stimulate and encourage among the Eastern Band of Cherokee Indians a keener interest in farming and to promote a desire for better homes and better living."

The ambivalence of the Cherokee Indian Agency toward traditional Cherokee culture was apparent in the exhibits and activities at the fair. In a letter to the press the first year of the fair, the agency superintendent took pride in the "Indian exhibit of baskets, beadwork and pottery," noting that the "most gratifying feature is that many of the old non-English-speaking Indians have brought in exhibits of their farm products and baskets"; but he also made it clear that the central purpose of the fair is "interesting the Indians in farming and cattleraising." Traditional practices of farming and raising children were not seen as adequate by the agency, and they wished to set a model to make the Cherokee more "modern."

European-American stringband music was incorporated into the Cherokee Fair in the early years, though it is unclear whether the interest derived primarily from the Cherokee Indian Agency or from the Cherokee themselves. In 1915, the agency superintendent wrote to Kelly Bennett, a well-known Bryson City pharmacist and musician, about the possibility of Bennett's band playing at the fair. At the end of his letter, he added, "A number of our Indians want to play and might aid you in the matter." In 1921, Superintendent Henderson wrote to John Tatham

Basketmaker demonstra-
ting in the early days of
the Cherokee Fair (Photo
courtesy of Lunsford scrapbook, Photographic Ar-
chives, Mars Hill College)

of Andrews, North Carolina, to tell him that the agency had decided to
hold an old time fiddlers contest at the fair, and that they wished to have
Tatham conduct it. He added, "Our mutual friend John Sneed has given
us the names of a number of fiddlers." (John Sneed, who had returned to
the Cherokee reservation two decades before, was the father of the well-
known fiddler, Manco Sneed.) Clogging was probably incorporated into

the fair's events a decade or so later, since teams from Cherokee were active in the Mountain Dance and Folk Festival in Asheville during the formative years of clogging in the 1930s.

Today the refashioned Cherokee Indian Fall Festival touts itself as "A Celebration of the Fall Season in the Ancient Cherokee Tradition." The 1993 festival program goes on to give this explanation of the festival's origin: "Following the occupation of these scenic mountains by the early English settlers, many Indian customs and traditions were lost forever. Among those that have persisted, the Fall Festival is the most prominent . . . a giving of thanks to U ne hla nv (The Creator) for a prosperous year and a bountiful harvest. Each year, as the Great Smoky Mountains don their glorious Autumn cloak of crimson, gold and brown, the seven clans of the great Cherokee Nation gather to offer their thanks with songs, feasting, dancing and contests." The program tends to emphasize events that are more distinctly Cherokee: competitions in archery and the use of blow guns, the playing of stickball and Indian dancing (including Plains-style fancy dance, as well as traditional Cherokee dancing). However, bluegrass, country music, and gospel are also a prominent part of the entertainment. A clogging contest is held every night of the four-day festival.

Despite the name change, the fall festival is much like many small rural fairs. Along with its varied cultural images, the Cherokee fair also has the country fair's inherent duality, encompassing both out-of-the-ordinary festivities (amusement rides, games of chance, pink cotton candy) and the celebration of traditional home values (crafts and skills, homemade food). The carnival aspects of the festival differ little from those of any fair, with the same rides, games, and food. In the exhibit hall, however, the complex nature of contemporary Cherokee culture is apparent. Most of the agricultural displays and assortments of baked and canned goods are interchangeable with those that might be found in any other rural fair in the region. The importance of Christianity is apparent, both in literature distributed and in specific Christian images used in artwork. Much of the artwork and a sizeable amount of the crafts displayed are not readily distinguishable as Cherokee. However, some crafts, such as the baskets, are distinctly Cherokee in nature, and some of the artwork uses imagery that makes specific reference to Indian identity. Most of these display a generalized Indian theme rather than a specifically Cherokee identity, although a few images of Sequoyah are found.

The food stands similarly display the duality between carnival and home values, as well as the various types of cultural identification. Youngsters—Cherokee and non-Indian alike—seem most attracted to the standard fair foods. On children's day, free hot dogs are given out. Tourists are especially attracted to the numerous stands featuring the standard Indian fair food: fry bread. "Indian tacos," taco fixings served on top of fry bread, are particularly popular. Older Cherokees veer toward the stands that serve "Indian dinners." These typically consist of pan-fried chicken, potatoes, and the choice of bean or chestnut bread. Since these booths serve the most home-like food (and generally have the oldest clientele), they are the ones most likely to provide seating. Older people sitting around one booth can be heard to bemoan the fact that they just don't have the time to cook in the traditional manner anymore.

The entertainment features a number of events typical of the small rural fair: a pet show, a bubble-gum-blowing contest, a turtle race, a pie-eating contest, "greasy pig," and several beauty contests. Although Gilliam Jackson saw the beauty contests as an imitation of Anglo ways, the 1990s versions of Cherokee beauty queens emphasize their Indian identity in appearance and through public statements. Miss Fall Festival 1992–93, along with being active in Teens for Christ and Students Against Drunk Driving, listed her hobbies as "doing beadwork, fancy shawl dancing, making new friends, traveling and making my own dance regalia."

For the tourist, the most novel aspect of the festival, aside from the Indian dance competitions, is probably the demonstration game of stickball. This sport, which was common among a number of Native American groups in the eastern United States, has long fascinated anthropologists, including Mooney, who documented Cherokee stickball in the late nineteenth century. Through the first several decades of the twentieth century, each township had a stickball team. However, the Cherokee Indian Agency took a dim view of the sport. Denying the request to send a ball team to play for tourists in Highlands, North Carolina, Superintendent Henderson wrote that "we do not favor sending out ball teams for Indian ball, for the reason that it interfers [sic] with their work and encourages idleness on the reservation." In the 1930s, the agency abolished the sport, ostensibly for the injuries and unruly behavior it caused, though the gambling and conjuring traditionally associated with the sport may also have been a factor. In subsequent decades, stickball was revived as a demonstration sport for the fair. In 1959 the chamber of commerce sponsored weekly exhibitions, though once again because of injuries the frequency of the games was restricted.

Even as a demonstration game, stickball is a fast-paced and rough sport. Played shoeless and shirtless, it involves some fast running and quite a lot of wrestling. Since the limits of the playing field are apparently not absolute, stickball players at the festival in 1993 sometimes got tackled in the gravel road and in some cases looked like they might end up in the fry bread stands. An announcer describes the rules of the game and explains what is happening throughout. The festival program also devotes a page to the game, including its historical traditions, and hastens to add,

Cherokee Indian ball-game, 1932 (Photo courtesy of Great Smoky Mountains National Park)

"The ballgame is played much the same way today, except that the rituals the night before and the gambling are no longer a part of the stickball game."

The annual fall event at Cherokee has always been shaped by private and public agendas. The theme of "progress" endorsed by the Cherokee Agency is no longer as central as the current theme of "tradition." Making money has always been a less overtly stated goal. Ironically, those who believe that the fall festival should be "more Indian" are probably promoting changes that would increase the tourist trade. While clogging and bluegrass might be inducements that bring tourists to other heritage events in the Smokies, most visitors want to see Indian items and events at the Fall Festival. Tourists, of course, frequently cannot distinguish between Native American traditions of vastly different cultural groups, but, perhaps unlike the "chiefing" along the main drag of Cherokee, the pan-Indianism of the festival does not cater solely to tourists with preconceived ideas. At the festival, the Cherokee celebrate their Indian identity and their connection to other Indian cultures.

Trying to distinguish between what is authentic and what is not at the

Fall Festival is a pointless task. Certain aspects of the festival are motivated by economics and others by the preservation of tradition. If clogging and beauty contests and amusement rides continue to form a part of the event, it's because the local people want them. They are part of the tradition of the event. Taken as a whole, the Cherokee Indian Fall Festival is representative of the complexity of Cherokee culture. Hot dogs and bean bread, gospel singing and stickball, clogging and Plains Indian fancy dance, rivercane baskets and Sunbonnet Sue quilts, Walker Calhoun's dance group and beauty queens all are authentic parts of the culture.

Dollywood

In some parts of the Smokies, the carnival atmosphere is not limited to yearly events. At amusement parks such as Dollywood, the carnival goes on every day of the tourist season. Dollywood is located in Pigeon Forge, Tennessee, which has recently become one long strip development of motels and hotels, amusements, and, most recently, outlet stores. As the town of Gatlinburg, wedged up against the park's boundary, began to hit critical mass, the commercial development of Pigeon Forge took up the overflow.

Dolly Parton, a Sevier County native, has played a prominent role in this development. In 1985, Parton joined up with the Herschend Enterprises of Missouri to transform an existing four-hundred-acre theme park, Silver Dollar City, into "Dollywood." The transformation points out the interchangeability of certain American images; "wild west," "Appalachian," "Victorian" are relatively undifferentiated in the theme park setting, providing a carnivalesque backdrop for the amusement rides and entertainment. An old-fashioned carousel (moved from Lancaster, Pennsylvania), pseudo-Victorian buildings, and the Smoky Mountain Rampage, an artificial whitewater raft trip, exist side by side with a considerable amount of Dolly iconography. Butterflies, Parton's logo, are a somewhat puzzling image at the park, and the relevance of the exhibit of birds of prey is not altogether clear, except insofar as it reflects Parton's personal interests and concerns.

The average visitor at Dollywood is typical of those who go to Gatlinburg and Pigeon Forge: white, Protestant, blue-collar homeowners. The entrance fee is not cheap (just under twenty dollars), but compared to rival tourist sites such as Disney World, it's a bargain. Once the entrance fee is paid, most of the rides and entertainments are free. However, much of Dollywood is devoted to selling products to tourists: vaguely country/western clothing, "authentic" crafts, outhouse salt and pepper shakers. Food concessions range from typical carnival food stands to sitdown places featuring beans and cornbread.

Unlike the local festivals and fairs, the establishments in Gatlinburg and Pigeon Forge are explicitly about making money. However, cultural display is typically part of this enterprise. Most utilize the most stereotypical hillbilly images. But Dollywood is different. There Dolly Parton is selling her own image, her own life story. She is careful not to denigrate her background. While there are hints of hillbilly stereotypes, particularly in the tackier souvenirs and in a sort of vaudeville-type skit featured on the train ride, for the most part these are not in evidence. Among the more noticeable absences are misspellings, grammatical errors, and backwards "s" 's in the signage. Dolly does not portray her kin as ignorant.

In some ways, Dollywood is a metaphor for Dolly's own image: glitzy and somewhat tacky on the surface but presumably with an authentic heart. Dolly Parton has her own brand of self-deprecating humor, which might include naming a theme park after herself. But, especially when it comes to her childhood, she also markets a pious sentimentality. Her sentimental side, however, is countered by a shrewd business sense; it is difficult to discern where one begins and the other leaves off.

Of course, one does not necessarily go to Dollywood to see "authentic" Smoky Mountains culture. Dollywood has been criticized as having a superficial commitment to its crafts program, as was Parton herself, who posed in a national advertisement for the area holding a foreign-made basket. The entertainment, for the most part, is composed of the slickest versions of precision clogging and country music. (Though, once a year, old harp singers are admitted free with their songbooks for an annual singing.) The most authentic aspect of the place, perhaps, is Parton's own life story, although it conveniently fits into a "rags to riches" fairy tale. Among the most popular attractions at Dollywood is the museum devoted to that story. Inside the museum, the most popular icon is the "coat of many colors" that inspired her most famous song about her childhood, although even here it is difficult to draw the line between artifice and reality. The original coat apparently wore out long ago and was not preserved.

The most compelling image of Parton's childhood is not at the museum but is backed up against an outdoor stage (where Parton's relatives sometimes perform) in the center of Dollywood. As architectural reconstructions go, the replica of Parton's childhood home leaves something to be desired. Air-conditioned for the comfort of the tourists, the structure, by necessity, is considerably more solid than the original small boxed house. The outside of the replica has neat board and battens, while pictures of the original indicate that it was simply sheathed in vertical boards. The sign outside the house makes another shrewd reference to a hit song, "My Tennessee Mountain Home," and the text has the usual overly sincere sentimentality: "These mountains and my childhood home have a special place in my heart. They inspire my music and my life. I hope being here does the same for you!"

What is compelling is not the authenticity of the physical reconstruction of the dwelling but the interior display. Parton is said to have had relatives help re-create what the home would have looked like when she was a child. This bit of self-documentation achieves something the National Park Service typically fails to do: it gives the tourist a feel for how the house was lived in. It's not an empty shell with a few artifacts inside. It also gives visitors a peek into an era that the Great Smoky Mountains National Park is reluctant to interpret. While Parton was born after the park removals, they were a recent memory during the period of her childhood. The replication of her home is a more accurate depiction of the way many lived in the Smokies when the park was created than any of the structures interpreted within the park's boundaries.

At the time of the park's creation, officials attempted to prevent the "peddling of wares by irresponsible mountain people." While the park service clearly failed at preventing commercial development at the gates of the Great Smoky Mountains National Park, they still retain some authority over the interpretation of "authentic" mountain culture. The savvier tourists may shop at the outlet stores and ride the amusement rides, but they depend on the park service to give them the real stuff, at least as far as cultural history is concerned. Others may not be so discerning; but those who stand in line to view "My Tennessee Mountain Home" are perhaps the richer for the fact that one poor little mountain girl with plenty of ambition and talent not only succeeded in peddling her wares but in giving the tourist a far more interesting account of domestic life in the Smoky Mountains region than the park service ever accomplished.

Who controls public interpretation of the folklife of the Great Smoky Mountains? Writers and scholars have played a major role in defining the folklife of the region. The federal government, particularly the Cherokee Indian Agency and the National Park Service, have attempted to control the expression and interpretation of traditional culture. Most of all, business interests have turned aspects of traditional culture into a commodity. But not all the sellers, or buyers, come from outside the region. People from the Smoky Mountains also make a buck from—and find new meanings in—their own folklife. While the people and the folklife of the Smoky Mountains have been affected by outside interpretations and interventions, culture is not something that can truly be appropriated. In the past two hundred years, people from the Smoky Mountains have lost their homes and their land, but not their culture. It may change, but it has not been stolen.

CHAPTER ONE

For a history of the Eastern Band of Cherokee, see John R. Finger, *The Eastern Band of Cherokees, 1819–1900* (Knoxville: University of Tennessee Press, 1984) and Finger's subsequent work, *Cherokee Americans: The Eastern Band of Cherokees in the Twentieth Century* (Lincoln and London: University of Nebraska Press, 1991).

Information on African-Americans in the southern mountains and their relationship to the Cherokee may be found in Theda Perdue's "Red and Black in the Southern Appalachians," in *Blacks in Appalachia*, eds. William H. Turner and Edward J. Cabbell (Lexington: University Press of Kentucky, 1985), pp. 23–29. For an exploration of the nature of slavery in the mountains, see John C. Inscoe's *Mountain Masters, Slavery, and the Sectional Crisis in Western North Carolina* (Knoxville: University of Tennessee Press, 1989). An examination of attitudes toward slaveholding in Cades Cove can be found in Durwood Dunn, *Cades Cove: The Life and Death of a Southern Appalachian Community 1818–1937* (Knoxville: University of Tennessee Press, 1988), pp. 125–26.

For a history of timbering in Appalachia, see Ronald D. Eller, *Miners, Millhands, and Mountaineers: Industrialization of the Appalachian South, 1880–1930* (Knoxville: University of Tennessee Press, 1982), pp. 86–127. Florence Cope Bush's *Dorie: Woman of the Mountains* (Knoxville: University of Tennessee Press, 1982) is a moving account of one woman's perspective on the changes wrought by industrialization in the Smokies during the early twentieth century.

Information on park opposition to the location of African-American Civilian Conservation Corps companies in the Smokies is found in the 1935 Superintendent's Reports, GSMNP Archives, Sugarlands Visitors Center. For a history of the treatment of African-Americans at the TVA's Fontana Dam project, consult Nancy L. Grant, *TVA and Black Americans: Planning for the Status Quo* (Philadelphia: Temple University Press, 1990), pp. 60–61.

Most histories of the Great Smoky Mountains were written by park supporters or were written directly under the auspices of the National Park Service. Typical are Carlos Campbell, *Birth of a National Park in the Great Smoky Mountains* (Knoxville: University of Tennessee Press, 1970);

Wilma Dykeman and Jim Stokely, *Highland Homeland: The People of the Great Smokies* (Washington D.C.: National Park Service, 1978); and Michael Frome, *Strangers in High Places: The Story of the Great Smoky Mountains* (Knoxville: University of Tennessee Press 1966, rev. ed. 1980). A recent critical reexamination of the creation of the park can be found in Margaret Brown's "Power, Privilege, and Tourism: A Revision of the Great Smoky Mountains National Park Story" (M.A. thesis, Department of History, University of Kentucky, 1990). For a contemporary (and not complimentary) account of the park removals, see W. O. Whittle, "Movement of Population from the Great Smoky Mountain Area," University of Tennessee Agricultural Experiment Station Bulletin, 1934.

A tape-recorded interview was conducted by the author with Bonnie Meyers, 29 July 1993, Cades Cove Visitors Center.

CHAPTER TWO

Two influential books that examine how Southern Appalachia has been defined are Henry Shapiro's *Appalachia on Our Mind: The Southern Mountains and Mountaineers in the American Consciousness, 1870–1920* (Chapel Hill: The University of North Carolina Press, 1978) and Allen W. Batteau's *The Invention of Appalachia* (Tucson: University of Arizona Press, 1990). See also W. K. McNeil's introduction to *Appalachian Images in Folk and Popular Culture* (Ann Arbor and London: UMI Research Press, 1989). The latter collection of essays includes "A Week in the Great Smoky Mountains," a travel account written by "R.," first published in the *Southern Literary Messenger* in 1860.

For a detailed account of Mooney's career, see L. G. Moses, *The Indian Man: A Biography of James Mooney* (Urbana and Chicago: University of Illinois Press, 1984). See also *Special Issue: A Tribute to James Mooney, Cherokee Ethnologist, Journal of Cherokee Studies* VII, no. 1 (1982). For Mooney's reflections on the non-Cherokee inhabitants of the Great Smoky Mountains region, see "Folk-Lore of the Carolina Mountains," *Journal of American Folk-Lore* II (1889):95–104.

The most detailed account of Horace Kephart's life is found in George Ellison's introduction to the new edition of *Our Southern Highlanders: A Narrative in the Southern Appalachians and a Study of Life among the Mountaineers*, reprinted in 1976 by the University of Tennessee Press.

Allen Batteau's assessment of Kephart's work is found in *The Invention of Appalachia*, pp. 89–91. For an opposing point of view, see the preface of Durwood Dunn's *Cades Cove: The Life and Death of a Southern Appalachian Community, 1818–1937* (Knoxville: University of Tennessee Press, 1988).

Horace Kephart's *The Cherokees of the Smoky Mountains* was reprinted in 1983 by the Great Smoky Mountains National Park. The new edition contains a useful introduction by John R. Finger.

The classic account of the crafts revival in Southern Appalachia is Allen Eaton's *Handicrafts of the Southern Highlands* (New York: Russell Sage Foundation, 1937). The work is illustrated with photographs taken by Doris Ullmann, whose romanticized images did much to shape popular conceptions of Appalachia. The work was reprinted in 1975 by Dover with an introduction by Rayna Green. Frances Louisa Goodrich's own account of the tradition she discovered and the revival she did much to spawn was published as *Mountain Homespun* (New Haven: Yale University Press, 1931). The book was reprinted in 1989 by the University of Tennessee Press, and Jan Davidson's lengthy introduction provides an excellent analysis of Goodrich's career.

Recent analyses of crafts revivals have examined the political and cultural complexities of the patron-craftsman interaction. For Appalachia (and for revivalism in general as it related to cultural intervention), David Whisnant's groundbreaking *All That is Native & Fine: The Politics of Culture in an American Region* (Chapel Hill and London: University of North Carolina Press, 1983) informs all subsequent analysis of craft revivalism in Appalachia. An excellent recent study of the crafts revival in the southern mountains is Jane Stewart Becker's, "Selling Tradition: The Domestication of Southern Appalachian Culture in 1930s America" (Ph.D. dissertation, Boston University, 1993).

Although somewhat defensive in tone, Garry Barker's *The Handicraft Revival in Southern Appalachia, 1930–1990* (Knoxville: University of Tennessee Press, 1991) provides something of a sequel to Eaton's classic study. Barker's book is a highly personal account of the author's own work to promote revival crafts in North Carolina and Kentucky. Also written as a sequel to Eaton by an individual involved in the revival, Helen Bullard's *Crafts and Craftsmen of the Tennessee Mountains* (Falls Church, Va.: Summit Press Ltd., 1976) is mostly a description of the individual craftspeople working in the region as part of the revival. Funded by the Tennessee and Kentucky humanities councils, Philis Alvic has studied the weaving program begun by Pi Beta Phi. Her pamphlet *Weavers of the Southern Highlands: Early Years in Gatlinburg* (Murray, Ky., 1991) provides a solid history of the program from its inception to the current day.

Other overviews of the crafts revival in the Great Smokies region are chapter XVII, "Social Workers in High Places," in Michael Frome's *Strangers in High Places: The Story of the Great Smoky Mountains*, and chapter 9, "Creating Community and Culture in Appalachia: Folk Schools and the Crafts Revival," in Henry D. Shapiro's *Appalachia on Our Mind*. Although it deals with the southern mountains in general, and not just the Smokies, Shapiro provides a thought-provoking analysis of how Goodrich and the other workers in the revival represent an important shift in the nature of mountain benevolence.

Historical information about the crafts revival on the Cherokee reservation can be found in John R. Finger's *Cherokee Americans: The Eastern Band of Cherokees in the Twentieth Century* (Lincoln and London: University of Nebraska Press, 1991). For the Cherokee response to the Indian New Deal, see also Larry R. Stucki, "Will the 'Real' Indian Survive?: Tourism and Affluence at Cherokee, North Carolina," in *Affluence and Cultural Survival: The 1981 Proceedings of The American Ethnological Society*, eds. Richard F. Salisbury and Elisabeth Tooker (Washington, D.C.: American Ethnological Society, 1984).

For early accounts of the music of the Smoky Mountains region, see Lila W. Edmunds, "Songs from the Mountains of North Carolina," *Journal of American Folk-Lore* 6 (1893):131–34 and Louise Rand Bascom, "Ballads and Songs of Western North Carolina," *Journal of American Folk-Lore* 22 (1909):238–50. An account of Olive Dame Campbell's career can be found in Whisnant's *All That Is Native & Fine*, chapter 2. Cecil Sharp's fieldwork experiences in the mountains are recounted in Maud Karpeles's preface and Sharp's introduction to *English Folk Songs from the Southern Appalachians*, 2d ed. (London: Oxford University Press, 1932) and in Maud Karpeles's *Cecil Sharp: His Life and Work* (Chicago and London: University of Chicago Press, 1967), chapters 6–8. See also chapter 10 of Shapiro's *Appalachia on Our Mind*.

Robert Winslow Gordon's fieldwork in western North Carolina is described in chapter 4 of Debora Kodish's *Good Friends and Bad Enemies: Robert Winslow Gordon and the Study of American Folksong* (Urbana and Chicago: University of Illinois Press, 1986). Dorothy Scarborough's own account of her fieldwork in the same area is found in *A Song Catcher in the Southern Mountains: American Folk Songs of British Ancestry* (New York: AMS Press, Inc., 1966) pp. 53–78.

The two best accounts of Bascom Lamar Lunsford's work are Loyal Jones, *Minstrel of the Appalachians: The Story of Bascom Lamar Lunsford* (Boone, N.C.: Appalachian Consortium Press, 1984) and David E. Whisnant, "Finding the Way Between the Old and the New: The Mountain Dance and Folk Festival and Bascom Lamar Lunsford's Work as a Citizen," *Appalachian Journal* 7 (1979–80):135–54.

Mildred Haun's 1937 thesis, "Cocke County Ballads and Songs," has never been published, but the original is available at Special Collections, Jean and Alexander Heard Library, Vanderbilt University, Nashville, Tennessee. On Haun's life and work, see the introduction by Herschel Gower to Haun's *The Hawk's Done Gone and Other Stories* (Nashville: Vanderbilt University Press, 1968). Vanderbilt's special collections also has the papers of George Pullen Jackson. His classic *White Spirituals in the Southern Uplands: The Story of the Fasola Folk, Their Songs, Singings, and "Buckwheat Notes"* was reissued by Dover Publications in 1965.

The extensive recordings of the Kirklands and Barnicle and Cadle were only cataloged during the 1980s. The Kirklands had moved to Florida in the 1940s, and Mary Kirkland had carefully preserved the collection after her husband's death. See Kip Lornell's liner notes to "The Kirkland Recordings: Newly Discovered Field Recordings From Tennessee and North Carolina 1937–39," released by the Tennessee Folklore Society (TFS–106). In 1983, while searching for Edwin and Mary Kirkland's field recordings at the University of Tennessee, Willie Smyth discovered an unknown cache of recordings made by Barnicle and Cadle and later found that Cadle had still more recordings. See Smyth's liner notes to "It's Just the Same Today: The Barnicle-Cadle Field Recordings From Eastern Tennessee and Kentucky, 1938–1949" (Tennessee Folklore Society–108) and Willie Smyth, "Bearing Up: Mary Elizabeth Barnicle and Folklore Recording," *Tennessee Folklore Society Bulletin* LII, no. 2 (summer 1986):34–45.

CHAPTER THREE

James Mooney described the dances and songs that accompanied the playing of stick ball in his article, "The Cherokee Ball Play," published in *American Anthropologist* III (1890):105–32. This article has been reprinted in the *Journal of Cherokee Studies* VII, no. 1 (1982):10–24.

Frank G. Speck and Leonard Broom's *Cherokee Dance and Drama*, first published in 1951, was republished in 1983 (Norman: University of Oklahoma Press). The new edition includes a foreword by Broom containing biographical information on Will West Long. Raymond D. Fogelson and Amelia B. Walker, in "Self and Other in Cherokee Booger Masks," *Journal of Cherokee Studies* 5, no. 2 (fall 1980):88–102, question Speck and Broom's assumption that the booger dance was primarily about the threat from non-Cherokees.

For a recent study of dance among the Eastern Cherokee, see Olivia Skipper Rivers, "The Changes in Composition, Function, and Aesthetic Criteria as a Result of Acculturation found in Five Traditional Dances of the Eastern Band of Cherokee Indians in North Carolina" (Ph.D. dissertation, University of Wisconsin, Madison, 1990). Rivers focuses more on the dance itself than the cultural contexts but makes useful comments on the distinction between "dances held" and "dances performed" and on the shared aesthetics of Cherokee dancers.

Diverging somewhat from its characteristic focus, *Old Time Herald* ran an article on Walker Calhoun by Michael Kline, "Where the Ravens Roost: Songs and Ceremonies of Big Cove" (August/October 1990, pp. 24–28). The article includes excerpts from a taped interview with Calhoun. Another article that focuses on the contributions of Calhoun is Jane Harris Woodside, "The Cherokee: Hungry for the Dance," *Now and Then* 6, no. 3 (fall 1989):22–25. A cassette tape, "Where the Ravens Roost: Cherokee Traditional Songs of Walker Calhoun," produced in 1991, is available from the Mountain Heritage Center, Western Carolina University, Cullowhee, North Carolina.

In her study *Snowbird Cherokees: People of Persistence* (Athens: University of Georgia Press, 1991), Sharlotte Neely devotes chapter 4 to an intensive study of the Trail of Tears Singing at Snowbird.

For Maud Karpeles's and Cecil Sharp's comments on the continuation of the ballad tradition, see Karpeles's preface and Sharp's introduction to *English Folk Songs from the Southern Appalachians*, 2d ed. (London: Oxford University Press, 1932).

The quotation about rural minstrels as precursors to country music artists is from Charles K. Wolfe's *Tennessee Strings: The Story of Country Music in Tennessee* (Knoxville: University of Tennessee Press, 1977), p. 8.

Ballad singers from Laurel Country were recorded in 1963 by Folkways; the resulting album was released as "Old Love Songs & Ballads from the Big Laurel, North Carolina" (Folkways Records, No. 2309). The liner notes are by John Cohen and Peter Gott. Despite the interest of folk song aficionados and public sector folklorists, almost no contemporary scholarly literature exists on the ballad tradition of this region. A tape-recorded interview with Doug Wallin was conducted by Michael Ann Williams, 11 March 1993, Sodom-Laurel, North Carolina.

For the classic history of shape-note singings, see George Pullen Jackson's *White Spirituals in the Southern Uplands: The Story of the Fasola Folk, Their Songs, Singings, and "Buckwheat Notes."* Dorothy D. Horn's *Sing to Me of Heaven: A Study of Folk and Early American Materials in Three Old Harp Books* (Gainesville: University of Florida Press, 1970) focuses on *The New Harp of Columbia*, as well as *The Southern Harmony* and *The Original Sacred Harp*. It is musicological in orientation and assumes the reader has prior technical knowledge of music. M. L. Swan's *The New Harp of Columbia* has been reprinted (Knoxville: University of Tennessee Press, 1978) with the addition of two excellent introductory essays: Dorothy D. Horn, "The New Harp of Columbia and Its Music in the Singing-School Tradition," and Ron Peterson and Candra Phillips, "East Tennessee Harp Singing."

A good source of information on current old harp singings is *The New Harp of Columbia Newsletter*, published biannually since 1988. It is available c/o Jubilee Community Arts, 1538 Laurel Avenue, Knoxville, Tennessee 37916. The newsletter contains news of area sings and local members, as well as historical information and the remembrances of older singers. Articles useful in the preparation of this chapter include Bruce Wheeler, "Burl Adams" (fall 1988); Lena Headrick, "Headrick's Chapel" (spring 1990); Eleanor Patty, "Wears Valley Old Harp Singing" (fall 1992); Bob Richmond, "Christian Harmony in Etowah, North Carolina: A Live Sister Tradition" (fall 1992); and "The Changing of the Tradition" (fall 1992). A 1950s recording of old harp singers is available from Smithsonian/Folkways Records (FA 2356).

The John C. Campbell Folk School (Rt. 1, Box 14A, Brasstown, N.C. 28902) has recently released a two CD (or cassette) collection, "Meeting in the Air: Sacred Music of the Southern Appalachians," based on field recordings, many of which were made in and around the Smoky Mountains region. The collection, which includes extensive notes, contains shape-note singing from the Christian Harmony, Sacred Harp, and Old Harp of Columbia traditions, as well as other forms of Anglo-American, African-American and Native-American sacred music.

The groundbreaking work that began to pose serious scholarly questions about the origin of the dulcimer is Charles Seeger, "The Appalachian Dulcimer," in *Journal of American Folklore* 71 (1958):40–51. A more recent attempt to come to grips with the issues raised by Seeger is found in L. Allen Smith, *A Catalogue of Pre-Revival Appalachian Dulcimers* (Columbia & London: University of Missouri Press, 1983). For an examination of contemporary dulcimer making, see Charles Winston Joyner, "Dulcimer Making in Western North Carolina: Creativity in a Traditional Mountain Craft," *Southern Folklore Quarterly* 39 (1975):341–46.

For an early-twentieth-century description of a fiddle contest, see Louise Rand Bascom, "Ballads and Songs of Western North Carolina," *Journal of American Folk-Lore* 22 (1909):238–50. Biographical information on the regional musicians is more likely to be found in publications that cater to aficionados than in scholarly journals. An exception is Blanton Owen, "Manco Sneed and the Indians: 'These Cherokee Don't Make Music Much,' " *North Carolina Folklore* 28, no. 2 (Nov. 1980):58–66. *Old Time Herald* is a good source of information on regional musicians. See Charles Wolfe, "Samantha Bumgarner: The Original Banjo Pickin' Girl" (winter 1987–88):6–9; Bob Carlin, "Whip the Devil Around the Stump— The Story of the Helton Brothers" (November–January 1989/90):14–44; and Wayne Martin, "The Legendary Dedrick Harris: New Facts Come to Light" (February–April 1991):32.

Though outdated in many of its ideas, a good source of information on Bill Hensley is David Parker Bennett, "A Study in Fiddle Tunes From Western North Carolina" (master's thesis, University of North Carolina at Chapel Hill, 1940). Much of the thesis is a detailed musical analysis of individual tunes in Hensley's repertoire.

Information on Carroll Best is found in the 1994 North Carolina Arts Council's Folk Heritage Award program and script for the awards presentation, as well as in the Folk Heritage Award Documentation Project. As part of the documentation, Alicia J. Rouverol conducted a tape-recorded interview with Carroll Best on 24 July 1993 in Upper Crabtree Valley, North Carolina.

For a study of popular images of the banjo, see Karen Linn, *That Half-Barbaric Twang: The Banjo in American Popular Culture* (Urbana and Chicago: University of Illinois Press, 1991). Cecelia Conway examines banjo traditions in Southern Appalachia in "Mountain Echoes of the African Banjo," *Appalachian Journal* 20 (1993):146–60.

For a broad overview of square dance and clogging, see Burt Feintuch, "Square Dancing and Clogging," in *Encyclopedia of Southern Culture*, eds. Charles Reagan Wilson and William Ferris (Chapel Hill and London: University of North Carolina Press, 1989), pp. 1033–34. For an examination of Bascom Lamar Lunsford's role in the development and popularization of clogging, see Loyal Jones's *Minstrel of the Appalachians: The Story of Bascom Lamar Lunsford* (Boone, N.C.: Appalachian Consortium Press, 1984), pp. 58–59, and David Whisnant, "Finding the Way Between the Old and the New: The Mountain Dance and Folk Festival and Bascom Lamar Lunsford's Work as a Citizen," *Appalachian Journal* 7, no. 1–2 (autumn–winter 1979–80):145–48. For his article, Whisnant interviewed members of two dance teams who performed in Lunsford's first festival in 1928 in order to assess the impact of the festival on local dance traditions. *Old-Time Herald* has a regular column, "The Dance Beat," which contains information on regional clogging; see three articles by Phil Jamison: "In the Old-Time Days: The Beginnings of Team Clogging" (winter 1987–88):18–19; "James Kesterson's Blue Ridge Mountain Dancers: Stepping Between Tradition & Precision" (Aug.–Oct. 1989):24–25, 27; and "The Green Grass Cloggers" (Aug.–Oct. 1988):22–24, 39. Also of interest are two articles that feature traditional dancers from just north of the Smoky Mountains region: Phil Jamison, "Willard Watson: Old-Time Flatfoot Dancer" (Feb.–April 1988):18–19; and Mike Seeger, "Two Western North Carolina Dancers" (Aug.–Oct. 1990): 4–5, 40.

Two of the best references tracing the development of traditional music to country music are Bill C. Malone's encyclopedic *Country Music, U.S.A.*, rev. ed. (Austin: University of Texas Press, 1985) and Charles K. Wolfe's more regionally specific *Tennessee Strings: The Story of Country Music in Tennessee* (Knoxville: University of Tennessee Press, 1977). See also these articles by Wolfe: "Early Country Music in Knoxville," *Old Time Music* 12 (spring 1974):19–31 and "George Reneau: A Biographical Sketch," *John Edwards Memorial Foundation Quarterly* XV, no. 56 (winter 1979):205–7.

For scholarly explorations of hillbilly music, see Archie Green, "Hillbilly Music: Source and Symbol," *Journal of American Folklore* 78 (1965):204–28 and Robert Cogswell, "Commercial Hillbilly Lyrics and the Folk Tradition," *Journal of Country Music* III, no. 3–4 (fall–winter 1973):65–106.

Information on Lulu Belle and Scotty Wiseman can be found in "Wiseman's View: The Autobiography of Skyland Scotty Wiseman," *North Carolina Folklore Journal* 33 (1985–86) and William E. Lightfoot, "Belle of the Barn Dance: Reminiscing with Lulu Belle Wiseman Stamey," *Journal of Country Music* XII (1987):2–15.

Articles on other 1930s musicians from the Smoky Mountains region are Ivan M. Tribe and John W. Morris, "J. E. and Wade Mainer," *Bluegrass Unlimited* 10, no. 5 (November 1975):12–21; Ivan M. Tribe, "Roy Hall and His Blue Ridge Entertainers: Almost Bluegrass," *Bluegrass Unlimited* 13, no. 3 (Sept. 1978):44–49; and Ivan M. Tribe, "Bill & Joe Callahan: A Great Brother Duet," *Old Time Music* 16 (spring 1975):15–22. The Country Music Foundation in Nashville also has files on the Wisemans and the Mainers, as well as a 1930s second edition *Souvenir of the Crazy Barn Dance and the Crazy Bands* (including the Crazy Mountaineers and the Smoky Mountain Boomers).

Information on Dr. John Brinkley can be found in Ed Kahn, "International Relations, Dr. Brinkley and Hillbilly Music," *John Edwards Memorial Foundation Quarterly* 9, part 2, no. 30 (summer 1973):47–55.

For a complete history of bluegrass music, see Neil V. Rosenberg, *Bluegrass: A History* (Urbana and Chicago: University of Illinois Press, 1985).

A tape-recorded interview with Raymond Fairchild was conducted by David Baxter, 1 April 1994, Canton, North Carolina. Articles about Fairchild include Ivan M. Tribe, "Someone Really Different: Raymond Fairchild," *Bluegrass Unlimited* 9, no. 4 (Oct. 1974):24–25; Wayne Erbsen, "Raymond Fairchild: Making His Own Way," *Bluegrass Unlimited* 16, no. 9 (March 1982):14–17; and Janice Brown McDonald, "Raymond Fairchild: Master of the Five-String," *Bluegrass Unlimited* 23, no. 11 (May 1989):22–27.

Dolly Parton has just released her autobiography, which is titled *Dolly: My Life and Other Unfinished Business* (New York: HarperCollins, 1994).

CHAPTER FOUR

For overviews of the folk houses of the region, see Michael Ann Williams, *Homeplace: The Social Use and Meaning of the Folk Dwelling in Southwestern*

North Carolina (Athens and London: University of Georgia Press, 1991) and John Morgan, *The Log House in East Tennessee* (Knoxville: University of Tennessee Press, 1990). More information on the cantilevered barns of the Smoky Mountains region can be found in Marian Moffett and Lawrence Wodehouse, *East Tennessee Cantilever Barns* (Knoxville: University of Tennessee Press, 1993).

Delce Dyer's master's thesis, "The Farmstead Yards at Cades Cove: Restoration and Management Alternatives for the Domestic Landscape of the Southern Appalachian Mountaineer" (M.L.A. thesis, University of Georgia, 1988), contains evidence of the historic appearance of farmsteads in the Smokies. See also E. Raymond Evans, "The Palen Fence: An Example of Appalachian Folk Culture," in *Appalachian Images in Folk and Popular Culture*, ed. W. K. McNeil (Ann Arbor and London: UMI Research Press, 1989).

Information on the significance of the boxed house in the Smokies can be found in Michael Ann Williams, "Pride and Prejudice: The Appalachian Boxed House in Southwestern North Carolina," *Winterthur Portfolio* 25, 4 (winter 1990):217–30. The quotation about the nature of boxed houses is from the author's tape-recorded interview with Jim Neal, Aquone community, Macon County, North Carolina, 2 August 1984. The story of the sister-in-law entering the boarding house business is from a tape-recorded interview with Pearl Caldwell, Maggie Valley, Haywood County, North Carolina, 24 July 1984.

Records of the industrial surveys conducted by the Bureau of Indian Affairs, Cherokee Indian Agency, are found at the Federal Records Center, East Point, Georgia. Information on housing among the Eastern Cherokee during the 1950s is from John Gulick, *Cherokees at the Crossroads* (Chapel Hill: Institute for Research in Social Science, University of North Carolina, 1960, rev. ed., 1973), pp. 48–52. The photographic evidence and Charles Grossman's survey material of structures within the park are found at the Great Smoky Mountains National Park Archives, Sugarlands Visitors Center.

The best published study of basketry among the Eastern Cherokee is Betty J. Duggan and Brett H. Riggs, *Studies in Cherokee Basketry*, Occasional Paper No. 9, Frank H. McClung Museum (Knoxville: University of Tennessee Press, 1991). The collection, published in cooperation with the Qualla Arts and Crafts Mutual, Inc., contains not only Duggan's and Riggs's excellent essay, "Cherokee Basketry: An Evolving Tradition" but also a reprint of Frank G. Speck's monograph, *Decorative Art and Basketry of the Cherokee*, originally published in 1920. Another thorough examination of Cherokee basketry, which places changes in the tradition in the context of several centuries of ecological and cultural change, is Sarah H. Hill, "Cherokee Pattern: Interweaving Women and Baskets in History" (Ph.D. dissertation, Emory University, 1991).

Information and quotations from Louise Goings are taken from a tape-recorded interview conducted by Michael Ann Williams in Goings's home, 8 August 1993.

The best overview of Appalachian white oak basketry is Rachel Nash Law and Cynthia W. Taylor, *Appalachian White Oak Basketmaking: Handing Down the Basket* (Knoxville: University of Tennessee Press, 1991). An earlier and somewhat less scholarly work, John Rice Irwin's *Baskets and Basket Makers in Southern Appalachia* (Exton, Pa.: Schiffer Publishing, 1982), contains information on the McCarter family's basketmaking tradition and on baskets owned by the Walker sisters of Little Greenbrier.

Laurel Horton's exploration of quilting during the nineteenth century in the mountains of North Carolina is found in "Nineteenth Century Middle Class Quilts in Macon County, North Carolina," *Uncoverings* (Research Papers of the American Quilt Study Group) 4 (1983):87–98. Also useful is Horton's exploration of the image of quilting in the southern mountains in "In Search of the Appalachian Quilt," *Now and Then* 6, no. 3 (fall, 1989):19–21.

Merikay Waldvogel's essay, "Southern Linsey Quilts of the Nineteenth Century" is in *Uncoverings* 8 (1987):87–103. Bets Ramsey and Merikay Waldvogel's *The Quilts of Tennessee: Images of Domestic Life Prior to 1930* (Nashville: Rutledge Hill Press, 1986) includes a number of quilts from the eastern part of the state. Particularly interesting is the chapter on the Blair family. The Blair sisters were quiltmakers in Roane County, just west of the Smoky Mountain region, who left a particularly well-documented family collection of bills, tools, letters, etc. Merikay Waldvogel's *Soft Covers for Hard Times: Quiltmaking & the Great Depression* (Nashville: Rutledge Hill Press, 1990) also draws on Tennessee examples. She includes one chapter on reusing cotton sacks and another based on oral interviews. Among those interviewed is Georgia Thomas Mize from Sevier County.

Suzanne Hill McDowell presented a preliminary paper at the Appalachian Studies Conference in spring 1993 on the regional patterns in quilts in southwestern North Carolina. Among the examples she documented were quilts from Jackson, Haywood, Swain, and Macon counties.

The section on the Baxter quilt is based on David Baxter, "The Baxter Family Quilt 1989–1990: A Study in Contemporary Tradition," term paper for Folk Studies 561, Western Kentucky University.

Chapter Five

Although it does not specifically discuss foodways of the Smoky Mountains, a good historical overview of southern foodways written for a popular audience is John Egerton's "Pass and Repast: A Gastronomical View of the South," in his *Southern Food* (New York: Alfred A. Knopf, 1987).

Some local cookbooks are produced for tourists; most are rather cornball and rely on "hillbilly" stereotypes. Local cookbooks, such as those produced by extension homemakers groups, reflect contemporary cooking in the region, though they tend to make a particular effort to appear up-to-date. A good historically oriented cookbook is Duane Oliver's *Cooking on Hazel Creek: The Best of Southern Mountain Cooking* (Hazelwood, N.C.: privately published, 1990). Oliver relied on information garnered from former residents of Hazel Creek in compiling the cookbook.

Privately produced memoirs such as Alice Hawkins Haynes's *Haywood Home: Memories of a Mountain Woman* (Tallahassee: Rose Printing Company, 1991) often include descriptions of regional foodways. Haynes's comments on community food sharing are found on pp. 43–44. Florence Cope Bush's *Dorie: Woman of the Mountains* (Knoxville: University of Tennessee Press, 1992), based on her mother's memories of growing up in the Smokies in the early twentieth century, has a number of descriptions of traditional foodways and folk medicine.

Quotations from tape-recorded interviews are from interview with John and Alberta Baxter, conducted by David Baxter, Somerset, Kentucky, 18 March 1994; interview with Bonnie Meyers, conducted by Michael Ann Williams, Cades Cove, Tennessee, 29 July 1993; interview with Letha Hicks, conducted by Michael Ann Williams, Big Bend, North Carolina, 8 September 1984.

For a 1935 study of the diets of people in the Southern Appalachians, including the Smoky Mountains region, see Lester R. Wheeler, "Changes in the Dietary Habits of Remote Mountain People since 1900," reprinted in *Appalachian Images in Folk and Popular Culture*, ed. W. K. McNeil (Ann Arbor: U.M.I. Research Press, 1989), pp. 255–62.

For a discussion of trout fishing in the region, see Jan Davidson, "Of Specks and Yallarhammers: North Carolina's Rich Trout Fishing History," *The FLYline* (Publication of the North Carolina Council of Trout Unlimited) II, no. 2 (summer/fall 1989):10–11, 16.

John R. Finger's description of Cherokee foodways, circa 1900, is found in *Cherokee Americans: The Eastern Band of Cherokees in the Twentieth Century* (Lincoln and London: University of Nebraska Press, 1991), pp. 7–8. Information about food at Cherokee boarding schools is found on pp. 60–61. For a historical examination of Cherokee corn, see Joan Greene and H. F. Robinson, "Maize was Our Life: A History of Cherokee Corn," *Journal of Cherokee Studies* XI, no. 1 (spring 1986):40–52. A discussion of Cherokee use of wild foods is found in Max E. White, "Contemporary Usage of Native Plant Foods by the Eastern Cherokee," *Appalachian Journal* 2 (1975):323–26.

The Fading Voices interviews, an oral history project conducted at Snowbird, have a number of references to traditional food preparation. The interviews are excerpted in a special issue of *Journal of Cherokee Studies*, XI (1989).

For a description of the Cherokee diet in the mid-twentieth century, see John Gulick, *Cherokees at the Crossroads* (Chapel Hill: Institute for Research in Social Sciences, 1960, rev. ed., 1973), pp. 74–79.

For a discussion of hematic herbs and folk hematology in Southern Appalachia, see Charles W. Logsdon, "Plant Medicine of the Southern Appalachians, I, Hematic Herbs ('The Tonics of Spring')," *Tennessee Anthropologist* XI, no.1 (spring 1986):55–68; and Anthony Cavender, "Folk Hematology in the Appalachian South," *Journal of Folklore Research* 29, no. 1 (Jan.–April 1992):23–36. For a discussion of ginseng, see also Charles W. Logsdon, "The Pharmacology of Folk Medical Use of *Panax* in the Southern Appalachians: An Overview with Suggested Applications for Further Study," *Tennessee Anthropologist* IX, no. 1 (spring 1984):66–79.

An examination of Cherokee healing in relation to religious belief can be found in Catherine L. Albanese, "Exploring Regional Religion: A Case Study of the Eastern Cherokee," *History of Religion* 23 (1984):344–71. For a brief exploration of Cherokee medical beliefs in the mid-twentieth century, see *Cherokees at the Crossroads*, pp. 94–97. Sharlotte Neely briefly discusses traditional medicine in *Snowbird Cherokees: People of Persistence* (London and Athens: University of Georgia Press, 1991), pp. 63–64.

CHAPTER 6

See Chapter XVI, "The Mountain Dialect," of *Our Southern Highlanders* for Horace Kephart's writing on the speech of the Smokies (and of the southern mountains generally). Linguist Frederic G. Cassidy specifically cites the use of "chimbly" for "chimney" as an example of epenthesis (an intrusive, excrescent or parasitic sound) in his essay "Language Changes Especially Common in American Folk Speech," in the introduction of the *Dictionary of American English, vol. 1, Introduction and A–C* (Cambridge, Mass., and London: Belknap Press, 1985), pp. xxxvi–xxxvii.

For Joseph Hall's scholarly work on the speech of the region, see *The Phonetics of Great Smoky Mountain Speech, American Speech Reprints and Monographs* no. 4. (New York: King's Crown Press, 1942). For a more popularized work, see Joseph Hall, *Sayings From Old Smoky* (Asheville, N.C.: Cataloochee Press, 1972). Another academic study is M. Jean Jones, "The Regional English of the Former Inhabitants of Cades Cove in the Great Smoky Mountains" (Ph.D. dissertation, University of Tennessee,

1973). This study, which focuses on five "elderly natives with little formal education," primarily stresses phonology.

A compilation of Cratis Williams's writing on the speech of the Southern Appalachians is found in *Southern Mountain Speech*, edited and with an introduction and glossary by Jim Wayne Miller and Loyal Jones (Berea, Ky.: Berea College Press, 1992).

Quotations from Jim Wayne Miller are from a tape-recorded interview conducted by David Baxter, 8 March 1994, in Bowling Green, Kentucky. Among the writings of Miller are *The Mountains Have Come Closer* (Boone, N.C.: Appalachian Consortium Press, 1980, rpt. 1991), a book of poems; and his two novels, *Newfound* (New York: Orchard books, 1989, rpt. 1991) and *His First, Best Country* (Frankfort, Ky.: Gnomon Press, 1993).

For material on the use of the Cherokee language during the 1950s, see John Gulick, *Cherokees at the Crossroads*, pp. 104–10; see also Sharlotte Neely's epilogue on educational changes, pp. 185–90. Information on the use of the Cherokee language at Snowbird is from Sharlotte Neely, *Snowbird Cherokees: People of Persistence* (Athens and London: University of Georgia Press, 1991), pp. 62–63, 147–48.

The first scholarly record of Jack tales in the southern mountains is found in Isabel Gordon Carter, "Mountain White Folk-lore: Tales from the Southern Blue Ridge," *Journal of American Folk-lore* 38 (1925):342–68. Popular attention to this genre was encouraged by the works of Richard Chase, who rewrote and bowdlerized versions of Jack tales collected from oral informants. See especially Richard Chase, *The Jack Tales* (Boston: Houghton Mifflin, 1948). For an exploration of the family connections among the Smoky Mountain Jack tale tellers, see James W. Thompson, "The Origins of the Hicks Family Traditions," *North Carolina Folklore Journal* 34, no. 1 (winter-spring 1987):18–28. A recent examination of Jack tales is found in William Bernard McCarthy, ed., *Jack in Two Worlds: Contemporary North American Tales and Their Tellers* (Chapel Hill and London: University of North Carolina Press, 1994); in this volume, see especially Bill Ellis, "The Gentry-Long Tradition and Roots of Revivalism: Maud Gentry Long," pp. 93–106, and Joseph Daniel Sobol, "Between Two Worlds: Donald Davis," pp. 204–12.

Stories (and some examples of local idioms) are quotations from tape-recorded interviews conducted by Michael Ann Williams with Zena Bennett, 18 October 1983, Iotla, North Carolina; with Letha Hicks, 8 September 1984, Big Bend, North Carolina; with Anna Collett, 13 October 1983, Aquone, North Carolina; and with Doug Wallin, 11 March 1993, Sodom-Laurel, North Carolina.

James Mooney's *Myths of the Cherokee and Sacred Formulas of the Cherokees* (19th and 7th Annual Reports B.A.E.) were reprinted (Nashville: Charles Elder Publisher, 1972). Portions of transcripts of the Fading

Voices interviews, translated from Cherokee, were published in *Journal of Cherokee Studies* XI (1989).

In "Exploring Regional Religion: A Case Study of the Eastern Chero-kee," *History of Religions* 23 (1984):344–71, Catherine L. Albanese pro-vides an interpretation of the importance of the Tsali legend as a unifying creation myth for the Eastern Cherokee.

Two compilations of Appalachian humor are Loyal Jones and Billy Edd Wheeler, *Laughter in Appalachia: A Festival of Southern Mountain Humor* (Little Rock: August House, 1987) and the subsequent volume, *Curing the Cross-Eyed Mule* (Little Rock: August House Publishers, 1989). In the latter volume, see especially William E. Lightfoot's "Esoteric-Exo-teric Dimensions of Appalachian Folk Humor." See also Jim Wayne Miller, "The Laughing Snake: A Serpentine Look at Appalachian Humor," in Loyal Jones and Billy Edd Wheeler, *More Laughter in Appala-chia* (Little Rock: August House, forthcoming [1995]).

CHAPTER SEVEN

Primary documents concerning the efforts of the National Park Service to preserve and present folk culture in the Great Smoky Mountains can be found in the archive at the Sugarlands Visitors Center. Relevant mate-rials can be found in the papers of H. C. Wilburn and Charles Grossman, the monthly reports of the park superintendent, and in the following re-ports: Alden B. Stevens, "A Preliminary Report on a General Museum Development Plan for Great Smoky Mountains National Park," 1935; H. C. Wilburn, C. S. Grossman, and A. Stupka, "Report on the Proposed Mountain Culture Program for Great Smoky Mountains National Park," 1938; Charles S. Grossman, "A Study for the Preservation of Mountain Culture in Field Museums of History," no date; Dr. Hans Huth, "Report on the Preservation of Mountain Culture in Great Smoky Mountains Na-tional Park," August 1941; H. W. Lix, "Short History of the Great Smoky Mountains National Park," 1958.

For information on the Walker sisters, see Robert R. Madden and T. Russell Jones, *Mountains Home—The Walker Family Homestead* (Washing-ton D.C.: U.S. Department of Interior, 1977).

Cherokee bear myths can be found in James Mooney's *Myths of the Cherokee*. For accounts of bear lore from the pre-park era, see Chapter IV, "A Bear Hunt in the Smokies," in Horace Kephart's *Our Southern Highlanders*, and Joseph S. Hall, "Bear-Hunting Stories from the Great Smokies," *Tennessee Folklore Society Bulletin* XXIII (1957):67–75. Early park superintendents' reports are found in the GSMNP Archives, Sugar-lands Visitors Center. The bear with the watermelon story is from a tape-recorded interview conducted by David Baxter with Norma Sizemore, Atwood Sizemore and Randy Sizemore, London, Kentucky, 15 March 1994.

For an examination of the National Park Service's effort to control tourism at the entrances of the Great Smoky Mountains National Park, see Jane Stewart Becker, "Selling Tradition: The Domestication of Southern Appalachian Culture in 1930s America," (Ph.D. dissertation, Boston University, 1993), pp. 428–31.

A critical examination of tourism that uses Sevier County, Tennessee, as a case study is Michal Smith, *Behind the Glitter: The Impact of Tourism on Rural Women in the Southeast* (Lexington, Ky.: Southeast Women's Employment Coalition). The otherwise insightful study is marred by its stereotypical portrayal of women's roles in mountain culture. *Now and Then* 8, no. 1 (spring 1991) offers a special issue on tourism that also looks specifically at Sevier County. See especially Pat Arnow's "Tourist Central: Scourge or Salvation?" and "Dollywood: Changing the Profile of Pigeon Forge." Also reprinted in this issue are an excerpt from Jeff Rennicke's *The Smoky Mountain Black Bear: Spirit of the Hills* (Great Smoky Mountains Natural History Association, 1991) and "Living with the Tourist Trade: Cherokee and the Tourists" from the *Cherokee One Feather* (December 17, 1975). See also Larry R. Stucki, "Will the 'Real' Indian Survive?: Tourism and Affluence at Cherokee, North Carolina," in *Affluence and Cultural Survival, 1981 Proceedings of the American Ethnological Society* (Washington D.C.: American Ethnological Society, 1984), for a critical examination of the development of tourism at Cherokee.

Chapter Eight

For an overview of the history of Cataloochee, see Wilma Dykeman and Jim Stokely, *Highland Homeland: The People of the Great Smokies* (Washington D. C.: National Park Service, 1978), pp. 7–18.

Robert H. Woody's essay, "Cataloochee Homecoming," was published in *South Atlantic Quarterly* 49, no. 1 (Jan. 1950):8–17.

The quotation by Joseph Hall on homecomings is from "Folk-lore and Folk History in the Great Smoky Mountains," January 29, 1940, report located in the GSMNP Archives, Sugarlands. Reports on attendance of the homecoming are found in superintendents' reports also in the GSMNP Archives.

For a detailed description of several structures at Little Cataloochee and their historical contexts, see Roy Carroll and Raymond H. Pulley, *Historic Structures Report: Little Cataloochee North Carolina* (Department of History, Appalachian State University for Great Smoky Mountains Natural History Association, 1976). The Cataloochee Auto Tour booklet available at the park is also a source of information on the existing structures.

The best historical account of Cades Cove is Durwood Dunn, *Cades Cove: The Life and Death of a Southern Appalachian Community, 1818–1937* (Knoxville: University of Tennessee Press, 1988). A tape-recorded interview was conducted by Michael Ann Williams with Bonnie Meyers, 29 July 1993, Cades Cove Visitors Center.

The most complete history of the Hazel Creek community, written by a descendant of one of the early settlers, is Duane Oliver's *Hazel Creek: From Then Till Now* (1989). It is privately published but is available at the Visitors Center at Sugarlands. See also Sam Gray, *Hazel Creek: Patterns of Life on an Appalachian Watershed*, an exhibition booklet published by the Mountain Heritage Center, Western Carolina University.

In Special Collections, Hunter Library at Western Carolina University, copies can be found of *The Hardwood Bark: For the Employees of the W. M. Ritter Lumber Company*, which reported on life in the individual camps and lumber towns. The quotation is from vol. 3, no. 4 (April 1923):9.

The Tennessee Valley Authority's relocation files for the Fontana Dam project are now in the Federal Records Center, East Point, Georgia. Relevant files are found in the Reservoir Property Management Division—Population Removal Records and the Division of Reservoir Properties—General Correspondence, Programs and Procedures Correspondence and Kodak Negative Files.

The story of the acquisition of the north shore lands by the park is told from the park's and park promoters' point of view in Carlos C. Campbell's *Birth of a National Park in the Great Smoky Mountains* (Knoxville: University of Tennessee Press, rev. ed., 1969), pp. 130–33.

For an analysis of issues concerning the perceived resources of the park, see David E. Carpenter, "The Great Smokies: Diverse Perceptions of the Park as a Resource," in *The Many Faces of Appalachia: Exploring a Region's Diversity. Proceedings of the Seventh Annual Appalachian Studies Conference*, ed. Sam Gray (Boone, N.C.: Appalachian Consortium Press, 1985), pp. 169–81.

Considerable information on the development of Elkmont may be found at the Great Smoky Mountains National Park Archives in the Appalachian Club, Wonderland Club, Chapman, Tennessee Condemnation, Great Smoky Mountains Conservation Association, and Elkmont files. Historic photographs and copies of brochures and newspaper articles are also at the archives. Deed records are located at the archives and at the Sevier County Courthouse.

For a consideration of the historical and architectural significance of Elkmont, see *The History and Architecture of the Elkmont Community*, Report

Prepared for the National Park Service Southeast Region (Nashville, Tenn.: Thomason and Associates Preservation Planners, 1993).

An overview of the history of the Appalachian and Wonderland clubs and their conflict with the National Park Service may be found in John Morrell, "A Brief History of the Appalachian and Wonderland Clubs Within the Great Smoky Mountains National Park," on file at the GSMNP Archives. Morrell, a former park ranger, however, can hardly be considered an objective guide to the situation.

Other sources of information on the development of Elkmont are Robert S. Lambert, "Logging on Little River, 1890–1940," *East Tennessee Historical Society Publications*, no. 33 (1961); Willard Yarbrough, "Elkmont, Rooted in Smoky Park History, is Proud of Tradition," *Knoxville News-Sentinel*, August 29, 1965; and Vic Weals, *Last Train to Elkmont* (Knoxville: Olden Press, 1991), which is a compilation of newspaper articles by the author.

The editorial on Elkmont, "Requiem for a Resort," was published by the *Knoxville News-Sentinel*, October 7, 1992.

The Knoxville Automobile Association's map of the proposed boundaries of the park was published as the frontispiece of Robert Lindsay Mason's *The Lure of the Great Smokies* (Boston and New York: Houghton Mifflin Co., 1927).

Quotations are from tape-recorded interviews conducted by David Baxter with Celia Baxter, 15 March 1994, Keavy, Kentucky; Nell and Jennifer Nelson, 15 March 1994, Keavy, Kentucky; Ken and Lee Baxter, 16 March 1994, Lexington, Kentucky; and John and Alberta Baxter, 18 March 1994, Somerset, Kentucky. The section is also based on "Baxter Family Fall Retreat: A Brief History and Outline" and "Family Sketch for David Baxter Interviews," both prepared by David Baxter.

Chapter Nine

For analyses of tourism, see citations for chapter 7.

Information on the history of the Cosby Ramp Festival and the quotation from the resolution presented to the Tennessee House of Representatives are from the 1993 40th Annual Cosby Ruritan Club Ramp Festival Program.

The quotation by Gilliam Jackson is from Gilliam Jackson, "Cultural Identity for the Modern Cherokees," *Appalachian Journal*, 2, no. 4 (summer 1975):280–83. Press releases, correspondence and newspaper articles from the early years of the Cherokee Fair are from the records of the Bureau of Indian Affairs, Cherokee Indian Agency, at the Federal Records Center, East Point, Georgia. Quotations are from the 1993 Cherokee

Fall Festival Program. A useful analysis of agricultural fairs and fair foods, which has some applicability to the Cherokee Fall Festival is Leslie Prosterman, "Food and Alliance at the County Fair," *Western Folklore* 40 (1981):81–90.

For another analysis of Dollywood, see Pat Arnow, "Dollywood: Changing the Profile of Pigeon Forge," *Now and Then* 8, no. 1 (spring 1991):8–10.